Causation
in
Early Modern
Philosophy

Causation in Early Modern Philosophy

Cartesianism, Occasionalism,
and Preestablished Harmony

Edited by Steven Nadler

The Pennsylvania State University Press
University Park, Pennsylvania

Library of Congress Cataloging-in-Publication Data

Nadler, Steven M., 1958–
    Causation in early modern philosophy : Cartesianism,
  Occasionalism, and pre-established harmony / edited by Steven
  Nadler.

       p.   cm.
    Includes bibliographical references and index.
    ISBN 0-271-00863-6 (alk. paper)
    1. Causation—History.   2. Philosophy, Modern—17th century.
  BD541.N33   1993
  122'.09'032—dc20
                                                                91-46809
                                                                    CIP

It is the policy of The Pennsylvania State University Press to use acid-free paper for
the first printing of all clothbound books. Publications on uncoated stock satisfy
the minimum requirements of American National Standard for Information
Sciences—Permanence of Paper for Printed Library Materials, ANSI Z39.48–1984.

Contents

Contributors

LOIS FRANKEL is an independent scholar in Mercerville, New Jersey.

DANIEL GARBER is Professor of Philosophy at the University of Chicago.

MARK A. KULSTAD is Professor of Philosophy at Rice University.

THOMAS M. LENNON is Professor of Philosophy and Dean of the Faculty of Arts at the University of Western Ontario.

STEVEN NADLER is Associate Professor of Philosophy at the University of Wisconsin—Madison.

EILEEN O'NEILL is Associate Professor of Philosophy at Queens College of the City University of New York.

DONALD P. RUTHERFORD is Assistant Professor of Philosophy at Emory University.

RICHARD A. WATSON is Professor of Philosophy at Washington University, St. Louis.

CATHERINE WILSON is Professor of Philosophy, University of Alberta.

MARGARET D. WILSON is Professor of Philosophy at Princeton University.

Abbreviations

The following abbreviations are used for works frequently referred to in the book. Additional abbreviations may appear in the notes for each chapter.

Works by Descartes:

AT   *Oeuvres de Descartes*, 11 vols., edited by C. Adam and P. Tannery (rev. ed., Paris: J. Vrin/C.N.R.S., 1964–76).

CSM   *The Philosophical Writings of Descartes*, 2 vols., translated by J. Cottingham, R. Stoothoff, and D. Murdoch (Cambridge: Cambridge University Press, 1985).

K   *Descartes: Philosophical Letters*, translated by A. Kenny (Oxford: Oxford University Press, 1970).

Works by Malebranche:

D   *Dialogues on Metaphysics*, translated by W. Doney (New York: Abaris, 1980).

LO   *The Search after Truth*, translated by T. M. Lennon and P. J. Olscamp (Columbus: Ohio State University Press, 1980).

OC   *Oeuvres complètes de Malebranche*, 20 vols., edited by A. Robinet (Paris: J. Vrin, 1958–70).

Works by Leibniz:

A   *G. W. Leibniz: Sämtliche Schriften und Briefe*, edited by the German Academy of Science (Darmstadt, Leipzig, and Berlin: Georg Olms and Akademie Verlag, 1923–).

AG   *G. W. Leibniz: Philosophical Essays*, translated by R. Ariew and D. Garber (Indianapolis, Ind.: Hackett, 1989).

C   *Opuscules et fragments inédits de Leibniz*, edited by L. Couturat (Paris, 1903).

G   *Die philosophischen Schriften von G. W. Leibniz*, 7 vols., edited by C. I. Gerhardt (Berlin, 1875–90; reprint, Hildesheim: Georg Olms, 1965).

GB   *Der Briefwechsel von Gottfried Wilhelm Leibniz mit Mathematikern*, edited by C. I. Gerhardt (Berlin, 1899; reprint, Hildesheim: Georg Olms, 1962).

GM   *Die mathematische Schriften von G. W. Leibniz*, 7 vols., edited by C. I. Gerhardt (Berlin and Halle, 1849–55).

Grua   *G. W. Leibniz: Textes inédits*, 2 vols., edited by G. Grua (Paris, 1948; reprint, New York: Garland, 1985).

H   *Theodicy: Essays on the Goodness of God, the Freedom of Man, and the Origin of Evil*, edited by A. Farrar, translated by E. M. Huggard (La Salle, Ill.: Open Court, 1985).

L   *Philosophical Papers and Letters*, edited and translated by L. Loemker (Dordrecht: D. Reidel, 1969).

LA   *The Leibniz-Arnauld Correspondence*, edited and translated by H. T. Mason (Manchester: Manchester University Press, 1967).

ML   *Malebranche et Leibniz: Relations personelles*, edited by A. Robinet (Paris: J. Vrin, 1955).

NE   *New Essays on Human Understanding*, translated by P. Remnant and J. Bennett (Cambridge: Cambridge University Press, 1981).

P   *Leibniz: Philosophical Writings*, edited by G.H.R. Parkinson (Totowa, N.J.: Rowman and Littlefield, 1975).

S   *"Monadology" and Other Philosophical Essays*, translated by P. Schrecker and A. M. Schrecker (Indianapolis, Ind.: Bobbs-Merrill, 1965).

Vorausedition *Gottfried Wilhelm Leibniz: Vorausedition zur Reihe VI—Philosophische Schriften—in der Ausgabe der Akademie der DDR*, edited by the Leibniz-Forschungsstelle der Universität Münster, Faszikel 1– (Münster, 1982–).

Steven Nadler

Introduction

I

Questions about the nature of causal relations occupy a central position in early modern philosophy. The prominence of this topic in seventeenth- and eighteenth-century thought can, in large measure, be traced to a specific historical problem: the need to reconcile an emerging scientific view of the natural world—mechanistic physics—with traditional beliefs about the relation between God and his creation. On the one hand, natural philosophers of the period see their task as one of identifying the underlying causal structures of observed phenomena and of framing explanations in terms of matter and motion alone. On the other hand, it is generally recognized that God is responsible not just for creating the world and its contents, but for sustaining them in existence as well. Against this background, in which philosophy, physics, and theology merge, the problem of causation arises in several contexts: in the realm of purely physical inquiry (how does one body produce changes in another body?); in regard to relations between the mind and the body (are mental events true causes of physical states of affairs, and do bodily states cause effects in the mind?); and in philosophical inquiry into the mind alone (are there causal relations among thoughts and other mental activities?). In all three contexts,[1] the answers to these specific questions hang upon the answer to the more general question as to how God's omnipotence and role in sustaining beings in existence can be reconciled with granting creatures true causal efficacy.

Three general accounts of causation stand out in early modern philosophy: Cartesian interactionism, occasionalism, and Leibniz's preestablished harmony. The chapters that follow examine these theories in their philosophical and historical context.[2] The authors were asked to address the theories both as specific answers to the above questions regarding causal relations and as they stand in relation to each other—in particular, to compare occasionalism and the preestablished harmony as responses to Descartes's metaphysics and physics and to the Cartesian account of causation. What significant differences and/or similarities are there between occasionalism and the preestablished harmony? What are Leibniz's objections to occasionalism? How do occasionalist objections to interactionism influence Leibniz's theory? How seriously were occasionalism and the preestablished harmony taken by contemporaries, and how do they hold up as philosophical accounts of causation?

In this introduction, I shall briefly summarize the three theories and show why these questions are important for our understanding of the development of early modern metaphysics and science.

II

One of the primary aims of Descartes's project in natural philosophy is to rid the physical world of the forms and qualities and occult powers of the Scholastics. According to the standard medieval Aristotelian account, a primary substance—a particular existent—is a compound entity made up of matter and an immaterial form. The substantial form of the substance is that from which its essential properties and characteristic behaviors derive. All motion and change, all causal and other powers are to be explained by reference to the specific form inhering in (and individuating) a parcel of

1. Questions about causal relations certainly arise in the seventeenth century in other contexts—social, psychological—that are not addressed by the essays in this book.
2. Most of the chapters were presented as papers at a conference on causation in early modern philosophy at the University of Wisconsin—Madison (April 1990).

matter. As Descartes notes, "[forms] were introduced by philosophers to explain the proper action of natural things, of which action this form is the principle and the source."[3]

By defining material substance as pure extension, Descartes eliminates at one stroke all forms and other soul-like beings from the physical world. A body is then nothing but extension in three dimensions, differentiated from other bodies not through some form but solely by means of local motion. It has no attributes other than the geometrical properties of outer shape, figure (which takes into account the interstices between its constituent particles), and size, along with mobility. All other properties (for example, weight and color) are nothing but relative properties or effects that arise when the body comes into contact either with other bodies or minds.[4]

With the banishment of forms from inanimate nature and the reduction of body to extension, however, Descartes has also thereby removed the primary causal mechanism of Aristotelian science—particularly with respect to the motion of bodies. And this seems to leave him with a rather difficult problem, namely, what then *does* cause the motion of bodies, and in what does their causal interaction consist? The motion of a body is one of its modifications (like its shape) and consists simply in its transference from the immediate vicinity of one set of contiguous bodies to that of another.[5] Moreover, one body affects another by collision alone—there is no action at a distance. But if a body just is a parcel of extension, inert and passive, then it must necessarily be devoid of any motive force. Whence, then, does its motion arise or change? How and by what power can it actively cause effects in other bodies (and in minds)? Descartes appears to treat physical causation as a matter of transference or communication of motion from one body to another.[6] But if the motion of a body is a mode of its being, and if modes cannot be transferred from one substance to another, how can one body cause motion in another body?[7] Finally, if mind and body are as radically different as Descartes's dualism demands, how can they causally engage one another and reciprocally bring about effects?

Thus, while Descartes frequently speaks of bodies and minds as real causal agents,[8] his metaphysics seems not to allow him to hold such a thoroughgoing interactionism. Descartes, I believe, recognizes this. With respect to body-body interaction his position is, as Daniel Garber suggests in his essay, basically an occasionalist one—he does refer to God as the

3. Letter to Regius, January 1642, AT III, 506; K 129.
4. *Principles of Philosophy* II.3–4.
5. Ibid., 25–27.
6. See *Principles of Philosophy* II.40.
7. Henry More raises this question for Descartes in his letter of 23 July 1649, AT V, 382.
8. See *Meditations* VI and *Principles of Philosophy* IV.187.

general and primary cause of motion[9]—although his occasionalism is limited and leaves room for finite minds as causes. Later Cartesians are split on this issue. Some (like Nicolas Malebranche and Géraud de Cordemoy) opt for a complete, others (like Antoine Arnauld and Louis de la Forge) for a restricted, occasionalist picture; while several physicists (Jacques Rohault, Pierre Sylvain Régis) continue to treat bodies as real causes of effects in other bodies.

III

Occasionalism (in its extreme version) is the theory that finite created beings—whether minds or bodies—have no causal efficacy whatsoever, no power to bring about changes in one another's states. Bodies do not cause effects in other bodies nor in minds; and minds do not cause effects in bodies, nor even within themselves. God is the only true causal agent and is immediately, proximately, and solely responsible for all events in nature. The pricking of my skin by a needle is not the true cause of the pain that I feel; rather, it is a mere "occasion" for God to cause a painful sensation in my soul, in accordance with the laws of mind-body union. Similarly, my volition to raise my arm is not the true cause of my arm's rising; rather, God causes the arm to rise on the occasion of that volition. And finally, the collision of a cue ball with a billiard ball is not the real cause of the second ball's motion, but rather the occasion for God to move the second ball, in accordance with the laws of physics.

Recent scholarship has made it clear that, contrary to the traditional textbook mythology, the occasionalism of such philosophers as Malebranche, Cordemoy, and Arnold Geulincx is not simply an ad hoc solution to a peculiarly Cartesian mind-body problem.[10] God's ubiquitous causal activity in the world is not employed merely as some deus ex machina to explain why mental events and bodily states are correlated. Occasionalism is just as much an account of body-body "interaction" as of mind-body "interaction." In fact, it is a full-bodied theory of causal relations generally, physical as well as psychophysical, and tries to reconcile in a single account a number of distinct and often competing philosophical, scientific, and theological considerations. At its basis lies both a philosophical analysis of

9. *Principles of Philosophy* II.36.
10. See T. M. Lennon, "Occasionalism and the Cartesian Metaphysic of Motion," *Canadian Journal of Philosophy*, Supplementary Volume no. 1 (1974): 29–40, and L. Loeb, *From Descartes to Hume* (Ithaca, N.Y.: Cornell University Press, 1981), ch. 5.

causation and an examination of certain essential limitations upon the causal power of finite creatures in the face of the omnipotence of God.

Malebranche claims that between a cause and its effect there must be a "necessary connection," apparently of a logical nature. Yet such a connection can never be discovered between any two finite events. Rather, only between the will of an infinite, omnipotent being (God) and its object can the requisite necessity be found; such is the nature of omnipotence.[11] Moreover, God's sustenance of the world involves its continuous re-creation from moment to moment, including the re-creation of beings with all their modes. The motion of a body, then, is simply its re-creation by God in different successive relative places (while its rest is its re-creation in the same relative place).[12] To believe that God has given real causal power to finite beings is simply to overlook the kind of absolute dependence creatures have upon God; it is to reason not on the basis of clear and distinct ideas, but rather on the misleading testimony of the senses.

One particularly fruitful way to regard occasionalism is as a way of dealing with the problems discussed above with respect to Descartes's theory of causation in the natural world, and as an attempt to provide a metaphysical foundation for explanations in Cartesian mechanistic physics. Motion can now be given a true causal ground in force, which in turn is identified with the will of God; and the laws of nature serve to determine (or describe) how God ordinarily moves things around. While the natural philosopher's task is still to seek the secondary or "occasional" causes of phenomena, there is no need to grant (within a Cartesian ontological framework) to bodies any active causal principles or powers.

IV

According to Leibniz, all the states of a substance follow from its own essential nature. Every body (or corporeal substance) and soul is itself the source of its own sequence of modifications, although God is responsible for choosing to create one compossible set of substances over all others and for "producing them continually by a kind of emanation."[13] Whatever state a body is in at any particular moment follows immediately and only from its own previous state, together with some immanent law of order or succession (which law "constitutes the individuality of each particular

11. See *De la recherche de la vérité* VI.2.iii.
12. See *Entretiens sur la métaphysique* VII.7, 11.
13. *Discourse on Metaphysics* §14.

substance").[14] A substance is thus characterized by a complete and perfect spontaneity. "In my opinion it is in the nature of created substance to change continually following a certain order which leads it spontaneously . . . through all the states it encounters."[15]

Thus, Leibniz, like the occasionalists, is committed to a complete noninteractionism among finite substances, mental and corporeal. On the spontaneity thesis, the state of one substance cannot be the true cause of the state of another substance. But, unlike the occasionalists, Leibniz is also committed to the real activity of substance, namely, in its production of its own modifications.

> Each substance is a world by itself, independent of anything else except God. . . . In a way, then, we might say, although it seems strange, that a particular substance never acts upon another particular substance, nor is it acted upon by it. That which happens to each one is only the consequence of its complete idea or concept, since this idea already involves all the predicates and expresses the whole world.[16]

Bodies and minds, for Leibniz, are genuinely active individuals. The causal generation of a corporeal substance's states is grounded in what he calls "force," an internal principle that, like the Aristotelian substantial forms to which Leibniz compares it,[17] is distinct from the body's extension or matter.

But if there is no interaction, how does Leibniz explain the apparent coordination in the states of substances; for example, the correlation between one's bodily states (the pricking of a finger by a pin) and one's mental states (pain), or that when one billiard ball strikes another, it loses a certain degree of motion while the other gains motion? Rather than attributing this feature of the world to the "constant intervention" of God (as Leibniz reads occasionalism), he claims that God, in his infinite wisdom, has so created and harmoniously coordinated substances that their sequences of states correspond to each other. Thus, there results a "grand concomitance," the unitary system of the world in which the phenomena are in agreement: "So there will be a perfect accord between all these substances which produces the same effect that would be noticed if they all

---

14. "Clarification of the Difficulties which M. Bayle has found in the New System of the Union of Soul and Body," G IV, 518.

15. Ibid.

16. *Discourse on Metaphysics* §14.

17. *A New System of the Nature and Communication of Substances, and of the Union of the Soul and Body*, G IV, 478–79.

communicated with each other."[18] The motions and changes in bodies (and between bodies and minds) are, thanks to this divine preordination, reciprocal and have the appearance of being causally related. This account is what Leibniz eventually calls the "system of preestablished harmony."

V

Writing to Leibniz in 1687, Arnauld claims that he can see no essential difference between Leibniz's views on causation and what the occasionalists say. For Arnauld, Leibniz's claim that the "wonderful but unfailing agreement of things" is the result of God's initial resolution at creation upon the sequence of all things in the universe

> is to say the same thing in other terms that those say who maintain that my will is the occasional cause for the movement of my arm and that God is its real cause; for they do not claim that God does this at the moment by a new act of will each time that I wish to raise my arm, but by a single act of the eternal will by which he has chosen to do everything which he has foreseen that it will be necessary to do, in order that the universe might be such as he has decided it ought to be.[19]

While it is not clear that Arnauld correctly understands the occasionalist position on God's causal activity, he nonetheless stands at the beginning of a long line of commentators who minimize the differences between the two theories and who claim either that occasionalism and the preestablished harmony are explicitly asserting the same thing or that the one ultimately reduces to the other.[20] Thus, Thomas Lennon has suggested that because Leibniz agrees with the Cartesians that there is only a conceptual distinction between creation and conservation in existence, it is natural to wonder "what the difference comes to between saying that God natures things in such a way that certain states in them are correlated but that those things are constantly recreated, and saying that God constantly recreates things in such a way that these same correlations obtain."[21]

18. Ibid., 484.
19. Arnauld to Leibniz, 4 March 1687, G II, 84.
20. The most recent representative of this view is D. Clarke, *Occult Powers and Hypotheses: Cartesian Natural Philosophy under Louis XIV* (Oxford: Clarendon Press, 1989), p. 121.
21. "Philosophical Commentary," in Malebranche, *The Search after Truth*, LO 825.

To be sure, there are important and unmistakable similarities between the two causal doctrines. Both deny that there is any real interaction among finite created substances. Both refer to God as the ultimate explanation as to why the sequences of things and their states are such as they are. Most important, perhaps, both doctrines are answers to the same problem bequeathed by Cartesian metaphysics—not, indeed, the mind–body problem,[22] but rather the problem of saving mechanistic explanations in physics. Both the occasionalist and Leibniz are, in essence, trying to give motion and its laws (as well as other dynamical properties of bodies) a firm causal and metaphysical foundation in force. Yet their respective solutions to this problem are sufficiently different to prevent confusion between the two. The occasionalist, for whom a body is nothing but extension, insists that force must be located outside of bodies, in the will of God. For Leibniz, on the other hand, there must be some force *in* bodies, some "vital principle superior to material notions" to explain why bodies behave as they do.[23] (Leibniz insists that if bodies were mere extension, then the laws of motion and the phenomena would be entirely different from what they, in fact, are.)[24] In the one case, then, certain aspects of Descartes's own metaphysics of matter and motion (including God's causal role therein) are made explicit.[25] In the other case, the Cartesian model is fundamentally revised.

Thus, one cannot but find irreconcilable differences between two theories, one of which grants to finite substances a genuine causal (albeit noninteractive) activity or power, the other of which denies that such substances have any causal efficacy whatsoever. And while God certainly plays an important causal role in both accounts, there is surely (or so Leibniz believes) no way of mistaking God's direct and immediate causal role under occasionalism for his somewhat indirect and mediate role in the preestablished harmony.

The chapters that follow are all new contributions to the project of illuminating seventeenth-century thought on causation. They range from studies of non-Cartesian interactionist models and of Descartes's own views on causation to analyses of occasionalism and the preestablished harmony; several of them engage in the important (but heretofore neglected) task of critically comparing the two doctrines. Taken together, the essays provide a rather broad and detailed picture of the nature of causal relations in early modern philosophy.

---

22. Although Leibniz himself believes that this is a problem that they are both intended to solve; see his letter to Arnauld of 30 April 1687.
23. *Specimen Dynamicum*, GM IV, 242.
24. *Discourse on Metaphysics* §21.
25. See, for example, *Principles of Philosophy* II.36.

Daniel Garber

Descartes and Occasionalism

The doctrine of occasionalism was, of course, central to seventeenth-century metaphysics. On this widely held view, the changes that one body appears to cause in another upon impact, the changes that a body can cause in a mind in producing a sensation, or that a mind can cause in a body in producing a voluntary action are all due directly to God, moving bodies or producing sensations in minds on the occasions of other appropriate events. And so, on this view, the tickling of the retina and subsequent changes in the brain are only the "occasional causes" of the sensory idea I have of a friend in the distance; the real cause is God, who directly moves my sense organs when the light approaches them, moves the parts of the brain when the sensory organs are moved, and then produces the sensory idea I have of another person's face in my mind when my sense organs and brain are in an appropriate state. Similarly, it is God who is the actual cause of my arm's movement when I decide to raise it to wave; my volition is only an occasional cause.

Now, occasionalism was widely held among many of Descartes's followers; it can be found in various forms in Clauberg, Clerselier, Cordemoy, La Forge, Geulincx, and, most notably, in Malebranche.[1] And throughout its seventeenth-century career it is closely associated with Descartes's followers.[2] But to what extent is it really Descartes's own view? To what extent is it fair to attribute this view to the founder of the Cartesian school? This is the question that I shall explore here.

I. A Letter to Elizabeth

I will begin my investigation with a passage from a letter that Descartes wrote to the Princess Elizabeth on 6 October 1645:

> All of the reasons which prove the existence of God and that he is the first and immutable cause of all of the effects which do not depend on the free will of men, prove in the same way, it seems to me, that he is also the cause of all of them that depend on it [i.e., free will]. For one can only prove that he exists by considering him as a supremely perfect being, and he would not be supremely perfect if something could happen in the world that did not derive entirely from him. . . . God is the universal cause of everything in such a way that he is in the same way the total cause of everything, and thus nothing can happen without his will.[3]

1. For general accounts of occasionalism among the members of the Cartesian school, see, for example, Joseph Prost, *Essai sur l'atomisme et l'occasionalisme dans la philosophie cartésienne* (Paris: Paulin, 1907); Henri Gouhier, *La vocation de Malebranche* (Paris: J. Vrin, 1926), ch. III; Jean-François Battail, *L'avocat philosophe Géraud de Cordemoy* (The Hague: Martinus Nijhoff, 1973), pp. 141–46; and Rainer Specht, *Commercium mentis et corporis: über Kausalvorstellungen im Cartesianismus* (Stuttgart–Bad Cannstatt: Friedrich Frommann Verlag, 1966), chs. II and III.

2. Indeed, when it first appears, it is closely associated with Descartes himself. It is an integral part of La Forge's commentary on Descartes's *Treatise on Man*, and it is one of the central points of a letter Clerselier, Descartes's literary executor, wrote to La Forge in December 1660, a letter that appeals to the authority of *"nostre Maistre"* on a number of occasions and that Clerselier published alongside Descartes's own letters in one of his volumes of the philosopher's collected correspondence. On La Forge, see Gouhier, *La vocation de Malebranche*, pp. 93–94; for the Clerselier letter, see Claude Clerselier, *Lettres de Mr Descartes . . . [tome III]* (Paris, 1667), pp. 640–46. I am indebted to Alan Gabbey for calling the Clerselier letter to my attention.

3. AT IV, 313–14 (K 180). This letter appeared in the first volume of Clerselier's edition of Descartes's correspondence in 1657.

This passage would seem to be quite clear in asserting that God is the real cause of everything in the world; if "nothing can happen without his will," as Descartes tells Elizabeth, then surely it is reasonable to infer that Descartes was an occasionalist.

He may, in the end, turn out to be an occasionalist, but I think that this passage is not so clear as it may look at first. When reading this, it is very important to place it in context, and understand what exactly Descartes was addressing in the passage. In this series of letters, Descartes is trying to console Elizabeth in her troubles. In a letter of 30 September 1645, she wrote:

> [The fact] of the existence of God and his attributes can console us in the misfortunes that come to us from the ordinary course of nature and from the order which he has established there [as when we lose some good through a storm, or when we lose our health through an infection in the air, or our friends through death] but not in those [misfortunes] which are imposed on us by men, whose will appears to us to be entirely free. . . .[4]

Descartes's reply, as quoted above, is that all things, including human beings acting freely, are under the ultimate control of an omniscient, omnipotent, and benevolent God. In saying this, Descartes does not take himself to be saying anything particularly original; it is, indeed, a theological commonplace. While these kinds of theological issues have led thinkers in various theological traditions to take the issue of occasionalism seriously,[5] it is not appropriate to infer the full-blown metaphysical doctrine of occasionalism from this commonplace observation, and conclude that Descartes held that God is the only real cause in nature; his words to Elizabeth are meant as consolation, not metaphysics.

The question of Descartes's occasionalism is still open. To settle it we have to turn to a more detailed investigation of his metaphysical and physical writings. I will divide the investigation into three parts, discussing first the case of body-body causation (one billiard ball hitting another), then mind-body causation (voluntary motions in human beings), and finally body-mind causation (sensation).

4. AT IV, 302.
5. For a recent discussion of some of this larger theological debate, see Alfred Freddoso, "Medieval Aristotelianism and the Case against Secondary Causation in Nature," in *Divine and Human Action: Essays in the Metaphysics of Theism*, ed. Thomas V. Morris (Ithaca, N.Y.: Cornell University Press, 1988).

II. The Case of Body-Body Causation

I will not pause (too) long over this case. It seems to me as clear as anything that, for Descartes, God is the only cause of motion in the inanimate world of bodies, that bodies cannot themselves be genuine causes of change in the physical world of extended substance. To understand why, let me turn for a moment to Descartes's reflections on motion and its laws.[6]

Descartes's conception of physics must be understood as being in opposition to an Aristotelian one, as a substitute for the kind of physics that was taught in the schools. Basic to the physics of the schools was the notion of a substantial form. According to the Aristotelian physics, each kind of thing had its own substantial form, and it was through this that the basic properties of things were to be explained. And so fire rises and stones fall because of their forms, for example. In this way, things were thought to have basic, inborn tendencies to behavior; physics consisted in finding out what these basic tendencies were and in explaining the manifest properties of things in those terms.

A basic move in Descartes's philosophy, something he shared with other contemporary adherents of the so-called mechanical philosophy, was the elimination of these substantial forms, these basic explanatory principles. But how, then, are we to explain the characteristic behavior of bodies? Descartes's strategy was simple; instead of locating the basic laws that govern the behavior of things in these forms, he placed them in God. That is, it is God, not substantial forms, that will ground the laws that govern bodies.

How God grounds the laws of motion is illustrated in the proofs that Descartes gives for them. These proofs are grounded in his celebrated doctrine of continual re-creation. Descartes writes in Meditation III:

> All of the time of my life can be divided into innumerable parts, each of which is entirely independent of the others, so that from the fact that I existed a short time ago, it does not follow that I ought to exist now, unless some cause as it were creates me again in this moment, that is, conserves me.[7]

Now, he argues,

6. For a fuller account of Descartes on the laws of motion, see Daniel Garber, *Descartes' Metaphysical Physics* (Chicago: University of Chicago Press, 1992).
7. AT VII, 49.

plainly the same force and action is needed to conserve any thing for the individual moments in which it endures as was needed for creating it anew, had it not existed.[8]

Clearly such a power is not in us; if it were, then, Descartes reasons, I would also have been able to give myself all of the perfections I clearly lack.[9] And so, he concludes, it must be God that creates and sustains us.[10] This conclusion, of course, holds for bodies as well as it does for us. It is not just *souls,* but *all* finite things that require some cause for their continued existence. And as with the idea of ourselves, "when I examine the idea of body, I perceive that it has no power [*vis*] in itself through which it can produce or conserve itself."[11] And so, we must conclude that the duration of bodies, too, must be caused by God, who sustains the physical world he created in the beginning.

This view of divine sustenance underlies Descartes's derivations of the laws of motion, both in *The World* of 1633 and in the *Principles of Philosophy* of 1644. Arguing for his conservation principle in the *Principles* (for example, the law that God maintains the same quantity of motion in the world), Descartes writes:

We also understand that there is perfection in God not only because he is in himself immutable, but also because he works in the most constant and immutable way. Therefore, with the exception of those changes which evident experience or divine revelation render certain, and which we perceive or believe happen without any change in the creator, we should suppose no other changes in his works, so as not to argue for an inconstancy in him. From this it follows, that it is most in harmony with reason for us to think that merely from the fact that God moved the parts of matter in different ways when he first created them, and now conserves the totality of that matter in the same way and with the same laws [*eademque ratione*] with which he created them earlier, he always conserves the same amount of motion in it.[12]

Similarly, consider his argument for the law that a body in motion tends to move rectilinearly, as that argument is given in the *Principles:*

8. Ibid.
9. See AT VII, 48, 168.
10. See AT VII, 49–50, 111, 165, 168, 369–70; and *Principles of Philosophy* I.21.
11. AT VII, 118; see also p. 110.
12. *Principles of Philosophy* II.36.

The reason [*causa*] for this rule is . . . the immutability and simplicity of the operation through which God conserves motion in matter. For he conserves it precisely as it is in the very moment of time in which he conserves it, without taking into account the way it might have been a bit earlier. And although no motion takes place in an instant, it is obvious that in the individual instants that can be designated while it is moving, everything that moves is determined to continue its motion in some direction, following a straight line, and never following a curved line.[13]

The picture in both of these arguments is reasonably clear: God stands behind the world of bodies and is the direct cause of their motion. In the old Aristotelian philosophy, the characteristic behavior of bodies was explained through substantial forms; in Descartes's new, up–to–date mechanism, forms are out, and God is in; in Descartes's new philosophy, the characteristic behavior of bodies is explained in terms of an immutable God sustaining the motion of bodies.

I think that it is reasonably clear, then, that in the material world, at least, God is the only genuine causal agent. There are some further subtleties in the argument that I will set aside for the moment, returning to at least one of them later. But before moving on to the somewhat more difficult cases of mind-body and body-mind causation, I would like to pause a moment and examine one complexity in the case.

Though it is clear that God is the real agent of change, the real cause of motion in the physical world, it is not at all clear how he does it, how he pulls it off. Though it is not appropriate to argue it in full detail here, it seems to me that there are at least two somewhat different models that one can find in Descartes for this.[14] On one model, God sustains the world by re-creating a succession of discrete, timeless world stages, one after another, like frames in a movie film. On this view, God is conceived to cause motion by re-creating bodies in different places in different frames of the movie, as it were. We might call this the *cinematic view* of how God causes motion. But Descartes sometimes suggests something a bit different. On this alternative view, what God sustains is a world of bodies existing continually in time. Now, in this world, some bodies are at rest, while others are in motion. Those in motion, Descartes sometimes suggests, receive a kind of impulse from God. Writing to Descartes on 5 March 1649, More asked if

13. *Principles of Philosophy* II.39.
14. For a fuller development of this idea, see Garber, *Descartes' Metaphysical Physics*, ch. 9, or Daniel Garber, "How God Causes Motion: Descartes, Divine Sustenance, and Occasionalism," *Journal of Philosophy* 84 (1987): 567–80.

matter, whether we imagine it to be eternal or created yesterday, left to itself, and receiving no impulse from anything else, would move or be at rest?[15]

Descartes answered:

I consider "matter left to itself and receiving no impulse from anything else" as plainly being at rest. But it is impelled by God, conserving the same amount of motion or transference in it as he put there from the first.[16]

On this view, what might be called the *divine-impulse view*, God causes motion by impulse, by a kind of divine shove.

It is interesting to try to understand how Descartes thought of God as a cause of motion. But this distinction I have tried to make between the *cinematic view* and the *divine-impulse view* of God as a cause of motion will come in very handy when we are discussing Descartes's thoughts on mind-body causation, to which we must now turn.

III. The Case of Mind–Body Causation

The problem of mind-body causation is, of course, a central concern of Cartesian scholarship; there are few issues in his philosophy about which more ink has been spilled. But my interest in it here is relatively narrow: To what extent does Descartes think that there can be genuine mental causes of motions in the physical world, and to what extent does he believe, with the majority of his followers, that God is the true cause of motion in the world of bodies?

Here, as on the issue of body-body causation, I believe that the case is reasonably clear: for Descartes, I think, mind can be a genuine cause of motion in the world, indeed, as genuine a cause as God himself.

But though the case is, in the end, clear, it is not without its complications. As a number of later philosophers have noted, Descartes's views on God's role as continual re-creator, that which underlies the derivation of the laws of motion, as we have seen, would seem to lead us directly to a strong version of occasionalism, where God can be the only cause of change

15. AT V, 316.
16. AT V, 404 (K 258).

in the physical world. The argument is formulated neatly by Louis de la Forge:

> I hold that there is no creature, spiritual or corporeal, that can change [the position of a body] or that of any of its parts in the second instant of its creation if the creator does not do it himself, since it is he who had produced this part of matter in place A. For example, not only is it necessary that he continue to produce it if he wants it to continue to exist, but also, since he cannot create it everywhere, nor can he create it outside of every place, he must himself put it in place B, if he wants it there, for if he were to have put it somewhere else, there is no force capable of removing it from there.[17]

The argument goes from the doctrine of continual re-creation, authentically Cartesian, to the conclusion that God can be the only cause of motion in the world. When God sustains a body, he must sustain it *somewhere,* and in sustaining it where he does he causes it to move or be at rest. And so, it seems, there is no room for any other causes of motion in the Cartesian world, in particular, mind; if mind is to have a role to play in where a given body is from moment to moment, it must work through God, who alone can sustain a body and who is ultimately responsible for putting a body one place or another.[18]

This argument is not decisive, I think. First of all, however good an argument it might be, I see no reason to believe that Descartes ever saw such consequences as following out of his doctrine of continual re-creation. But, more than that, I do not think that the argument is necessarily binding on Descartes. It is certainly persuasive, particularly if one takes what I called

17. Louis de la Forge, *Oeuvres Philosophiques*, ed. Pierre Clair (Paris: Presses Universitaires de France, 1974), p. 240. A similar argument can also be found in Dialogue VII of Malebranche's *Dialogues on Metaphysics*.

18. Though the argument concerns motion, states of body, and their causes, it would seem to hold for the causes of states of mind as well, insofar as the divine sustainer must sustain minds with the states that they have as much as he must sustain bodies in the places that they occupy. To these arguments from continual re-creation, one might also call attention to the several passages in which Descartes uses the word '*occasion*' to characterize particular causal relations (see Prost, *Essai*). But as argued in Gouhier, *La vocation de Malebranche*, pp. 83–88, this is hardly worth taking seriously as an argument. See also Jean Laporte, *Le rationalisme de Descartes* (Paris: Presses Universitaires de France, 1950), pp. 225–26. For general discussions of the term, see Battail, *L'avocat philosophe*, pp. 141–46, and Géraud de Cordemoy, *Oeuvres philosophiques*, ed. P. Clair and F. Girbal (Paris: Presses Universitaires de France, 1968), p. 322, n. 10; for a general discussion of the language of indirect causality in Descartes and the later Scholastics, see Specht, *Commercium mentis et corporis*, chs. II and III.

the cinematic view of God as a cause of motion, the view in which God causes motion by re-creating a body in different places in different instants of time. But the argument is considerably less persuasive if one takes what I earlier called the divine-impulse view of God as a cause of motion. On that view, God causes motion by providing an impulse, much as we take ourselves to move bodies by our own impulses. If this is how God causes motion, then his activity in sustaining bodies is distinct from his activity in causing motion, and there is no reason why there cannot be causes of motion distinct from God.[19]

There *can* be causes of motion for Descartes other than God. But it still remains to be shown that he thought that there *are* such causes. The question comes up quite explicitly in Descartes's last response to Henry More:

> That transference that I call motion is a thing of no less entity than shape is, namely, it is a mode in body. However the force [*vis*] moving a [body] can be that of God conserving as much transference in matter as he placed in it at the first moment of creation or also that of a created substance, like our mind, or something else to which [God] gave the power [*vis*] of moving a body.[20]

Descartes is here quite clear that some created substances, at the very least our minds, have the ability to cause motion. Furthermore, there is no suggestion in this passage that minds can cause motion in bodies only with God's direct help, as the occasionalists would hold. Indeed, our ability to cause motion in the world of bodies is the very model on which we understand how God does it, Descartes sometimes argues. Writing to Henry More in April 1649, he remarks:

> Although I believe that no mode of acting belongs univocally to God and to his creatures, I confess, nevertheless, that I can find no idea in my mind which represents the way in which God or an angel can move matter, which is different from the idea that shows me the way in which I am conscious that I can move my own body through my thought.[21]

It would then be quite strange if Descartes held that minds are only the occasional causes of motion in the world. At least two passages in the

19. This argument is developed at greater length in Garber, "How God Causes Motion."
20. AT V, 403–4 (K 257).
21. AT V, 347 (K 252).

Principles also suggest that he meant to leave open the possibility that, in addition to God, minds could cause motion in the world. In defending the conservation principle, for example, Descartes argues that we should not admit any changes in nature "except for those changes, which evident experience or divine revelation render certain, and which we perceive or believe happen without any change in the creator."[22] Such a proviso would certainly leave open the possibility that finite substances like our minds can be genuine causes of motion. Similarly, in presenting his impact law (law 3) in the *Principles* II.40, Descartes claims that the law covers the causes of all changes that can happen in bodies, "at least those that are corporeal, for we are not now inquiring into whether and how human minds and angels have the power [*vis*] for moving bodies, but we reserve this for our treatise *On Man*."[23] Again, Descartes is leaving open the possibility that there may be incorporeal causes of bodily change, that is to say, motion. And so, I think, we should take him completely at his word when on 29 July 1648 he writes to Arnauld:

> That the mind, which is incorporeal, can set a body in motion is shown to us every day by the most certain and most evident experience, without the need of any reasoning or comparison with anything else.[24]

Minds can cause motion in Descartes's world; there is genuine mind-body causation for him, it would seem. But before going on to examine the last case, that of body-mind causation in sensation, I will pause for a moment and examine a question raised by the passage from the letter to More that we have been examining: What is the "something else to which [God] gave the power [*vis*] of moving a body" to which Descartes refers? Angels are certainly included, the passage from *Principles* II.40 suggests; angels are also a lively topic of conversation in the earlier letters between Descartes and More. Indeed, when Descartes is discussing with him how we can comprehend God as a cause of motion through the way we conceive of ourselves as causes of motion, Descartes explicitly includes angels as creatures also capable of causing motion, like us and like God.[25] It is not *absolutely* impossible that Descartes meant to include bodies among the finite substances that can cause motion.[26] But I think that it is highly

---

22. *Principles of Philosophy* II.36.
23. *Principles of Philosophy* II.40.
24. AT V, 222 (K 235).
25. See AT V, 347 (K 252).
26. P.H.J. Hoenen, "Descartes's Mechanism," in *Descartes*, ed. Willis Doney (New York: Doubleday, Anchor, 1967), pp. 353–68, esp. p. 359, claims that he did include bodies here.

unlikely. If Descartes really thought that bodies could be causes of motion like God, us, and probably angels, I suspect that he would have included them *explicitly* in the answer to More; if bodies could be genuine causes of motion, this would be too important a fact to pass unmentioned. As I noted earlier, Descartes's whole strategy for deriving the laws of motion from the immutability of God presupposes that God is the real cause of motion and of change of motion in the inanimate world of bodies knocking up against one another; this reading of Descartes's view of inanimate motion seems too secure to be shaken on the basis of a possibly oblique remark in a letter.

Before going on to discuss the next case, I will take up one more brief issue. It is a standard view that, for Descartes, mind cannot cause motion in a body because to do so would violate his conservation law, that the total quantity of motion in the world must always remain constant. And so, it is claimed, minds can change the direction with which bodies move but cannot change the actual motion that they have. This is certainly a position that many of Descartes's later followers held. But I see no reason to believe that he himself ever maintained such a view. The argument is a bit complex, and I cannot develop the details here.[27] But briefly, there is no passage in Descartes that suggests in any but the weakest way that he ever held such a position, and there are other passages that strongly suggest that he did not. Furthermore, Descartes's conception of the grounds of the laws of motion in divine immutability would seem to impose no constraint on finite causes of motions, like minds. As I noted earlier, Descartes grounds the laws of motion in God's immutability; because God is immutable, he cannot add or subtract motion from the world. But though the conservation principle may constrain God's activity, it does not in any way constrain ours; in our mutability and imperfection, we are completely free to add or subtract motion from the world.

IV. The Case of Body-Mind Causation

We have established, I think, two reasonably clear cases: for Descartes, God is responsible for all motion in the inanimate world; while in the world of

27. In Daniel Garber, "Mind, Body, and the Laws of Nature in Descartes and Leibniz," *Midwest Studies in Philosophy* 8 (1983): 105–33, I argue that, in fact, the laws of motion that Descartes posits for inanimate nature do not hold for motion caused by minds, and that, in this way, animate bodies, bodies attached to minds, stand outside the world of physics. I argue that the position widely attributed to Descartes, that the mind can change the direction in which a body is moving but not add or subtract speed (thus apparently violating the conservation principle) is not actually his view.

animate creatures, creatures like us who have souls, minds can cause motion in bodies. The last case we have to take care of is that of body-mind causation, the situation in which the motion of a body causes sensations in a mind. Again, our question is this: Is there genuine causality in this circumstance, or must God link the cause to the effect?

Here, unfortunately, I know of no easy way of settling the question about Descartes's views. It seems to me that he should be committed to the position that the body cannot be a genuine cause of sensation in the mind. It seems to me that if the motion of bodies is due directly to God, and if bodies cannot be genuine causes of changes in the states of other bodies, then it would seem to follow that bodies cannot be genuine causes of changes in minds either. This, at least, is the logic of Descartes's position. While, to the best of my knowledge, there is no passage in his writings that settles the question with assurance, there is some reason to believe that this is a view that Descartes may have come to hold by the late 1640s, at least.

The evidence I have in mind is connected with the proof Descartes offers for the existence of a world of bodies. The argument first appears in 1641 in Meditation VI:[28] "Now there is in me a certain passive faculty for sensing, that is, a faculty for receiving and knowing the ideas of sensible things. But I could make no use of it unless a certain active faculty for producing or bringing about those ideas were either in me or in something else." So the argument begins. Descartes's strategy is to show that the active faculty in question is not in me (i.e., my mind), or in God, or in anything but bodies. "This [active faculty] cannot be in me, since it plainly presupposes no intellect, and these ideas are produced without my cooperation, and, indeed, often involuntarily," he writes. "Therefore it remains that it is in some substance different from me. . . . This substance is either body, or corporeal nature, namely, that which contains formally everything which is in the ideas [of bodies] objectively, or it is, indeed, in God, or some other creature nobler than body in which it [i.e., corporeal nature] is contained eminently." To show that bodies really exist, Descartes will eliminate the latter two possibilities, and show that the active faculty must be in bodies themselves, or else God would be a deceiver.

The argument in Meditation VI clearly asserts that bodies have an "active faculty" that corresponds to the "passive faculty" of sensation; the clear implication is that the body that exists in the world is the cause of my

---

28. The quotations below all come from AT VII, 79–80; for fuller treatment of the argument, see Martial Gueroult, *Descartes' Philosophy Interpreted According to the Order of Reasons*, trans. Roger Ariew (Minneapolis: University of Minnesota Press, 1984), vol. II, ch. XIV; Daniel Garber, "*Semel in Vita*: The Scientific Background to Descartes's *Meditations*," in *Essays on Descartes' "Meditations*," ed. Amélie Rorty (Los Angeles and Berkeley: University of California Press, 1986), pp. 104–7.

sensation of it. The same basic argument comes up again, a few years later, in part II, section 1, of the *Principles of Philosophy* of 1644, where it begins as follows:

> Now, it can scarcely be doubted that whatever we sense comes to us from some thing which is distinct from our mind. For it is not in our power to bring it about that we sense one thing rather than another; rather, this [i.e., what we sense] plainly depends upon the very thing that affects our senses.

As in the *Meditations,* Descartes goes on to examine the question as to whether the sensation might proceed from me, from God, or from something other than bodies. Talking about that from which the sensory idea proceeds, he says:

> [W]e clearly understand that thing as something plainly different from God and from us (that is, different from our mind) and also we seem to ourselves clearly to see that its idea comes from things placed outside of us, things to which it [i.e., the idea] is altogether similar, and, as we have already observed, it is plainly repugnant to the nature of God that he be a deceiver.

And so, Descartes concludes, the sensory idea proceeds from a body.

The argument in the *Principles* is obviously similar to the one in the *Meditations.* But there is at least one crucial difference. The argument in Meditation VI starts with the observation that I have "a certain passive faculty for sensing"; what we seek is the active faculty that causes the sensations I have, and the ultimate conclusion is that that active faculty is found in bodies. But, interestingly enough, in the argument of the *Principles* there is no appeal to an active faculty. Indeed, the terminology Descartes uses to describe the relation between our sensation and the body that is the object of that sensation seems studiously noncausal; we all believe, Descartes tells us, that "whatever we sense comes to us [*advenit*] from something which is distinct from our mind," that the idea of body "comes from [*advenire*] things placed outside of us." The concern I have attributed to Descartes here is suggested further by a variant that arises between the Latin version of *Principles* II.1, which we have been discussing, and the French version published three years later in 1647. In the Latin, the crucial phrase reads as follows:

> . . . We seem to ourselves clearly to see that its idea comes from things placed outside of us. . . .[29]

29. *Principles of Philosophy* II.1, Latin version.

In the French translation, the phrase reads:

> . . . it seems to us that the idea we have of it forms itself in us *on the occasion of* bodies from without.[30]

One must, of course, be very careful drawing conclusions from variants between the Latin text and Picot's French translation; while some alternatives are clearly by Descartes, it is often unclear whether a given change is due to the author or to his translator. But this change is consistent with the trend already observed between Meditation VI and *Principles* II.1, Latin version, and weakens the causal implications further still. Rather than asserting that the idea *comes from* the thing, the French text says only that it "forms itself in us on the occasion of bodies from without." Furthermore, while it is by no means clear how to interpret the word *'occasion'* in Descartes's vocabulary, the word is certainly suggestive of what is to become a technical term in later Cartesian vocabulary, that of an occasional cause, a cause whose effect is produced through the activity of God.[31]

It is difficult to say for sure why the two arguments differ in this respect, and one should always be open to the explanation that, as Descartes suggests in a number of places, metaphysical issues are taken up in the *Principles* in a somewhat abbreviated and simplified fashion, and that the *Meditations* must be regarded as the ultimate source for his considered views in that domain.[32] But it is tempting to see in this variation the shadow of an important philosophical question Descartes was facing. It is possible that he eliminated the reference to an active faculty precisely because he was no longer certain that bodies could correctly be described as active causes of our sensations. The language he substitutes is, of course, consistent with bodies being active causes of sensations, as he may well have believed; but it is also consistent with a weaker view, on which our sensations *come from* bodies, but with the help of an agent, like God, distinct from the bodies themselves, which, in the strictest sense, are inert.

There is another place that is sometimes thought to support the attribution of occasionalism to Descartes. The passage I have in mind is the celebrated one from the *Notae in Programma* (1647):

> Nothing reaches our mind from external objects through the sense organs except certain corporeal motions. . . . But neither the motions

---

30. *Principles of Philosophy* II.1, French version; emphasis added.

31. See the reference given in note 18 above in connection with the word *'occasion'*.

32. On the relations between the *Meditations* and Part I of the *Principles*, see, for example, AT III, 233 (K 82), 259; AT V, 291 (K 246); and AT IX-2, 16.

themselves nor the shapes arising from them are conceived by us exactly as they occur in the sense organs, as I have explained at length in my *Dioptrics*. Hence it follows that the very ideas of the motions themselves and of the shape are innate in us. The ideas of pain, colors, sounds, and the like must be all the more innate if, on the occasion of certain corporeal motions, our mind is to be capable of representing them to itself, for there is no similarity between these ideas and the corporeal motions.[33]

The use of the word 'occasion' in this context (as well as in a previous sentence on the same page) does lend some support to the claim that the use of the corresponding French word in the French translation of the *Principles,* published in the same year, is no accident, and may be significant for the way in which Descartes is thinking about body–mind causality. But it is important to recognize that the claim that the sensory idea is innate in the mind is, I think, irrelevant to the issue of Descartes's occasionalism. His worry here is not (primarily) the *causal connection* between the sensory stimulation and the resulting sensory idea; what worries him is their utter *dissimilarity,* the fact that the sensory idea is nothing like the motions that cause it. To make an analogy, consider, for example, a computer with a color monitor capable of displaying complicated graphics and pictures. Suppose that if I tap in a certain sequence of keystrokes, a picture of the Notre Dame in Paris appears on the screen. One might perhaps want to point out that the actual sequence of motions (i.e., the keystrokes) that causally produce the picture in no way "resembles" the picture, and one might infer from that fact to the claim that the picture must be innate in the machine, that is, stored in its memory. But one probably would not want to infer from that that the keystrokes are not in some sense the direct cause of the picture's appearing, that the keystrokes did not really elicit the picture; and one *certainly* would not want to infer that it was God who somehow connected the keyboard with the screen of the monitor. I think that the situation is similar with respect to Descartes's point in the passage quoted from the *Notae in Programma;* in this case, as in the computer case, Descartes's main point is simply that sensory ideas cannot come directly from the motions that cause them, but must, at best, be innate ideas that are elicited by the motions communicated to the brain by the sense organs.

But even though this passage does not lend much support to the view that Descartes may have come to see God as connecting bodily motions with sensations, neither does it detract from the evidence I presented earlier. And so, while the evidence is not altogether satisfactory, it seems reasonable

33. AT VIII-2, 359.

to think that while Descartes may have seen bodies as genuine causes of sensations at the time that the *Meditations* was published in 1641, by the publication of the *Principles of Philosophy* a few years later he may have changed his view, holding something closer to what his occasionalist followers held, that God is the true cause of sensations on the occasion of certain motions in bodies.

V. Was Descartes an Occasionalist?

In the earlier parts of this chapter we have examined three different sorts of causal relations as treated by Descartes in his thought. While it seems clear that mind can be a genuine cause of motion in the physical world, it also seems clear that God is the real cause of change in the inanimate world of physics, and it seems probable that God is the real cause behind body-mind interaction, the causation of sensations in the mind. It thus seems clear that while Descartes may share some doctrines with the later occasionalists of the Cartesian school, he is not an occasionalist, strictly speaking, insofar as he does allow some finite causes into his world, minds at the very least.

Might we say, on this basis, that Descartes is a quasi-occasionalist, an occasionalist when it comes to the inanimate world, though not in the world of bodies connected to minds? The doctrine of occasionalism is certainly flexible enough to allow this. But even if we choose to view Descartes in this way, we must not lose sight of an important difference between Descartes and his occasionalist followers.

For many of Descartes's later followers, what is central to the doctrine of occasionalism is the denial of the efficacy of finite causes simply by virtue of their finitude. Clerselier, for example, argues for occasionalism by first establishing that only an incorporeal substance can cause motion in body. But, he claims, only an infinite substance, like God, can imprint new motion in the world "because the infinite distance there is between nothingness and being can only be surmounted by a power which is actually infinite."[34] Cordemoy argues similarly. Like Clerselier, he maintains that only an incorporeal substance can be the cause of motion in a body, and

---

34. Clerselier, *Lettres de M' Descartes . . . [tome III]*, p. 642. Clerselier argues that while a finite incorporeal substance, like our mind, cannot add (or destroy) motion in the world, it can change its direction, because, unlike motion itself, "the determination of motion . . . adds nothing real in nature . . . and says no more than the motion itself does, which cannot be without determination" (ibid.). This, though, would seem to conflict with what Descartes himself told Clerselier in the letter of 17 February 1645, that motion and determination are two modes of body that "change with equal difficulty" (AT IV, 185).

that this incorporeal substance can only be infinite; he concludes by saying that "our weakness informs us that it is not our mind which makes [a body] move," and so he determines that what imparts motion to bodies and conserves it can only be "another Mind, to which nothing is lacking, [which] does it [i.e., causes motion] through its will."[35] And finally, the infinitude of God is central to the main argument that Malebranche offers for occasionalism in his major work, *De la recherche de la vérité*. The title of the chapter in which he presents his main arguments for the doctrine is "The most dangerous error in the philosophy of the ancients."[36] And the most dangerous error he is referring to is their belief that finite things can be genuine causes of the effects that they appear to produce, an error that, Malebranche claims, causes people to love and fear things other than God in the belief that they are the genuine causes of their happiness or unhappiness.[37] But why is it an error to believe that finite things can be genuine causes? Malebranche argues as follows:

> As I understand it, a true cause is one in which the mind perceives a necessary connection between the cause and its effect. Now, it is only in an infinitely perfect being that one perceives a necessary connection between its will and its effects. Thus God is the only true cause, and only he truly has the power to move bodies. I further say that it is not conceivable that God could communicate to men or angels the power he has to move bodies. . . .[38]

For these occasionalists, then, God must be the cause of motion in the world because only an infinite substance can be a genuine cause of anything at all.

But, as I understand it, Descartes's motivation is quite different. He seems to have no particular worries about finite causes as such. If I am right, he is quite happy to admit our minds and angels as finite causes of motion in the world of bodies. Indeed, it is through our own ability to cause motion in our bodies that we have the understanding we do of God and angels as causes of motion. When God enters as a cause of motion, it is simply to replace a certain set of finite causes, the substantial forms of the Schoolmen, which, Descartes thinks, are unavailable to do the job. He argued that the substantial forms of Scholastic philosophy were improper impositions of mind onto matter and must, as such, be rejected. But, one

35. Cordemoy, *Oeuvres philosophiques*, p. 143.
36. Malebranche, *De la recherche de la vérité* VI.2.iii: OC I, 643; LO 446.
37. OC I, 643–46; LO 446–48.
38. OC I, 649; LO 450.

might ask, if there are no forms, what can account for the motion that bodies have, for their characteristic behavior? What Descartes turns to is God. In this way he seems less a precursor of later occasionalism than the last of the Schoolmen, using God to do what substantial forms did for his teachers.[39]

39. Portions of this essay will also appear in Garber, *Descartes' Metaphysical Physics*.

Eileen O'Neill

Influxus Physicus

There is hardly anyone who does not imagine the Soul as a
little Angel lodged in the brain, where it contemplates the
species which come to it from objects, like so many diverse
little pictures which represent to it all that happens outside.
—Louis de la Forge, *Traité de l'esprit de l'homme*

I. The Problem

Leibniz appears to have originated the tripartite division of "systems" of
change in created substances, which Wolff popularized, and which the

The initial stages of research for this chapter were made possible by a Fellowship for Recent
Recipients of the Ph.D. from the American Council of Learned Societies and by a grant from
the PSC–CUNY Research Award Program of the City University of New York. Final stages
of research were supported by a University of Pennsylvania Mellon Fellowship in the Humanities. I thank Seth Kaster, director of the Rare Books Collection at Union Theological Library,
for making materials available to me. I also thank Elizabeth Beckwith for her invaluable critical
comments on my translations of Latin texts. I am indebted to Alan Gabbey, James Ross, Gary
Hatfield, and Fred Freddoso for helpful suggestions, and to Daniel Garber and Stephen Menn
for detailed comments on an early draft of this chapter.

This essay is dedicated to the memory of my friend Professor Charles Gillespie (1958–1991),
University of Wisconsin–Madison.

The editions frequently cited, in addition to those listed in the front of the book, will be

nineteenth century remembered because of its appearance in the *Critique of Pure Reason*. These three systems include the "hypothesis of occasional causes,"[1] the preestablished harmony,[2] and "the common hypothesis of influx" [*Hypothesis vulgaris influxus*][3] or of "physical influence" [*influence physique*].[4] Most of the essays in this book focus on aspects of occasionalism or the preestablished harmony. This is understandable, since these systems are the innovative responses in early modern philosophy to the system of physical influence.

But what precisely *is* this system that both the occasionalists and Leibniz sought to subvert? And *who* explicitly advocated "the way of influence"? An examination of present-day scholarship on these questions is far from illuminating. To begin with, a critical history of *influxus physicus* has yet to appear.[5] The glosses that scholars have given so far have been based solely on the analysis of a relatively narrow range of texts by Leibniz, Male-

---

abbreviated as follows:

PG   *The Selected Works of Pierre Gassendi*, translated by C. Brush (New York and London: Johnson Reprint, 1972).

RB   *Roger Bacon's Philosophy of Nature*, edited and translated by D. Lindberg (Oxford: Oxford University Press, 1983).

SCG   *Saint Thomas Aquinas: Summa Contra Gentiles*, translated by Pegis et al. (Notre Dame, Ind.: University of Notre Dame Press, 1975).

ST   *St. Thomas Aquinas: Summa Theologica*, translated by the Fathers of the English Dominican Province (New York: Benziger, 1947).

V   *Francisco Suarez: Opera Omnia*, edited by L. Vives (Paris, 1856–78).

Except for material from the English-language editions listed here and in the front of the book, the translations used in this chapter are my own, unless otherwise noted.

1. L 269(C 521); L 338(G II 58); L 457(G IV 483); L 494(G IV 520). This system is also known as the "way of assistance" L 460(G IV 499).

2. This system is also termed "the hypothesis of agreement" L 458(G IV 485); L 494(G IV 520), "the hypothesis of concomitance" L 269(C 521); L 338(G II 58), and "the hypothesis of the correspondence of substances" L 338(G II 580).

3. L 269(C 521).

4. NE 135(G V 123); H 155(G VI 135). Leibniz also refers to this as the "way of influence" L 460(G IV 498); L 494(G IV 520); L 574(G IV 554), the "hypothesis of impression" L 338(G II 58), and the view of the "transmission of species or qualities" L 457(G IV 484).

5. Alan Gabbey is one of the few scholars who has noted our lack of understanding regarding the notion of "influx" and the importance of clarifying this notion if we are to understand divine causation in the work of Descartes. See his "Force and Inertia in the Seventeenth Century: Descartes and Newton," in *Descartes: Philosophy, Mathematics, and Physics*, ed. Stephen Gaukroger (Sussex: Harvester Press, 1980), p. 301, n. 31. See also the helpful contribution by Leo Sweeney, S.J., in "*Esse Primum Creatum*, in Albert the Great's *Liber de Causis et Processu Universitatis*," *The Thomist* 44 (1980): 609–13, where the notion of "influx" in the Neoplatonic-Aristotelian work of Albertus Magnus is discussed at some length. Finally, Allison Laywine has some very useful material in manuscript on *influxus physicus* in the period from Leibniz to Kant.

branche, and select "Cartesians." These texts, however, have not proven decisive, as is evident in the wildly different interpretations of the system that able scholars have proposed in recent years. To wit, some have read it as "causal interactionism," and a subset of these have pictured interaction through a "transference model." All of the aforementioned have viewed it as obvious that Leibniz attributed the system of physical influence to Descartes.[6]

Other commentators target an unspecified group of "Scholastics" as the proponents of the system.[7] Some of these scholars maintain that Leibniz included Descartes among those who opted instead for occasionalism.[8] Finally, there are those who suggest that the "common hypothesis" was the position of the atomists.[9]

My aim here is to reconstruct what Leibniz meant by the term *'influxus physicus'* by providing the groundwork for a history of the system. With something of its genealogy in hand, I believe that we shall be in a better position to appreciate what Leibniz and the occasionalists saw themselves as standing in opposition to.

Tracing the history of physical influx and its proponents has seemed to me not unlike chronicling the adventures of the Rosicrucian fraternity. Clues for decoding the system are seemingly everywhere, but avowed adherents are nowhere to be found. In what follows, I shall argue that the solution to this puzzle is that Leibniz is the originator of the system of *influxus physicus*.

Leibniz may have gotten the name for the system from Daniel Stahl, a colleague of Leibniz's teacher Jacob Thomasius, who, in 1662, had defined 'physical cause' [*causa physica*] as "any efficient cause, related to the effect, into which the cause produces a true influx [*influxum*]."[10] Or it is possible

6. See Daisie Radner, "Is There a Problem of Cartesian Interaction?" *Journal of the History of Philosophy* 23 (1985): 35–49, and Joseph Gredt, O.S.B., *Elementa Philosophiae Aristotelico-Thomisticae* (Freiburg, 1937), vol. 1, p. 413. T. E. Wilkerson, in *Kant's "Critique of Pure Reason": A Commentary for Students* (Oxford: Oxford University Press, 1976), pp. 107–8, also equates "physical influence" with "causal interaction," and reads Kant's criticism of this view as directed at Descartes.

7. See Stuart Brown, *Leibniz* (Minneapolis: University of Minnesota Press, 1984), pp. 32–33, and Hide Ishiguro, "Pre-Established Harmony versus Constant Conjunction: A Reconsideration of the Distinction between Rationalism and Empiricism," in *Rationalism, Empiricism, and Idealism*, ed. Anthony Kenny (Oxford: Oxford University Press, 1986), pp. 65–66.

8. See Peter Machamer, "The Harmonies of Descartes and Leibniz," *Midwest Studies in Philosophy* 8 (1983): 135–42.

9. See *Leibniz: The "Monadology" and Other Philosophical Writings*, ed. Robert Latta (London: Oxford University Press, 1971), pp. 42–43, 219, n. 10.

10. Daniel Stahl, *Regulae Philosophicae explicatae & Orationes aliquot* (1662), Part II, § 9, of "Theses Concerning Efficient Cause and Some of Its Distinctions," pp. 576–90.

that he got the name from Suarez, who may well have been its originator. I want to stress, however, that although '*influxus*' appears throughout Suarez's endless discussions of 'cause', and in countless discussions of 'cause' after Suarez, the only place where I have found mention of '*influxus physicus*' is in an extremely brief passage in his *Metaphysical Disputations*:

> Physical cause in this case is not taken for corporeal or natural cause, acting by means of a corporeal or material motion, but it is taken more universally for a cause truly and really inflowing into an effect; for just as we said above that 'nature' sometimes signifies any essence, so *influxus physicus* sometimes is called 'that which happens by means of a true and real causality, essentially and per se'. And in this way, even God is the physical cause while he creates, and an angel, when it brings about motion either in the heavens or also in itself, and the intellect, when it brings about understanding, and the will, [when it brings about] volition, and so on for other cases.[11]

In 1658, Gassendi had held that a "real" or "physical action" on a body was one where the cause "influenced" the body. He glossed this influence on the body in terms of touching, taking hold, overpowering, moving, and impelling.[12] But Gassendi's corpuscular influx model is obviously going to be quite different from any picture Suarez may have of how the intellect brings about understanding. Our question, then, is this: Which influx model, or which elements of distinct models, did Leibniz have in mind when he spoke of the system of physical influence? Let us begin by examining the range of influx models with which Leibniz would have been familiar.

The first such model is that of astrological influx. I shall give a cursory treatment of it, since, for our purposes, I think that it is something of a red herring. In rule 9 of the *Regulae*, when Descartes is considering whether a natural power [*potentia*] can pass instantaneously to a distant point, he says,

> I shall not immediately turn my attention to the magnetic force, or the influence of the stars [*astrorum influxus*], or even to the speed of light . . . for I would find it more difficult to settle that sort of question than the one at issue.[13]

The reference here is to an influx model from the astrological and alchemical traditions. These traditions attributed the formation of metals, the sponta-

11. Francisco Suarez, *Disputationes Metaphysicae*, Disp. XVII, section II, 6.
12. Pierre Gassendi, *Syntagma*, "Physics," section 1, book 4, in PG 414.
13. CSM I 34, AT X 402. See Gabbey, "Force and Inertia," p. 301, n. 31.

neous generation of "lower" forms of animal life, the generation of plants and "higher" animals, magnetism, the tides, and the course of a disease to the motion, light, and "influence" [*influentia*] of the celestial bodies. This influence was described by the fourteenth-century Parisian astronomer Themon Judaeus as "a certain quality, or virtue, diffused through the whole world, just as the species of heat or light is multiplied."[14]

But we need not detain ourselves in trying to separate the distinct strands of Aristotelian cosmology, Neoplatonism, hermeticism, cabbalism, and natural magic that seem to have contributed to this astrological picture of natural change; nor is it crucial for us to produce the major features of this model. At least as early as the sixteenth century, the influx of the celestial bodies was distinguished from the broader class of "influx of causes." Thus, in a medical treatise of about 1520, Paracelsus tells us that

> [t]he *entia*, the active principles or influences, which govern our bodies and do violence to them are the following. The stars have a force and efficacy that has power over our body. . . . This virtue of the stars is called *ens astrorum*, and it is the first *ens* to which we are subjected.[15]

But aside from the astral *ens*, Paracelsus claims that there is also the influence of poison, the influence of our natural constitution [*ens naturale*], spiritual influence, and the influence of God. This distinction between the notion of purely "astral influence" and the broader notion of an "influx of causes or causal factors" continues to be made throughout the seventeenth and eighteenth centuries. For instance, in their respective lexicons, Micraelius (1653) distinguishes the occult *influentia* of the stars from the *influxus* of a cause, and Chauvin (1692) gives separate entries for 'the *influxus* of a cause' and 'the *influxus* of the stars'.[16]

When Leibniz proposes *influxus physicus* as an overall system of natural change, he surely is using 'influxus' in its broader signification, and is not

---

14. *Questions on the Meteors*, Bk. 1, question 1, fol. 155v, in *L'Oeuvre Astronomique de Themon Juif*, ed. Henri Hugonnard-Roche (Geneva, 1973); English translation in Edward Grant, *Studies in Medieval Science and Natural Philosophy* (London: Variorum Reprints, 1981), p. 290.

15. *Paracelsus, Sämtliche Werke*, ed. Sudhoff (Munich: R. Oldenbourg, 1922–33), Part I, vol. I, pp. 216–17; English translation in *Paracelsus: Selected Writings*, ed. Jacobi (New York: Pantheon, 1958), pp. 75–76. See also *Sämtliche Werke*, Part I, vol. I, pp. 202–3; Jacobi, *Paracelsus*, p. 40: "Two influences operate in man. One is that of the firmamental light. . . . The second influence emanates from matter."

16. Johannes Micraelius, *Lexicon Philosophicum Terminorum Philosophis Usitatorum* (Jena, 1653); reprint in (Düsseldorf: Stern-Verlag Janssen, 1966), p. 619; Stephan Chauvin, *Lexicon Philosophicum* (Rotterdam, 1692); reprint in (Düsseldorf: Janssen, 1967), p. 318.

suggesting a purely astrological picture of such change. So, I propose that we examine the range of influx models of causation in general, which would have been available to Leibniz.

II. Neoplatonic Model

Neoplatonic influx models go back at least as far as Plotinus's doctrine of emanation. According to this doctrine, all being proceeds from the overflow of the essence of the One, into Intellect, then into Soul, and successively into all the levels of being, in much the same way as light flows from the sun.

> The visible universe, then, is properly called an image always in process of being made. . . . As long as Intellect and Soul exist, the forming principles will flow into this lower form of soul, just as, as long as the sun exists, all its rays will shine from it.[17]

I want to suggest that three of the four main elements of the Neoplatonic influx model are implicit in this passage from the *Enneads*:

1. *What flows is distinct from the substance of the agent; it is a likeness or replica,* or, as Plotinus calls it, an "image."

2. *Influx is from the more perfect to the less perfect*, that is, from higher things like Intellect and Soul to the lower form of soul.

3. *The effect brought about by the influx is coexistent with the activity of the agent,* as in the case where the light of the rays lasts just so long as the sun shines.

The final element of this influx model is clear in this passage from the *Elements of Theology* of Proclus, where he argues that all beings imitate the One insofar as

> every producer remains as it is, and its consequent proceeds from it without change in its steadfastness. . . . For the product is not a parcelling-out of the producer: that is not a character[istic] even of physical generation or generative causes. Thus the engenderer is established beyond alteration or diminution, multiplying itself in

17. Plotinus, *Enneads*, ed. A. H. Armstrong (Cambridge, Mass.: Harvard University Press, 1979), II, 3, 18: vol. II, p. 101.

virtue of its generative potency and furnishing from itself secondary substances.[18]

The final element, then, is this:

4. *The agent is in no way diminished in the act of inflowing; it loses nothing of its virtue, power, or essence.*

This Neoplatonic tradition, which would play such a central role in the development of Western causal concepts, was widespread in Arabic philosophy. For example, as David Lindberg has shown, Avicebron, in the *Fons Vitae*, utilizes the model of emanative influx in his account of the *metaphysical* action of one simple substance (a separate intelligence) on another. And al-Kindi, in *De Radiis*, uses the model to picture natural change in the purely corporeal realm, as in the transmission of heat by fire and the phenomenon of magnetic attraction.[19]

In the Latin West, the extremely influential *Liber de Causis* and some of the many commentaries on this book, like the *Liber de Causis et Processu Universitatis* of Albertus Magnus, also make use of the Neoplatonic influx model. By the seventeenth century, the Cambridge Platonists, among others, utilize the emanative influx model to picture how a spiritual force, originating in God, inflows into the descending orders of being and is eventually infused into, and vitally united with, matter. Henry More, with his "Spirit of Nature," and Ralph Cudworth, with his "Plastic Nature," seek to replace the purely mechanical picture of natural change with a model of vital matter, that is, matter infused with spirit. Nathanael Culverwel uses the model in his account of the generation and maintenance of human reason (the "Candle of the Lord"). These early modern Platonists explicitly endorse the four features of the emanative influx model, as do their medieval predecessors. The model and the textual support for each of its features are as follows:

1. *What flows is distinct from the substance of the agent; it is a likeness or replica.*
Albertus Magnus, *Liber de Causis et Processu Universitatis* (1270), I.4.2:
> Only that flows which is of a single likeness [*formae*] in the flowing agent and in that in which the influx is made.

Liber de Causis, III, § 27–31:
> Every noble soul has three operations: a vital operation, an intellectual operation, and a divine operation. . . . And the soul performs

---

18. Proclus, *The Elements of Theology*, ed. and trans. E. R. Dodds (Oxford: Clarendon Press, 1963), pp. 31–33; reprinted in RB xliii.

19. RB xliv–xlv; xlvi–xlviii.

these operations only because it is itself an example of the higher power.[20]

Henry More, *The Immortality of the Soul*, Bk. III, Ch. XVI, 8:

[The Soul] may be said to be a Ray of Him, as the rest of the Creation also; but in no other sense that I know of, unless of likeness and similitude, she being the Image of God, as the Rays of Light are of the Sun.

2. *Influx is from the more perfect to the less perfect.*

Liber de Causis, IX, §99:

Everything receives what is above it . . .

Liber de Causis, XXII, §173:

And, just as God, the blessed and most high, overflows perfections upon things, similarly Intelligence overflows knowledge upon the things that are under it.[21]

Ralph Cudworth, *The True Intellectual System of the Universe* (1678):

In the things Generated from Eternity, or Produced by way of natural Emanation, there is no progress upwards, but all Downwards, and still a Gradual Descent into Greater Multiplicity. . . . 'That which is Generated or Emaneth, immediately from the First and Highest Being, is not the very same thing with it, as if it were nothing but that Repeated again and Ingeminated; and as it is not the same, so neither can it be Better than it.' (Plotinus, *Enneads*, 5, Bk. 3, Ch. 15). From whence it follows, that it must needs be Gradually Subordinate and Inferiour to it.[22]

3. *The effect brought about by the influx is coexistent with the activity of the agent.*

Liber de Causis, XXV, §188:

The First Cause does not cease illuminating its effect.[23]

Albertus Magnus, *Liber de Causis et Processu Universitatis*, I.4.2:

A flux is always in becoming.

Henry More, *The Immortality of the Soul*, Bk. I, Ch. VI, 2:

An Emanative Effect is coexistent with the very substance of that which is said to be the Cause thereof. This must needs be true,

20. *The Book of Causes [Liber de Causis]*, trans. Brand (Milwaukee, Wis.: Marquette University Press, 1984), p. 21.

21. Ibid., pp. 29, 38.

22. Ralph Cudworth, *The True Intellectual System of the Universe* (London, 1678); facsimile reprint (1964), p. 581.

23. *The Book of Causes [Liber de Causis]*, p. 24.

because that very Substance which is said to be the Cause, is the adequate and immediate Cause, and wants nothing to be adjoined to its bare essence for the production of the Effect; and therefore by the same reason the Effect is at any time, it must be at all times, or so long as that Substance does exist.[24]

4. *The agent is in no way diminished in the act of inflowing; it loses nothing of its virtue, power, or essence.*

Liber de Causis, XIX, §155–56:

The First Cause governs all things without intermingling with them. This is because its governance does not weaken or destroy its unity, which is exalted above everything. . . .[25]

Nathanael Culverwel, *An Elegant and Learned Discourse of the Light of Nature* (1652):

The soul . . . was not framed and carv'd out of the essence of a Deity, but rather sprung from the dilatation, and diffusion of his power and goodnesse, as beams from the Sun. . . . [Y]ou must neither imagine that there is the least division, or diminution, or variation in the most immutable essence of God; nor that the creature does partake the very essence of the Creatour, but that it hath somewhat of his workmanship, obvious and visible in it, and according to the degree of its being, doth give fainter or brighter resemblances of its Creatour.[26]

In his "Considerations on Vital Principles and Plastic Natures" (1705), Leibniz describes these "celebrated authors who by their vital principles and plastic natures have occasioned the present controversy" as those who "believed that souls have an influence on bodies."[27] Leibniz obviously had More, Cudworth, and other Platonists in mind. I suggest that the Neoplatonic influx model, as I have characterized it, plays a central role in Leibniz's construction of *influxus physicus*. But we need to look at the other influx models, with which Leibniz would have been familiar, to be able to see precisely what that role is.

24. Compare Cudworth's discussion of the "essential dependence" of a recipient on an agent in *The True Intellectual System*, pp. 172, 888.

25. *The Book of Causes* [*Liber de Causis*], p. 35.

26. Nathanael Culverwel, *An Elegant and Learned Discourse of the Light of Nature* (London, 1652); facsimile reprint (1978), pp. 100–101. Compare Albertus Magnus, *Liber de Causis et Processu Universitatis*, I.4.2.

27. L 586–87 (G VI 539 ff.).

III. Scholastic Model

It is clear that the Scholastic influx model, as we find it in Saint Thomas Aquinas, derives in part from the Neoplatonic influx model, which I just examined:

1. *What flows is distinct from the substance of the agent; it is a likeness or replica.*
Summa Contra Gentiles, II, ch. 6, 6:
> God wills to communicate His being to other things by way of likeness.

Summa Contra Gentiles, II, ch. 85, 14–15:
> Some wished to infer that the soul is of the very nature of God. . . . But the likeness in question is no proof that man is a part of the divine substance, for man's understanding suffers from many defects—which cannot be said of God's. This likeness, then, is rather indicative of a certain imperfect image than of any consubstantiality.

2. *Influx is from the more perfect to the less perfect.*
Quaestiones Quodlibetales, III, Art. VII:
> Whence, the more superior angels are able to act on inferior angels and on our souls . . . and an action of this kind is called 'influx'.[28]

3. *The effect brought about by the influx is coexistent with the activity of the agent.*
Summa Contra Gentiles, III, Pt. 1, ch. 65, 7:
> Now, whatever belongs to the nature of a higher type of being does not last at all after the action of the agent; light, for instance, does not continue in a diaphanous body when the source of light has gone away. Now, *to be* is not the nature or essence of any created thing, but only of God. . . . Therefore, no thing can remain in being if divine operation cease.

Summa Contra Gentiles, II, ch. 67, 3:
> [God] has not merely granted operative powers to [things] when they were originally created, but He always causes these powers in things. Hence if this divine influence [*influentia*] were to cease, every operation would cease.

4. *The agent is in no way diminished in the act of inflowing; it loses nothing of its virtue, power, or essence.*

---

28. Cf. ST, Pt. I, Q. 84, Art. 6, where this general causal condition is stated: "The agent is more noble than the patient."

Summa Contra Gentiles, III. Pt. 1, ch. 69, 12:
> God is not changed by the fact that He operates in different things.

Summa Contra Gentiles, II, ch. 85, 6:
> In God there is absolutely no variation, either through himself, or by accident.

But the model also adds these three further elements:

5. *Influx does not take place through a contact of surfaces.*
Summa Contra Gentiles, Bk. II, ch. 56, 8–9:
> If there are any agents not in contact by their quantitative extremities, they nevertheless will be said to touch, so far as they act. . . . For intellectual substances, being immaterial and enjoying a higher degree of actuality than bodies, act on the latter and move them. This, however, is not contact of quantity, but of power.

6. *There is no time at which influx takes place.*
Summa Contra Gentiles, Bk. III, Pt. I, ch. 65, 8:
> If things have eternally emanated [*effluerunt*] from God, we cannot give a time or instant at which they first flowed forth from God.

Quaestiones Quodlibetales, III, Art. VI:
> Actions of this kind [i.e., influx] are beyond place and time, which are in corporeals.

7. *There is no locus of influx.*
Quaestiones Quodlibetales, III, Art. VII:
> Moreover, what is position in the case of bodies is order in the case of spirits; for position is a certain order of corporeal parts in conformity with location; and for that reason, the order itself of spiritual substances is, in turn, sufficient for this: that one [substance] inflow [*influat*] into the other, and it does not there require a corporeal or local medium. . . .

Leibniz most frequently mentions the "Scholastic philosophers" and "Peripatetics" when speaking of those who support the system of *influxus physicus*.[29] But there is a problem. There do not seem to be any prominent Schoolmen who used this Scholastic influx model to account for such things as sensation or purely corporeal change. It would be hard to see how they could, given features 5 through 7. The model only seems to have been

---

29. H 155(G VI 135); L 586(G VI 540); L 575(G IV 554); L 494(G IV 520).

used to picture how God or the higher intelligences could act on lower beings.

St. Thomas has a completely different picture for natural change. On the Aristotelian–Scholastic influx model, the activity of the agent passes over to the recipient: act comes out of act. But the Scholastics believed that natural change was a process of act coming to be out of potency. In other words, nothing passes over to the recipient. A body brings about a change in another body, or in a substantially united composite of body and soul, by educing it out of the patient's own potentiality. As St. Thomas puts it: "A natural agent does not hand over its own form to another subject, but it reduces the passive subject from potency to act."[30] For this reason, St. Thomas is at pains to set his picture of how we come to have knowledge of sensible things in opposition to the views that he attributes to Avicenna, on the one hand, and Democritus, on the other. He rejects the atomistic influx model (which I shall sketch in a moment) as a picture of how the sensible species are produced in us:

> The operations of the sensitive part [of the soul] are caused by the impression of the sensible on the sense: not by a discharge [per modum defluxionis], as Democritus said, but by some kind of operation. For Democritus claimed that every operation [actionem] is by way of an influx [influxionem] of atoms. . . .[31]

And St. Thomas rejects Avicenna's Neoplatonic emanative influx model, especially insofar as it is used to account for the production of intelligible species:

> Avicenna maintained that all substantial forms flow forth [effluere] from the agent intellect.[32]

> In accord with what [Avicenna] says about the generation of natural things . . . he asserts that the actions of all lower agents have merely the effect of preparing matter to receive the forms which flow into their matters from the separate agent intellect. So, too, for the same reason, he holds that the phantasms prepare the possible intellect, and that the intelligible forms emanate from a separate substance . . . [a] position contrary to the judgment expressed by Aristotle in Metaphysics VII. . . . For the human soul would seem to be not less

30. SCG III, Pt. 1, ch. 69, 28.
31. ST Pt. 1, Q. 84, Art. 6.
32. SCG III, Pt. 1, ch. 69, 4.

perfectly fitted for understanding than the lower things of nature for their proper operations.[33]

In short, St. Thomas simply does not use any of the available influx models to account for natural change, and he explicitly pits his "natural eduction out potentiality" model against them.

If St. Thomas and his followers are not the "influxionists" Leibniz has in mind, then whom is he targeting? Perhaps Suarez. After all, Suarez seems to have coined the term 'influxus physicus', and as early as 1670 Leibniz had stated in print:

> Whether terms are popular or technical, they ought to involve either no figures of speech or few and apt ones. Of this the Scholastics have taken little notice, for . . . their speech abounds with figures. What else are such terms as 'to depend', 'to inhere', 'to emanate', and 'to inflow'? On the invention of the last word Suarez prides himself not a little. . . . [H]e defined 'cause' as 'what flows being into something else', a most barbarous and obscure expression. . . . [T]his 'influx' is metaphorical and more obscure than what it defines.[34]

But notice that Leibniz's point here is not that Suarez's influx model is the wrong model for natural change. He is annoyed with the use of the *term* 'influx'; he seems to be suggesting that it is a figure of speech that could give people the impression that they actually had a causal model in mind, when, in fact, their ideas were completely obscure.

If this is Leibniz's point, I have to confess that I am quite sympathetic with his view. Any attempt to set out the main features of an influx model at work in Suarez's *Metaphysical Disputations* appear to be undercut by Suarez's remarks to the effect that he is not proposing a new model at all. He frequently suggests that his use of the term 'inflow' *is just* a figure of speech, and that causality is still to be thought of in terms of such standard models as those of "dependency," "participation," and the "communication" of perfections. Here is Suarez, in this vein, in the passage just following the definition that Leibniz quotes:

> However, the word 'inflow' ought not to be taken strictly . . . but more generally as equivalent to the verb 'to give', or 'to communicate being to another.'[35]

33. SCG II, ch. 76, 11.
34. L 126 (G IV 148).
35. Suarez, *Disputationes Metaphysicae*, Disp. XII, section II, 4.

A few paragraphs later he adds:

> I said that the cause is what inflows being into another; for with these words the same thing is revealed which is introduced in the verb 'to depend'. . . .[36]

Incidentally, in the seventeenth-century philosophical lexicons it was standard practice to explicitly mark as metaphorical the use of the term 'inflow' to characterize a cause.[37]

Moreover, once we move from Suarez's attempts at providing a unified definition of the four Aristotelian causes and turn to his own discussions of natural change, it is clear that he does not explicitly make use of an influx model. Following St. Thomas, he opts instead for a "natural eduction out potentiality" model. For example, in his *De Anima*, Suarez explicitly rejects an influx model to account for the production of our knowledge of sensible things:

> The determination [of the agent intellect by the phantasm] does not happen through some influx [*per influxum*] of the phantasm itself, but by furnishing the matter and, as it were, the exemplar for the agent intellect, from the power of the union which they have in the same soul.[38]

We are left, then, with this question: Why did Leibniz characterize the Scholastics as having an influx model for all natural changes? I shall return to this problem and propose a solution after we have completed our survey of influx models.

IV. Atomistic-Corpuscular Model

At this point in our examination, we have discovered one general influx model for all natural changes: the Neoplatonic model. It can be characterized as one of *replicative* influx: something is transmitted to the recipient, but what is transmitted is not in any way a part of the agent, but is rather a

---

36. Ibid., 7.

37. See, for example, the lexicon of Micraelius, *Lexicon Philosophicum . . .* , p. 620, and Rodolphus Goclenius, *Lexicon Philosophicum, Quo Tanquam Clave Philosophiae Fores Aperiuntur* (Frankfurt, 1613), p. 238.

38. *De Anima*, "De Potentia Intellectiva," Bk. IV, Ch. II.

likeness or replica of it. However, Roger Bacon, in *The Multiplication of Species* (1250–60), gives us quite a different characterization of an influx model of natural change. He tells us that such a model has two main features. First, it requires the continuous activity of the agent.[39] This, as we have seen, is a feature of Neoplatonic influx. Second, what is transmitted in an influx must either be an accident or a piece of the substance of the agent.[40] And since accidents must always inhere in a substance, this second requirement entails that what is transmitted in an influx is "continuous with the substance of the agent."[41] This second requirement is clearly *not* a feature of Neoplatonic influx.

I believe that the model which Bacon has described is, in fact, the atomistic–corpuscular influx model. This model, which was introduced by the ancient atomists, was the model of natural change used by seventeenth-century corpuscularians like Gassendi, Charleton, and Boyle to account for magnetic attraction and for the attractive force of static electrical materials like wax and amber. And it was used by a wide range of philosophers to account for the production in us of sensation. For example, the first feature of this model—the requirement for the continuous activity of the agent—is exemplified in Kenelme Digby's account:

> There is a perpetuall fluxe of litle partes or atomes out of all sensible bodies that . . . can not choose but gett in at the dores of our bodies, and mingle themselves with the spirits that are in our nerves. . . .[42]

The second feature, namely, that what flows must be continuous with the substance of the agent, is clear in John Sergeant's claim:

> Those *Effluviums* sent out from Bodies, have the *very Natures* of those Bodies in them, or rather are themselves Lesser Bodies of the *Self-Same* Nature, (as the smallest imperceptible parts of Bread and Flesh, are truly Bread and Flesh).[43]

A more detailed sketch of the atomistic–corpuscular influx model, with textual support, is as follows:

39. RB 257.
40. RB 45.
41. RB 257.
42. Kenelme Digby, *Two Treatises* (Paris, 1644); facsimile reprint (1978), p. 278.
43. John Sergeant, *Solid Philosophy Asserted, Against the Fancies of the Ideists* . . . (London, 1697); facsimile reprint (1984), p. 69.

1a. *The efflux is* not *distinct from the substance of the agent; it is a substantial effluxion direpted from the surface of a compound body.*
Walter Charleton, *Physiologia Epicuro-Gassendo-Charltoniana* (1654):
> Species . . . are direpted from the extreams of solid bodies.

> Witness only one, and the noblest of senses, the Sight: which discerns the exterior forms of objects, by the reception . . . of certain Substantial, or Corporeal Emanations. . . .[44]

1b. *The efflux from an agent bears an analogy or likeness to this body.*
Walter Charleton, *Physiologia*:
> In the University of Nature are certain most tenuious Concretions, or subtle Contextures, holding an exquisite analogy to solid bodies.[45]

3. *The effect brought about by the efflux is coexistent with the activity of the agent.*
Walter Charleton, *Physiologia*:
> If the object be removed, or eclipsed by the interposition of any opace body, sufficiently dense and crass to terminate them, the Images thereof immediately disappear. . . .

> Material is emitted from the Loadstone to Iron, which by continuity may Attract it.

> The attraction of all electrics is performed by the mediation of swarms of subtle Emanations, or Continued Rayes of exile particles. . . .[46]
Pierre Gassendi, *De Motu* (1642):

44. Walter Charleton, *Physiologia Epicuro-Gassendo-Charltoniana* (London, 1654); facsimile reprint (1966), pp. 137, 136.
45. Ibid., p. 137.
46. Ibid., pp. 344–45. I originally formulated this feature as "The efflux from a body is coexistent with the activity of the agent." Steven Nadler rightly pointed out that this is simply not a feature of the atomistic-corpuscularian model—at least according to Charleton. I have reformulated the feature, although I am not sure Nadler would accept this version.
  Charleton does say, "If the object be removed . . . the images thereof immediately disappear" [*Physiologia*, p. 138]. So the *effect* of the efflux, namely, the images, requires the continuous activity of the agent. But it is also clear that the material *effluvia* can continue to exist even when the continuous efflux stops (i.e., when the agent is no longer active):
> And the reason, why by the mediation of a small remainder of light, after the intersection of its fluor from the Lucid fountain, we have an imperfect and obscure discernment of objects; is no more then this: that only a few rayes, here and there one, are incident upon and so reflected from the superfice therof, having touched upon only a few scattered particles, and left the greater number untoucht; which therefore remain unperceived by the eye, because there wanted Light sufficient to the illustration of the whole, and so to the Excitement and Emission of a perfect species. [*Physiologia*, p. 145]

Because [corpuscles] are emitted continuously, these magnetic rays can be imagined better than the other conjectures as maintaining the rigidity of a tiny rod or at least of tight cables. . . .[47]

4. *The agent is in some way diminished in the production of the efflux.*
Walter Charleton, *Physiologia*:
> That a continual Efflux of substance must minorate the Quantity of the most solid visible . . . by the continual perdition of so many particles. . . . [is] solved by two reasons: (1) the decay is prevented by the apposition and accretion of other minute particles succeeding into the rooms of the effluxed; . . . (2) the tenuity of these Emanent Images is Extreme; and therefore the uninterrupted Emission of them . . . can introduce no sensible . . . minoration of Quantity.[48]

5. *All natural changes* require *the contact of surfaces between the agent and the recipient.*
Walter Charleton, *Physiologia*:
> No cause can act but by Motion. . . . [N]o body can move another, but by contact Mediate or Immediate, i.e. by the mediation of some continued organ, and that a Corporeal one too, or by itself alone.[49]

6. *The efflux from a body takes place over time.*
Walter Charleton, *Physiologia*:
> We conceive it impossible that any Moveable should be transferred to a distant place, in an indivisible moment, but in some space of time, though so short as to be imperceptible; because the Medium hath parts so successively ranged, that the remote cannot be pervaded before the vicine.[50]

7. *The efflux from a body has spatial location.*
Walter Charleton, *Physiologia*:
> Those Images, which are direpted from the extreams of solid bodies, do conserve in their separated state the same order and position of parts, that they had during their united.[51]

---

47. PG 133–34.
48. Charleton, *Physiologia*, pp. 140–41.
49. Ibid., p. 343. Cf. Pierre Gassendi, *De Motu*, in PG 132; *Syntagma*, "Physics," Section I, Book IV, Chapter 8, in PG 412–14.
50. Charleton, *Physiologia*, p. 144.
51. Charleton, *Physiologia*, p. 137. Cf. Robert Boyle, *Origin of Forms and Qualities*, in *Selected Philosophical Papers of Robert Boyle*, ed. Stewart (Manchester: Manchester University Press, 1979), p. 51: "When divers [minute particles of bodies] are considered together, there will

8. *The efflux from a body brings about change in the recipient precisely by an incursion into the recipient body.*

Walter Charleton, *Physiologia*:

> The Act of Vision . . . cannot be conceived to be effected otherwise then by an Impression; nor that Impression be conceived to be made, but by way of Incursion of the Image . . .[52]

Pierre Gassendi, *De Motu*:

> Magnetic rays . . . , when they strike iron, penetrate . . . wherever there are little pores and apertures, but one penetrates directly . . .[53]

Notice, by the way, that this is *not* the model used by the corpuscularians to account for the linear motion imparted to a body by a moving body. Among the ways that their model for that type of change differs from the model before us is in the rejection of feature 3. For the corpuscularians, linear motion is an effect that *can* endure *without* the continuous activity of the agent.

We now have two general influx models of natural change that Leibniz may have been considering in his construction of *influxus physicus*: a Neoplatonic model and a corpuscular model.[54] According to both, natural change

---

necessarily follow here below both a certain position or posture in reference to the horizon . . . , and a certain order or placing before or behind or besides one another. . . . And indeed these several kinds of location (to borrow a scholastic term), [are] attributed . . . to the minute particles of bodies."

52. Charleton, *Physiologia*, p. 152.

53. PG 134.

54. In response to this essay, Richard Watson suggested that an important influx model (possibly the "Ur" influx model) was missing from my presentation—namely, one from biology.

There is, indeed, another causal model, according to which natural change results from something flowing from the agent into the recipient of change: the contagion model. While the term 'contagion' originally referred to the communication of disease by direct contact, Girolamo Fracastoro (a classmate of Copernicus at the University of Padua) in his *De Contagionibus* (1546) distinguished three ways in which a contagious disease could be transmitted: (1) by direct contact; (2) by the influx of "effluvia" from intermediaries, like garments; and (3) by infection at a distance. As a proto-corpuscularian, Fracastoro believed that causality generally requires contact. Thus, he postulated a rudimentary theory of germs, or *seminaria*— seeds that propagate themselves and that help to explain how (2) is possible. But in his explanation of infection at a distance, as well as of magnetic attraction, he allowed for spiritual effluvia. Thus, he acknowledged a contagion model of causality according to which the patient who will undergo natural change receives inflowings from the cause, without any direct or indirect material contact.

Giambattista della Porta, in his *Natural Magick* (London, 1658) used the contagion model to account for such disparate cases of causation as the production of magnetic attraction and the influence of the very sight of our companions on our character: "Some natural things have not only such properties in themselves, but they are apt also to communicate them to others. A

results from something flowing from the agent into the recipient of change. The models share two main features: what flows bears a likeness or analogy to the agent, and the existence of the effect, brought about by the flux, requires the continuous activity of the agent. The most important difference between the models concerns the ontological status of what is transmitted in the flow. On the Neoplatonic model, what inflows is distinct from the substance of the agent; on the corpuscular model, the efflux is continuous with this substance.

V. Multiplication-of-Species Model

In early modern treatments of the source of our ideas of sensible things, yet another causal model is discussed, which John Norris calls "the way of the Optical Men."[55] According to this model, "the Light that is reflected to us from any Body . . . by that Reflection [has] its Rays cast into such a System as to express the Form, or carry a material Resemblance of that Body. . . ."[56]

Harlot is not only impudent in herself, but she also naturally infects . . . so that if as man do often behold himself in her glasse . . . it will make him impudent and lecherous as she is" (p. 19). According to the contagion-influx model, as in the case of the Neoplatonic and corpuscularean versions, natural change results from something that flows from the agent into the recipient of change. But the contagion model differs from the other two in that it does not require that the effect of the efflux be coexistent with the activity of the agent. For example, there need not be a continuous efflux from a sick agent in order for the effect to exist in the patient. (You need not keep sneezing upon me for the cold you gave me to persist.) However, in the case of the magnet, the piece of iron will move toward the magnet only so long as the magnet continues to impress its power upon, or flow its virtue into, the iron. This feature of magnetism, then, does not fit the contagion model. Small wonder that by the time William Gilbert is surveying the possible models for magnetic attraction in his *De Magnete* (1600) the contagion model is dismissed. In fact, by the seventeenth century, the contagion model is mainly used for the spread of disease and for animal generation.

William Harvey, in 1651, used this model in *Anatomical Exercises on the Generation of Animals*. Having agreed with his teacher Hieronymous Fabricius that the "male semen" could not reach the "female semen" in the uterus, Harvey argued that the male semen "carries with it a fecundating power by a kind of contagious property; the woman after contact with the spermatic fluid *in coitu*, seems to receive influence and to become fecundated without the cooperation of any sensible corporeal agent, in the same way as iron touched by the magnet is endowed with its powers and can attract other iron to it" (*Works*, trans. Robert Willis [London, 1847], pp. 533–34). Since the contagion model came to have a limited application by the seventeenth century, I have eliminated detailed discussion of it as a major influence on Leibniz's *influxus physicus*.

55. John Norris, *An Essay Towards the Theory of the Ideal or Intelligible World* (London, 1701–4); facsimile reprint (1978), pp. 359, 369.

56. Ibid., p. 358.

Charleton also discusses a model, which he characterizes as Aristotelian, according to which visible species are "changed and multiplied by propagation."[57] A model shaped in part by Aristotelianism, extremely influential in the history of optics, and which provided a general picture of natural change through the propagation of species was Roger Bacon's "Multiplication of Species" model. Its main features are:

1. *What is immediately produced by the agent [species] is distinct from the substance of the agent; it is a likeness or replica.*
Roger Bacon, *The Multiplication of Species* (1250–60):

> If a species were a body or a flow [*defluxus*] from a body, . . . which we disproved above, . . . it would necessarily exit from the agent, and it would be continuous with the substance of the body.

> [A species] is called 'similitude' and 'image' with respect to the thing generating it, to which it is similar and which it imitates.[58]

2. *In generating a complete effect, the species is produced by an agent more perfect than the recipient.*
Roger Bacon, *The Multiplication of Species*:

> For the generation of complete effect . . . the agent has greater power than the recipient in order to prevail over it. . . .[59]

3. *The continuous action of the agent is* not *required for the effect to last.*
Roger Bacon, *The Multiplication of Species*:

> It is inquired whether a species disappears in the absence of that which generated it. And it cannot be said that it disappears with its generator . . . for that would be the case only if a species were a body or a flow from body . . . which we disproved above.[60]

4. *The agent is in no way diminished in the act of inflowing; it loses nothing of its virtue, power, or essence.*
Roger Bacon, *The Multiplication of Species*:

> Acting does not destroy and corrupt an agent, but perfects it, since . . . a thing is perfect when it is able to produce a like thing.[61]

5. *Natural change* requires *the contact of surfaces between the agent and the recipient.*

57. Charleton, *Physiologia*, p. 140.
58. RB 257, 5.
59. RB 83.
60. RB 257.
61. RB 45.

Roger Bacon, *The Multiplication of Species*:
> The agent and recipient must be joined without intermediary, as Aristotle says. . . . [T]he agent need come no closer to the recipient than for their surfaces to be in contact. . . .[62]

6. *The generation of species takes place over time.*
Roger Bacon, *The Multiplication of Species*:
> Next it must be known that the multiplication of virtue occupies time, as Alhazen says in *Perspectiva*, book ii. . . .[63]

7. *A species does not require spatial location* per se.
Roger Bacon, *The Multiplication of Species*:
> A species does not require place, as does body, but requires a subject, and that subject need not be numerically one, but can be constantly different, because a species generated in one part of the medium can produce its like in another part of the medium; and therefore, there is no acquisition of place as a body acquires place, but there is a renewing of the species by generation in various parts of the medium.[64]

8. *The agent brings about change in the recipient by inducing it to actualize its potentiality and not by any incursion into the recipient.*
Roger Bacon, *The Multiplication of Species*:
> The generation of species occurs . . . by a true alteration and bringing forth out of the active potentiality of the recipient matter.[65]

Bacon maintains that his "multiplication of species" is *not* an influx model, for two main reasons. First, he rejects a central feature of the influx models that we have examined so far: *The effect brought about by the efflux is coexistent with the activity of the agent.* He claims that the images of things would disappear in the absence of the generating agent only if an image were a "body or a flow from [*defluxus*] a body."[66] We saw earlier that when Bacon speaks of influx, he has in mind the atomistic model. In rejecting this central feature, he sees his multiplication–of–species model as pitted against the atomistic model.

Second, he explicitly denies the possibility of the influx of similitude,

---

62. RB 63.
63. RB 221.
64. RB 185.
65. RB 47.
66. RB 257.

species, form, or likeness from the causal agent to the recipient of change. His denial of influx rests on the following argument. For an influx to occur, one of several possibilities would have to be true. Either (a) the species is emitted by the agent as a type of corporeal effluvia, or (b) the agent takes the species from outside itself and passes it on to the recipient, or (c) the agent creates the species ex nihilo. Since (b) is "ridiculous" and (c) is impossible, this leaves only (a). But (a) can only be true if either some of the substance of the agent, or at least one of its accidents, is emitted. Either case would entail an alteration and diminution of the agent, which is inconsistent with a fundamental aspect of Bacon's picture of natural change: *The agent is in no way diminished in the act of inflowing; it loses nothing of its virtue, power, or essence.* Bacon concludes:

> Therefore, it is badly and improperly said that the agent dispatches something to the recipient, which flows into it, for in that case something would enter the recipient from outside; but this cannot occur.[67]

On the other hand, Bacon repeatedly speaks of the "influence of the agent" [*influentia agentis*], which he defines as the "action of the agent in natural matter."[68] Moreover, he explicitly endorses an influx model when he states:

> For the production of natural things from the potency of the recipient matter, first an influence [*influentia*] of the agent rushes into [*incurrit*] this matter so that from the potency of such matter natural effects are produced.[69]

So while the multiplication-of-species model is clearly different from the atomistic-corpuscular influx model, it begins to look like a type of influx model nonetheless. But which feature(s) do the Neoplatonic, atomistic-corpuscular, and multiplication-of-species models share? It *cannot* be that an influx model requires what is transmitted to be distinct from the substance of the agent, for this is not true of the atomistic-corpuscular model. *Nor* can the continuous activity of the agent be essential to an influx model, since this does not characterize the multiplication-of-species model. I believe that Bacon himself hits the nail on the head:

> The wise and the foolish differ concerning many things in their knowledge of species, nevertheless they agree in this, that the agent flows [*influit*] a species into the matter of the recipient.[70]

67. RB 45.
68. RB 345.
69. RB 345.
70. RB 6; my translation.

Bacon's view that "a species cannot exist from [*exire*] or be emitted [*emitti*] by the agent itself, since neither accident nor a piece of substance can depart from a subject without corruption of the whole substance,"[71] leads him to the Aristotelian aspect of his model: species come into existence through an eduction out of the matter of the recipient. Yet despite Bacon's insistence on this Aristotelian picture of change, his description of how this process of natural alteration commences makes use of a Neoplatonic image of something flowing from the agent into the recipient, which influx brings about the appropriate alteration in the recipient. So, in the end, the optical model of the multiplication of species makes use of some notion of transmission on the part of a created agent, just as the Neoplatonic replication model and the atomistic–corpuscular direption model do.

VI. The Proposed Solution

Now we are in a position to see why Leibniz took the Scholastic picture of natural change to be an influx model. St. Thomas, Suarez, and others, like Bacon, saw their Aristotelian models as standing in opposition to a transmission picture of change. But Leibniz presses the Scholastics to produce the details of the model—to show *precisely* what the alternative is to a transmission picture. How, for example, are we to conceive of the means by which a body produces a likeness of itself? How precisely does the species get into the sense organ? After all of the talk about eduction, it looks as if the Scholastics ultimately rely on a transmission model. Consider Suarez on the sensible species:

> It is known by many experiences that species shoot forth [*provientes*] from an object. The first is, because we see ourselves in another's pupil, which cannot be understood to happen otherwise than by some little form [*formula*] which represents me having been impressed [*impressa*] on the other's pupil. [*De Anima*, III, 5][72]

In addition, Leibniz challenges the Scholastics to provide the picture that will make intelligible how a sensible species or a phantasm (i.e., a corporeal) can bring about a change in the soul (an incorporeal). Suarez, interestingly enough, denies that these corporeals are efficient causes of our knowledge

71. RB 45.
72. V 164.

of sensible things. In fact, he seems to endorse some sort of harmony model:

> The phantasm and also the intellect of man are rooted in one and the same soul. For, here it turns out that they have a wonderful order and agreement in their operation, whence . . . for the same reason that the intellect operates, the imagination also senses. Therefore, in this way, I think . . . there is spiritual force in a rational soul for bringing about, in the possible intellect, species of these things . . . , while sensible cognition itself does not at all concur efficiently to that action. [*De Anima*, IV, II, 12][73]

For Suarez, then, the concomitance between the "corporeal species" and the alteration in the soul known as the "intelligible species" is due to "the power of the union" of sense and intellect. But what is the model for this union? Seventeenth-century philosophers found the matter troublesome. Descartes, when pressed by Princess Elizabeth on this question, eventually said that our notion of union was a primitive given to us in sensation. Henry More conceded that "a firm union of Spirit and Matter is very possible, though we cannot conceive the manner thereof."[74] In a journal article, Leibniz concluded that this union is "not a phenomenon, and . . . no one has ever given an intelligible notion of it."[75] Lacking any intelligible notion of union, Leibniz notes that we form the "bad habit" of "thinking as if our soul received certain 'species' as messengers and as if it had doors and windows."[76] In short, Leibniz agrees with the remark of La Forge with

---

73. V 719.

74. Henry More, *The Immortality of the Soul* (London, 1662), I, Ch. VII, 5.

75. AG 197(G VI 595–96); cf. L 539(G II 281). Marleen Rozemond has rightly pointed out that Suarez is not faced with quite the same difficulties in making conceivable the "power of the union" of sense and intellect as the Cartesians are in making mind-body union intelligible. Suarez attempts to ground union in the fact that sense and intellect are operations of one and the same soul; no such move, however, is open to the Cartesian dualists for mind-body union. Still, I think there is something to Leibniz's skepticism about the ultimate explicability of Suarez's notion of union. Very roughly, Suarez's account of perception is this: The phantasm is the nonefficient, exemplar cause of the intelligible species, whose efficient cause is the active intellect, which educes the intelligible species out of the potency of the possible intellect. Since the phantasm and active intellect are rooted in the same soul, and since soul is what provides the *ratio* or rational account of the behavior of things, Suarez takes it that this natural union accounts for the concomitance between the sensible species of the phantasm and the intelligible species of the intellect. But for Leibniz, this account of concomitance comes to no more than saying that it is the nature of the soul for there to be a sympathy between imagination and intellect—which, he thinks, is to explain nothing. It remains, of course, for Leibniz to show how his own account of perception, and of natural change in general, is intelligible and explanatory in the ways he thinks Suarez's model is not. See n. 82.

76. L 320(G IV 451).

which I began this chapter: in the seventeenth century there was hardly anyone who, in the end, did not imagine little images coming into the soul for it to contemplate. And there was hardly a metaphysician, of whatever stripe, who failed to challenge the intelligibility of this picture. John Sergeant's invective was typical of these attacks:

> The Schoolmen . . . invented their *Species Intentionales*; which, if . . . they were *Corporeal*, they could only affect the Soul by way of *Local Motion*; of which, being *Spiritual*, she is not capable. And, if they were *Spiritual* it will be ask'd, How they *came* to be such, being caused by a *Corporeal* Agent; as also, *how* being sent from a *Body*, they could get into the Soul, or by what Vehicle?[77]

But Leibniz is not just concerned with the Scholastics' lack of an intelligible model for psychophysical change. He finds equally baffling how they can provide an intelligible nontransmission model for body–body change. The dialectic goes like this. St. Thomas says:

> Again, it is laughable to say that a body does not act because an accident does not pass from subject to subject. For a hot body is not said to give off heat in this sense, that numerically the same heat which is in the heating body passes over [*transeat*] into the heated body. Rather, by the power of the heat which is in the heating body, a numerically different heat is made actual in the heated body, a heat which was previously in it in potency.[78]

Leibniz, as we have seen, demands the details of this picture of reduction from potency to act. St. Thomas paints a picture in which the world is filled with physical natures, each of which has causal powers. For example, fire has the causal power to heat suitably disposed bodies with which it makes contact. And so, we can see why wood in a state of privation with respect to heat, and having the natural disposition to be heated by suitable agents, will be heated when it is thrown into the fire, *ceteris paribus*. But Leibniz finds this utterly obscure. He argues that if an angel came to him to explain the cause of magnetic declination and said simply that "this is the nature of the magnet or that there is a certain sympathy or a kind of soul in the magnet by which it happens" this would be totally unsatisfactory. So how have the Scholastics done any better?[79]

77. Sergeant, *Solid Philosophy Asserted*, p. 60; cf. Norris, *An Essay*, vol. II, p. 346.
78. SCG, Bk III, Pt. I, Ch. 69, 28.
79. L 176(G VII 265).

With respect to purely bodily change, Leibniz has his Lockean interlocutor in the *New Essays* maintain that "we can have no other conception, but of the passing of motion out of one body and into another; which I think is as obscure and unconceivable, as how our minds move or stop our bodies by thought."[80] Leibniz agrees that, *at the metaphysical level*, this is "as inconceivable as an accident's passing from one subject to another." Nonetheless, "we can easily conceive of both the emission and the reception of parts in matter."[81] In short, *at the phenomenal level* of description, the only clearly conceivable model we can have is some sort of transmission model for bodies.

I do not want my remarks here to suggest that I think Leibniz was correct in concluding that the Scholastics had no intelligible model of natural change. It may turn out that Harré, Madden, and their successors will convince us that the Scholastics were closer to an adequate picture of causation than we post-Humeans. But I think that Leibniz is to be commended for raising the level of discussion among his contemporaries by demanding that the Scholastics show precisely how their characterization of change in terms of potency, act, privation, disposition, and the life differs from a mere appeal to "occult powers" rooted in the natures of things.[82]

80. NE 224 (G V 208).
81. L 459 (G IV 486).
82. Robert C. Sleigh, Jr., has posed an extremely important question (possibly one of the most difficult questions that Leibniz must face, in light of his rejection of *influxus physicus*): Precisely how has Leibniz's account of natural change done better than that of the Scholastics? Adequately responding to this thorny issue is much too big a project for me to take on here; I simply note the following. Leibniz thinks that explanation of *phenomena* through "natures" and "forms" explains nothing. So one problem with the Scholastics' picture of natural change is that it simply is not an acceptable explanatory model for phenomena—which it purports to be. Furthermore, when the Scholastics get past their vacuous talk, they ultimately have to fall back upon a transmission model. Even Suarez, who provides us with a limited-harmony model for the production of sense ideas, relies upon an influx picture of how the sensible species get into the phantasm. Leibniz thinks there is nothing wrong with a transmission model as long as it is used to account for purely bodily change at the macro level. So another problem with the Scholastics is that they were confused about levels of explanation; they made use of a transmission picture, suited to the phenomenal level, and then plugged substances into the model. Leibniz believes that he has arguments to show that any model of natural change that relies on transmission between *substances* is unintelligible. Some of these arguments were well rehearsed in the Aristotelian-Scholastic tradition and had a history going back at least as far as Roger Bacon.

On the other hand, Leibniz argues that mechanism gives us a satisfactory explanatory model for *phenomena*. Nonetheless, a proper analysis of bodies will show us that body must ultimately be grounded in substances. And mechanism does *not* give us an intelligible model for change at the metaphysical level of *substance*. (No transmission of parts or contact of surfaces is possible with respect to immaterial, simple substances.) So mechanism is an improvement over the Scholastic model of change, but it is not the whole story. A complete expansion of

To recap, Leibniz explicitly recognizes the Scholastics, Peripatetics, and Neoplatonists as proponents of the system of physical influence, but, as I have attempted to show, the Scholastic, the optical, and the Neoplatonic models have some crucially different features. Nonetheless, the Neoplatonic replicative-influx model and the corpuscular direptive-influx models picture natural change through transmission. I have argued that the multiplication-of-species model from the optical tradition tries to avoid, but ultimately falls back upon, a transmission picture. And I have suggested that Leibniz saw the Scholastics as equally unable to escape this picture of natural change. He christened this complex of transmission models "the system of *influxus physicus.*"

VII. Coda

This leads me to two final questions. First, if this is the proper genealogy of *influxus physicus*, why is it that Leibniz never mentions the corpuscula-reans as proponents of this system? I have suggested that the way of influence is an artificial construction, not a particular position that had avowed supporters. I now want to suggest that Leibniz's triad of systems was artfully contrived. His purpose was to set up the options in such a way that the opposition would stand out in relief. Leibniz believed that at the most fundamental metaphysical level—that of simple unities or sub-stances—there were only two intelligible models of change: his and the system of occasionalism. He also believed that he had telling arguments against the occasionalists and ways to show the superiority of his system over theirs. With respect to such Neoplatonists as More and Cudworth, and the Scholastics, Leibniz challenged the very intelligibility of the models. So the occasionalists, the Neoplatonists, and the Scholastics were all Leibniz's opponents. But he had a more complex relation to the corpuscularians. Insofar as they applied their model to alterations that involved true unities (e.g., purely mental change, or mind-body change) or insofar as they used

---

natural change will have to account for substantial change and, as we have seen, Leibniz thinks the Scholastics have failed to provide such an intelligible account, since theirs is fundamentally a transmission model.

The thorny problems arise in showing, in detail, whether Leibniz's doctrines of monadic expression, preestablished accommodation, and "world-apart" (as Sleigh terms it) can consti-tute a concomitance model that is itself purely intelligible. Such a project will require, inter alia, carefully examining the role of "the law of the continuation of the series" in the harmony model to see just how it can escape the intelligibility problems that Leibniz ascribed to the Scholastic models.

mechanism to provide a model for purely bodily change at the deepest metaphysical level, Leibniz did see the corpuscularians as "mere influxionists," who held an inconceivable position.[83] But Leibniz also believed that the corpuscular-transfer models were, on the level of phenomena, the only intelligible models of body-body change. His basic strategy was to show that while it was inconceivable that part of a simple substance (either part of its substance or a detached accident) should be transmitted to or from another substance, since true substances have no parts, there is no such problem with respect to body-body change at the macro level. Since bodies are aggregates, we can conceive of the transfer of parts. Leibniz, in fact, makes this explicit in his first published statement of his system in *A New System of Nature*:

> The action of one substance upon another is not an emission or a transplanting of some entity, as is commonly supposed. . . . It is true that we can easily conceive of both the emission and the reception of parts in matter and can in this way reasonably explain all the phenomena of physics mechanically. But since material mass is not a substance, it is clear that the action of substance itself can be only what I have described [i.e., the preestablished harmony].[84]

So, the corpuscular influx model, as a picture of body-body change at the macro level, does not stand in opposition to the preestablished harmony in the way that the Neoplatonic and the Scholastic models do. I believe that it is for this reason that Leibniz does not mention the corpuscularians when listing the influxionists.

The final double question is: Does Leibniz take Descartes's model of natural change to be that of *influxus physicus*, and is Leibniz correct? This set of questions clearly merits an extended and separate treatment, so I will close with a brief observation.

Although there may be some difficulties in setting out the details of Descartes's model for body-body change, I think there will be no problem in showing that his model was one of physical influx—as I have characterized it. Providing the details of Descartes's model for voluntary motion, I think, will be more challenging. Leibniz certainly found Descartes's remarks on the matter obscure. He likened the soul, on Descartes's account, to a rider who,

> though giving no force to the horse he mounts, nevertheless controls it by guiding that force in any direction he pleases. But as that is

---

83. L 459(G IV 486); H 156(G VI 136); L 530(G II 251).
84. L 459(G IV 486).

done by means of spurs and other material aids, it is conceivable how that can be; there are, however, no instruments such as the soul may employ for this result.[85]

At one point, I thought that Peter Machamer was on the right track in suggesting that Descartes might have made use of Suarez's model of union in his accounts of voluntary motion and sensation.[86] I had hoped to show that, far from having an influx model for mind–body and body–mind change, Descartes held a version of Suarez's picture of concomitance. But Margaret Wilson's recent work on Descartes's views on sensation has convinced me that, with respect to body–mind causality, Descartes just did not have a consistent position; he waffled on the causal role body plays in the production of sensation.[87] And so, it now seems to me that perhaps Leibniz had Descartes pegged correctly, citing the *Cartesians* as occasional-ists, but never attributing the position to Descartes. But neither does he attribute the system of *influxus physicus* to Descartes. On the contrary, he states: "As far as we can know from his published writings, Descartes gave up the struggle over this problem."[88]

85. H 156(G VI 136).

86. See Peter Machamer, "Harmonies of Descartes and Leibniz."

87. Margaret Wilson, "Descartes on the Origin of Sensation," *Philosophical Topics* 19 (1991): 293–323.

88. L 457(G IV 483).

Steven Nadler

The Occasionalism
of Louis de la Forge

I

Louis de la Forge (1632–66) is generally recognized as playing an important
role in the genesis of occasionalism, the doctrine that finite created beings—
minds and bodies—have no causal efficacy and that God alone is a true
causal agent. Along with Géraud de Cordemoy (1626–84), he is usually
credited with being the first to argue in a systematic way for that doctrine.[1]
The lines of influence here, however, are not very clear. We know that

---

1. La Forge and Cordemoy published their most important philosophical works within a
year of each other—La Forge's *Traité de l'esprit de l'homme* appeared in late 1665 and Cordemoy's
Le discernement de l'âme et du corps in 1666. La Forge's friend Jacob Gousset, in fact, considers
La Forge to be the true founder of occasionalism, based on certain conversations they had in
the late 1650s; see Gousset's *Causarum primae et secundum realis operatio rationibus confirmatur et
ab objectionibus defenditur* (Leuwarden: François Halma, 1716). Occasionalism does have its
ultimate roots in Descartes—see, for example, *Principles of Philosophy* II.36–42—and more-
ancestral precedents in medieval theories of causation and divine sustenance.

Nicolas Malebranche (1638–1715), perhaps the most important and well-known occasionalist, read his fellow Parisian Cordemoy.[2] Did he also read La Forge? We can be pretty sure of it. It was Malebranche's reading of Descartes's *Traité de l'homme* in 1664 that inspired him to pursue philosophy; and, as Prost reminds us, the edition he read contained La Forge's *remarques*—editorial notes in which La Forge refers to his own *Traité de l'esprit de l'homme* (to appear in a year), in which he would complete Descartes's project.[3] Malebranche, in his initial enthusiasm for this new philosophy, cannot have failed to have had his interest stimulated in this forthcoming work. As expected, a copy of La Forge's *Traité* is found among the books in Malebranche's library.[4]

And, yet, the story is complicated by the fact that Arnold Geulincx and Johannes Clauberg had, by 1664, already published major works in which apparently occasionalist elements play an important role,[5] although it has been persuasively argued that neither exerted a significant influence upon either La Forge or Cordemoy[6]—nor, I suspect, upon Malebranche. Finally, while it is certainly possible that Cordemoy may have had some influence upon La Forge,[7] it is more likely that both Cartesians formulated their views on causation independently.

Thus, in spite of the flurry of occasionalist activity taking place in the 1660s, and in spite of the fact that we have yet to figure out the exact details of his influence and of his intellectual and personal relations to other occasionalists, there is widespread agreement on La Forge's originality and importance in the development of the occasionalist doctrine. By contrast, there is very *little* agreement on what precisely is the nature and extent of La Forge's occasionalism. Is he a consistent and thoroughgoing occasional-

2. Malebranche cites Cordemoy in *De la recherche de la vérité* I.10.

3. J. Prost, *Essai sur l'atomisme et l'occasionalisme dans la philosophie cartésienne* (Paris: Henry Paulin, 1907), pp. 187–88.

4. See Malebranche, OC XX, 237, 267. Both Gouhier and Battail give Cordemoy primary influence on Malebranche. See H. Gouhier, *La philosophie de Malebranche* (Paris: J. Vrin, 1948), p. 106, and J.-F. Battail, *L'avocat philosophe Géraud de Cordemoy* (The Hague: Martinus Nijhoff, 1973), pp. 147–48.

5. The first volume of Geulincx's *Ethica* and the first edition of Clauberg's *Corporis et animae conjunctio* both appeared in 1664.

6. See Prost, *Essai*, pp. 150–53, and Battail, *L'avocat philosophe*, pp. 143–46. La Forge read Clauberg (he cites him several times in the *Traité*) and corresponded with him.

7. This is Prost's suggestion; see *Essai*, pp. 103–4, 135–36. He suspects that such influence would have been transmitted through mutual friends like de Montmor and Clerselier. In addition to Prost's book, the best study of La Forge's contribution to the development of occasionalism is P. Clair, "Louis de la Forge et les origines de l'occasionalisme," *Recherches sur le XVIIème siècle* 1 (1976): 63–72.

ist, extending that theory to cover all three causal contexts—body-body, mind-body, and within the mind itself? Or is his occasionalism of a more restricted variety? I argue that La Forge's occasionalism is quite limited, and that he employs God's constant causal activity to explain only body-body relations. I then discuss the more general significance of this conclusion for our understanding of seventeenth-century occasionalism, both its theses and its historical development.

Before proceeding, two preliminary remarks are necessary. First, I am limiting the scope of my investigation to La Forge's mature thought on causation as it is found in the *Traité*, which he published in 1665 (although my conclusions are supported by La Forge's notes to the edition of Descartes's *Traité de l'homme* that he published with Clerselier in 1664). I do not consider La Forge's early (and unpublished) views as they are reported by Gousset.[8] It is clear that there is some development in La Forge's thinking between 1658, when he reportedly revealed his somewhat extreme ideas to Gousset, and the mid-1660s. But this lies outside the scope of my concern here.[9]

Second, I want to make it clear that by 'occasionalism' I mean a doctrine according to which God is actively, constantly, and ubiquitously engaged causally in the world. For an event or state of affairs x (and this might apply to every event or state of affairs, or only some, depending upon the scope of one's occasionalism), there is a discrete volition in God, a volition whose content is specific and that is causally responsible for the occurrence of that event or state of affairs: "Let x occur at t." It is important to make this point because there is a misinterpretation of occasionalism prevalent in some current scholarship according to which the God of occasionalism wills *not* particular events, but only general laws or correspondences (e.g., "Let minds and bodies . . .").[10] Contrary to this interpretation, occasionalism is significantly different from a preestablished harmony—at the very least, in that it requires of God an ongoing causal participation in things. God is actually and immediately moving individual bodies around and producing particular mental events, although God does always act in accordance with certain general laws and never arbitrarily. This difference is important for my argument.

8. *Causarum primae et secundarum realis operatio.*
9. See Prost, *Essai*, ch. 6, and Clair, "Louis de la Forge."
10. See, for example, C. J. McCracken, *Malebranche and British Philosophy* (Oxford: Clarendon Press, 1983), pp. 100–101, and N. Jolley, *The Light of the Soul: Theories of Ideas in Leibniz, Malebranche, and Descartes* (Oxford: Clarendon Press, 1990), pp. 106–7. I argue at length against this misinterpretation of occasionalism in "Occasionalism and General Will in Malebranche," *Journal of the History of Philosophy* (forthcoming).

II

The question, then, is: What is the nature and extent of La Forge's occasionalism? Is he a thoroughgoing or a limited occasionalist? Since, as I show, there is no question that La Forge's account of body-body relations is strictly occasionalist, one's answer to this question ultimately depends upon how one reads La Forge's account of the union and "interaction" of mind and body. And the scholarly literature on La Forge appears to be quite divided (and subdivided) on this issue. On the one hand, there are those who offer an extreme reading and claim that La Forge is a complete occasionalist: there are no real causal relations between any finite substances; bodies cannot act on other bodies or on minds, and minds cannot act on bodies. God moves bodies on the appropriate material or mental occasions, and God causes mental events on the appropriate bodily or mental occasions.[11]

On the other hand, there are those who argue that La Forge's account of the mind-body relation is more like a preestablished harmony than an occasionalism, with God willing once and for all that bodily states and mental events should arise and correspond in such and such a way. The correlation between mind and body, on this reading, results not from a constant causal activity on God's part, nor from some real interaction, but rather from God's initial establishment of the union of the two substances. Thus, Stein claims that "La Forge is not quite an occasionalist in the strict sense, since he traces the mutual influence of the two substances back to a single, creative, primary volition of God."[12] Still others, while agreeing with the claim that La Forge is not a complete occasionalist, argue this by showing that there *is* real causal interaction (in one way or another) between the two substances. Norman Kemp Smith, for example, states that "De la Forge still holds that the human will is the direct and efficient cause of voluntary movement,"[13] while Richard A. Watson claims that for La Forge there is "real causality" between mind and body, with each efficaciously

11. See Prost, *Essai*, ch. 6; F. Bouillier, *Histoire de la philosophie Cartésienne*, 2 vols. (Paris: Durand, 1854), vol. 1, pp. 503, 513; McCracken, *Malebranche and British Philosophy*, p. 95; T. M. Lennon, "Philosophical Commentary," in Malebranche, *The Search after Truth*, LO 811.

12. L Stein, "Zur Genesis des Occasionalismus," *Archiv für Geschichte der Philosophie* 1 (1888): 55. See also H. Seyfarth, *Louis de la Forge und seine Stellung im Occasionalismus* (Gotha: Emil Behrend, 1887), ch. 3. This is also A.G.A. Balz's view, if I read him correctly; see *Cartesian Studies* (New York: Columbia University Press, 1951), pp. 97–98. Prost argues against this "preestablished harmony reading" on the basis of God's atemporality—there is no "pre-" for God—and immutability; see *Essai*, pp. 125–26.

13. N. Kemp Smith, *Studies in the Cartesian Philosophy* (New York: Russell and Russell, 1902), p. 87, n. 2.

influencing the other, although such real secondary causality has its ultimate source in God.[14]

This deep division among scholars over just what La Forge thinks about mind–body relations is not surprising. He employs the language of both occasionalism and interactionism, thus making it easy to be caught off guard. But his real position is neither a strict occasionalism nor an interactionism that involves transitive, two-way efficient causation between mind and body. Nor is it accurate to call it a preestablished harmony, given Leibniz's appropriation of this term for the relationship between two causally active (but noninteractive) substances whose sequences of states flow spontaneously but (thanks to God) in correlation. For La Forge, mind and body do causally interact, but not in the way transitive, efficient causes were ordinarily (especially by Aristotelians) supposed to bring about their effects. Nothing literally passes from cause to effect here; nor does the cause itself "create" something in the effect. Rather, God has established that certain bodily motions should occasion the soul to produce certain ideas and that the mind, through its volitions, should move the body. Bodies do not "push" minds or pass ideas into them, and minds do not communicate or transfer motion to bodies. But that does not mean that minds and bodies do not stand in a real, nonoccasionalist causal relationship.[15]

III

Let us first look at the body–body context. In this case, La Forge's occasionalism is clear and straightforward. A body consists in nothing but

14. "As for the question of how mind and body interact causally, La Forge takes the hard Cartesian line that the animal spirits of the body (somehow) influence the mind and are influenced by the mind in the pineal gland. . . . [T]his is clearly not occasionalism" (*The Breakdown of Cartesian Metaphysics* [Atlantic Highlands, N.J.: Humanities Press International, 1987], p. 174). Watson's overall view, however, is a bit unclear, since he earlier expresses no disagreement with Bouillier's assessment that La Forge is a "complete occasionalist" on mind-body interaction (see p. 86). H. Gouhier also sees limits to La Forge's occasionalism, with real causal interaction between mind and body; see *La vocation de Malebranche* (Paris: J. Vrin, 1926), pp. 88–95, 101.

15. Thus, Smith is right to say that the will is the efficient cause of motions in the body, but his account is incomplete in that he does not see that for La Forge the body is also a "cause" (but not an efficient cause) of mental operations. And Watson's account is correct as long as the real causal relationship he refers to is not two-way efficient causality—a mental event (volition) is an efficient cause of bodily motions, but not vice versa—and definitely not transitive causality. There is also some truth to the Stein/Seyfarth reading, as I show, but not without admitting a real causally interactive relationship between mind and body.

pure extension, devoid of any spiritual properties (thoughts, desires) or sensuous qualities (heat, color, etc.). As such, a body is inert and passive, and has absolutely no motive force, no power to put itself in motion. Bodies cannot move themselves, and, consequently, they cannot move other bodies. "God is the first, universal, and total cause of movement," and the local contact of one body with another is only an occasion for God to modify the motion of the first body and to put the second body into motion, as dictated by the laws of nature (*Traité*, 241).[16] To be sure, we can still consider bodies as "particular" or secondary causes of the motions of other bodies, but only in the sense that "they determine and oblige the first cause to apply his motive force and virtue upon those bodies upon which he would not otherwise have exercised it . . . following the laws of motion" (*Traité*, 242).

La Forge offers four main arguments to the effect that bodies have no motive force, no power to cause or sustain motion either in themselves or in other bodies. First, our clear and distinct concept of body, which includes only extension and its properties, represents body as purely passive and does not contain any such active force. In fact, we cannot clearly conceive or imagine how such a force *could* be included among or derived from the properties of extension, which include only size, shape, internal figure, divisibility, and mobility (*Traité*, 237–38). Second, the motion of a body is simply a mode of it, and (on the Cartesian ontology) modes cannot pass from the substance to which they belong to some other substance. Thus, real transitive causation—whereby one body would communicate or transfer its motion to another body—is ruled out. Nor could one body create motion in another body, since this would be to attribute to bodies a creative power, which La Forge considers an obvious absurdity (*Traité*, 238–39). Third, La Forge believes that motive force, *la force qui transporte un corps d'un voisinage dans un autre,* must be distinguished from the body to which it is applied and that it moves. But this means that motive force is not inherent in bodies, and hence that "no body has the power to move itself"— otherwise, this power would not be distinguished from the body moved. Moreover, if a body cannot move itself then it is also evident that it cannot move another. "Thus, it is necessary that any body that is in motion must be pushed by something entirely distinct from itself, which thing is not a body" (*Traité*, 238). Finally, La Forge claims that God is required, not just to create the world ex nihilo, but to sustain it in existence from moment to moment by a kind of continuous production. This applies, as well, to all the particular substances in the world. When God creates or sustains a body

---

16. All page references to La Forge's *Traité* are to the *Oeuvres philosophiques*, ed. P. Clair (Paris: Presses Universitaires de France, 1974).

at a given time, he must do so in some relative place or another, in some specific relation of distance to other bodies. But it follows, then, that the motion of a body is just its being sustained or re-created by God from one moment to the next in different successive relative places, and its rest is its being re-created in the same relative place. The force that moves that body is and can be only the will of God.

> I maintain that there is no creature, spiritual or corporeal, that can change [the position of a body] or that of any of its parts, in the second instant of its creation if the Creator does not do it himself, for it is he who has produced this part of matter in place A. For example, not only is it necessary for him to continue to produce it if he wants it to continue to exist, but also, since he cannot create it everywhere, nor outside of any place whatsoever, he must himself put it in place B if he wants it to be there, for if he were to put it somewhere else, there is no force that would be capable of removing it from there. (*Traité*, 240).

This is as strong an argument as one could hope for that bodies have no power to move themselves or other bodies, and that God is the primary cause of the motion and rest of bodies (it also appears that the argument rules out the action of mind on body—"no creature, *spiritual* or corporeal . . ."—but I argue below that, in fact, it does not).[17] It is an unequivocal statement of occasionalism in the context of body–body relations.[18]

IV

Things are not so clear cut when we turn to the mind-body/body-mind context. First, let us consider the body-mind relation. There is an undeniable correspondence between certain bodily motions and certain thoughts (*pensées*) in the mind. More particularly, when an external material object communicates motions through a material medium, these motions eventually strike the sense organs. The sense organs, in turn, communicate the motions, via the nerves and the animal spirits, to the brain (all of this takes place in an occasionalist manner, since it involves only matter and motion).

17. See note 30 below.
18. This argument also appears in Malebranche's *Entretiens sur la métaphysique* VII; it has its immediate source in Descartes's doctrine of divine sustenance (see *Meditations* III and *Principles of Philosophy* I.21, II.36–42).

When the motions reach the brain, they are followed by certain ideas and sensations. This correlation is constant, lawlike, universal, and involuntary.

What, then, is the relationship, in causal terms, between the motions in the body and the corresponding thoughts in the mind? Is it, like the body-body relationship, an occasionalist one, whereby God, on the occasion of the relevant brain motions, causes an idea and sensations to be present to the mind? This is what *seems* to be suggested by some of La Forge's remarks. For example, he tells us that "he who wanted to unite [the mind and the body] . . . had to resolve at the same time to give to the mind the thoughts that we notice come to it on the occasion of motions in its body" (*Traité*, 244). Immediately after this, he warns us that "we must not think, nonetheless, that it is God that does everything and that the body and the mind do not truly act upon one another, since if the body had not had such a motion, the mind would not have had such a thought." Such a warning would appear to make sense only on the condition that La Forge is laying out an occasionalist account of body-mind relations and that he is concerned to remind us that on such an account bodies are still "occasional causes" and necessary conditions for the mental effects wrought immediately by God. La Forge, furthermore, insists that mind-body interaction is no more nor less problematic than body-body interaction: in neither case do we know clearly how the cause would bring about its effect (*Traité*, 235f.). If the body-body relation is an occasionalist one, does not this parallel suggest that so must be the body-mind relation?

And yet, in spite of these appearances, the details of La Forge's explanation of mind/body union present a different, nonoccasionalist picture of the body-mind relation. La Forge distinguishes between two kinds of causes of ideas of bodies in the mind: the principal and efficient (*effective*) cause, and the remote (*éloignée*) and occasional cause. The principal and efficient cause of any idea is the mind itself. The mind is an active substance and has the power to produce thoughts through its *faculté de penser*. Often, the mind produces ideas voluntarily, as occurs in pure rational thinking and imagination.[19] On many (if not most) occasions, however, thoughts are present to the mind without there being a volition to think of anything. Sensations and ideas of extension occur involuntarily when the senses are at work, normally on the occasion of the presence of some external material object. What happens, according to La Forge, is that the motions communicated to the brain by the object, which are the remote and occasional cause of the

19. This also demonstrates that La Forge rejects occasionalism in the realm of the mental alone. The mind, through the will, has the power to produce ideas spontaneously; see *Traité*, 176–79.

sensible idea, give the principal and efficient cause—the mind—occasion to produce an idea.

> While it can be said that the bodies that surround our own, and generally everything that can compel us to think of bodies, or even of minds, when this does not result from our own will, are in some manner the cause of the ideas that we then have, because we would not have them [the ideas] on all of the occasions that we have them if they [the bodies] did not act upon our body; nonetheless, because these are material substances, whose action does not extend as far as the soul, in so far as it is simply a thing that thinks; but in so far as it [the soul] is united to a body . . . they can at most be only the remote and occasional cause of them [the ideas] that, by means of the union of the mind and the body, compels our faculty of thinking and determines it to produce those ideas of which it is the principal and efficient cause. (*Traité*, 176)

He later claims that "all of our ideas considered in themselves in so far as they are only different ways of thinking, need . . . no cause for their production other than our mind" (*Traité*, 177). The mind, with its faculty of thinking, contains within itself (and he insists that he is speaking here of something *dedans l'Ame*) the sole efficient cause of its ideas, "that which has the power to determine and give form to [the mind's] thoughts" (*Traité*, 177).

Now to say that the external material body—or, more precisely, the motions it communicates to the brain—is the "occasional" cause of the idea does not commit La Forge to an occasionalism here. First, note that these motions do not serve *God* as an occasion to cause an idea; rather, they serve the mind itself, which is endowed with an active causal power. Second, one can call the bodily motions an "occasional cause" and still insist that they are not without a kind of causal efficacy. Here La Forge clearly parts company with occasionalists like Malebranche, who refuse to grant that occasional causes have any kind of causal efficacy. For La Forge, as well as for others, an occasional, remote, or accidental[20] cause is still a cause: an inferior type of cause when compared to an efficient cause, to be sure, but a real cause nonetheless.[21] As he claims, "one must not conclude that the body is not the cause of thoughts which arise in the mind on its occasion"

20. This is the term Descartes uses to describe how bodies occasion the mind to produce ideas; see *Comments on a Certain Broadsheet*, AT VIII-2, 360; CSM I, 305.

21. See Clair, "Louis de la Forge," for a discussion of the use of the term 'occasional cause' in seventeenth-century philosophy.

(*Traité*, 213). The bodily motions do really occasion or elicit the mind's own efficient causality. It is in this sense that La Forge thinks he can still speak of the "power" (*puissance*, or *force*) the body has to excite thoughts.

La Forge knows that this is the same account of the causal origin of ideas that Descartes offers in his response to Regius. In reply to Regius's claim that the mind has no need of innate ideas, Descartes says that in fact "there is nothing in our ideas which is not innate to the mind or the faculty of thinking." External objects do not transmit ideas to our mind through the sense organs. Rather,

> they transmit something which, at exactly that moment, gives the mind occasion to form these ideas by means of the faculty innate to it. Nothing reaches our mind from external objects through the sense organs except certain corporeal motions. . . . But neither the motions themselves nor the figures arising from them are conceived by us exactly as they occur in the sense organs. . . . Hence it follows that the very ideas of the motions themselves and of the figures are innate in us. The ideas of pain, colors, sounds, and the like must be all the more innate if, on the occasion of certain corporeal motions, our mind is to be capable of representing them to itself.

And to make this better understood, Descartes employs a distinction between the primary and proximate cause of a thing (in the case of an idea, the mind itself) and a remote and accidental cause (the bodily motions):

> Something can be said to derive its being from something else for two different reasons: either the other thing is its proximate and primary cause, without which it cannot exist, or it is a remote and merely accidental cause, which gives the primary cause occasion to produce its effect at one moment rather than another.[22]

La Forge adopts exactly this schema from Descartes. It is not occasional-ism—it is occasional causation,[23] which, for La Forge, is a secondary but

22. *Comments on a Certain Broadsheet*, AT VIII-2, 358–60; CSM I, 304–5. This account also appears in the *Port-Royal Logic* (A. Arnauld and P. Nicole, *La logique ou L'art de penser* [Paris: Flammarion, 1970], pp. 71–72).

23. I am using the phrase 'occasional causation' to denote the entire process whereby one thing, *A*, occasions another thing, *B*, to exert its efficient causal power. It relates *A* not just to *B* but also to the effect, *e*, produced by *B* (i.e., *A*, not *B*, is the occasional cause of *e*). In the case I am concerned with, it relates the body to the idea. In a sense, occasionalism can be regarded as a species of occasional causation—that species, namely, in which the proximate and efficient cause that operates on the occasion of the remote or occasional cause is God. But

real causal relation. The two causes—the remote, occasional cause (the body) and the proximate, efficient cause (the mind, not God)—each play a necessary but different role in the production of the idea.[24]

And yet how is it possible for a body, which is pure passive extension and is devoid of any active moving force, to enter into a causal relationship (however secondary) with *anything*, much less with an unextended thinking substance? How can the body occasion the mind to produce an idea when it lacks the power even to move itself or another body?

In fact, this lack of moving force in bodies—a point essential to La Forge's body-body occasionalism—is completely immaterial in the case of body-mind relations. If you take away moving force from bodies, then one body cannot *move* itself or another body. But La Forge is not asking the body literally to move the mind, to put it in motion (of which the mind is not capable). As he insists, it is a matter of *equivocal*, not univocal, causation: the effect does not resemble the cause.[25] "The body does not act on the mind by communicating to it some motion, because the mind cannot be moved. . . . It thus must be as an equivocal cause that . . . the body, in moving, occasions [*donne occasion à*] the mind to produce some thought" (*Traité*, 213). The presence or absence of moving force in the body is thus irrelevant in this context. While denying that bodies have moving force might commit you to occasionalism in the body-body case, it certainly does not commit you to occasionalism in the body-mind case, particularly if you grant that the soul has an active power to produce its own ideas (lest bodies should be required to produce ideas as their efficient causes, which would be to give to bodies a force even more incompatible with pure extension than moving force).

But an important question still remains: How is it that human bodies and minds are, in fact, engaged in this causal relationship? Why do bodily motions occasion the mind to produce thoughts? At one level, La Forge has no answer to this question, and thus his claim that body-mind interaction

---

the proximate and efficient cause that operates may also, in other species of occasional causation, be something other than God. In the case under consideration, it is the mind. Descartes also offers the example of workers (the "primary and proximate causes of their work") and those who give them orders or promise to pay them ("accidental and remote causes"); see *Comments on a Certain Broadsheet*, AT VIII-2, 360; CSM I, 305.

24. "Si le Corps n'avoit eu un tel mouvement, jamais l'Esprit n'auroit eu une telle pensée" (*Traité*, 245).

25. "Entre les causes, les unes sont equivoques, quand l'effet ressemble à sa cause, & les autres equivoques, quand il ne lui ressemble pas" (*Traité*, 213). For a body in motion to cause motion in another body is a case of univocal causation; for a body in motion to occasion not motion but thought in a mind is a case of equivocal causation. The distinction is a medieval one, and can be found, for example, in Duns Scotus, *Opus oxoniense* (*Ordinatio*) I, dist. II, q. 1, art. I, part 2.

is no more nor less understood than body-body interaction: both cases are equally opaque. We see nothing in the nature of things—neither in the nature of body nor in that of mind—that dictates that one should be the occasional cause of effects in the other (*Traité*, 213, 227). At a more general, metaphysical level, however, La Forge insists that the source of the relationship can only be God. In establishing the union of the two substances in a human being, God wills that the body should, under certain conditions, occasion the mind to produce thoughts; God wills, moreover, that *particular* motions in the body should occasion the mind to produce *particular* thoughts. God is the "total and proximate cause" of the union of mind and body, and "one cannot deny that he who joined our mind and our body was able, at the same time, to unite all the thoughts that we have on the occasion of external objects to the corporeal motions that do not at all resemble them" (*Traité*, 163). God, in uniting the body to the mind, has ordained that certain *pensées* should follow (be occasioned or elicited by) certain *mouvements*, and that is all there is to the matter.

Although this solution, like occasionalism, employs a divine cause as the ultimate explanatory principle for an apparently incomprehensible *explanandum*, it still does not amount to occasionalism. For La Forge, God establishes the causal relationship between body and mind once and for all.[26] God is not required to act constantly to cause mental effects on the occasions of bodily motions. God institutes the mind-body union, and "the power [*force*] . . . that the body has to excite various thoughts in the soul [is] a necessary consequence of this union" (*Traité*, 244). Deus ex machina? Yes. Occasionalism? No.

V

The other side of the mind/body context is the mind-body relation, particularly as it is manifested in voluntary movements of the body. While certain aspects of La Forge's account are somewhat confusing, nonetheless, as in the body-mind case, it does *not* amount to occasionalism.

La Forge, on several occasions, recognizes in the soul *une force du mouvoir le corps* (also described as *une puissance du mouvoir [le corps]*),[27] and grants the will (*la volonté*) "the power [*le pouvoir*] to unite our thoughts to movements that do not resemble them" (*Traité*, 163). The mind moves the body by exerting this power over the position of the pineal gland, which in

---

26. Here lies the truth in the views of Stein and Seyfarth.
27. *Traité*, 145, 152, 244.

turn controls the direction or course (but not the speed) of the animal spirits. These material spirits are communicated through the nerves to the muscles in the limbs, which are then moved.[28] There is no indication that this is anything but a real causal relationship, with the mind the *efficient* cause of the movement of the gland—and thus, ultimately, of the body's limbs. As La Forge claims, "the will can very well be the efficient cause of all things in this [mind-body] alliance that we notice depend immediately upon it" (*Traité*, 227).

Because the mind, unlike the body, is an *active* substance, it may not be thought surprising that it can act on and move the body. And yet, while the mind is active, it is nevertheless not spatial or extended; hence, local contact with the body is ruled out. Nor is the mind literally in motion (since motion can be a mode only of body). Thus, La Forge suggests, there is some prima facie force to the question as to how the mind can "push" or move an extended body. His response is that just as moving force is irrelevant in trying to understand how the body can occasion the mind to act, so local contact—which is essential in trying to understand how one body could move another—is irrelevant in trying to understand how the mind moves the body. La Forge hopes to eliminate "from the minds of many"

> the unfortunate prejudice of thinking that if the soul [is] not corpo-real, it [does] not have the force to move the body, because, they say, it cannot do this without touching it, and, as the Poet says, "no thing can touch or be touched except body." As if motion could only be communicated by means of contact [*l'attouchement*]. (*Traité*, 236)[29]

Like the body-mind case, and unlike the body-body case, it is a matter of equivocal causation.

Ultimately, however, the mind-body causal relation is, on its own naturalistic terms, no more comprehensible than body-mind or body-body relations. Once again, God is required to step in—not, as in the body-body case, in an occasionalist manner, but, as in the body-mind case, in establish-ing the union of mind and body and its laws. God, as the cause of this union, "has made the movements of the one depend upon [*a fait dependre*]

28. See *Traité*, ch. 24–26, passim. This account comes right from Descartes's *Traité de l'homme*, for which La Forge provided editorial *remarques*.

29. Descartes makes a similar point in one of his letters to Princess Elizabeth (28 June 1643), in which he cautions her against using concepts proper to the material world to try to understand matters in the psychophysical realm; see AT III, 690.

the thoughts of the other" (*Traité*, 210). If La Forge employs the "universal cause" to explain what he calls the "mutual and reciprocal dependence" of volitions and motions, it does not appear that he does so as an occasionalist.

I say above that I find La Forge somewhat confusing on the question of voluntary movements of the body. This is because he is not always clear about how this causal relation takes place. While, for the most part, he sticks to the account just outlined involving efficient causation by the will, he has one momentary but apparently significant lapse into the language of occasionalism. Thus, we find him saying that

> [w]hile God is the universal cause of all the motions that occur in the world, I do not hesitate, nonetheless, to recognize bodies and minds as particular causes of these same motions, not to be sure by producing any *impressed* quality, as the Schools explain it, but by determining and obliging the first cause to apply his force and motive virtue on those bodies upon which he would not have exercised it without them, following the manner according to which he resolved to govern himself regarding bodies and minds, that is to say, for bodies following the laws of motion . . . and for minds following the extension of the power that he desired to give to the will. The virtue that bodies and minds have to move consists in this alone. (*Traité*, 242)

This is the only statement regarding the mind–body relation that employs the occasionalist idiom so starkly. In all other cases, God's role is that of the first establishing (and sustaining) cause of the union of mind and body. While God is immediately and directly responsible in an ongoing and constant way for moving bodies when they collide with other bodies, there is still room in this schema for another cause that can move certain bodies. While inanimate bodies are always moved by God alone, and animate (i.e., for a Cartesian, human) bodies are also moved by God on an indefinite number of occasions (whenever they are "interacting" with other bodies in accordance with the laws of physics), animate human bodies are also moved by human minds.[30]

What, then, to do with the above passage? Perhaps La Forge does not intend the scope of this occasionalist claim to include animate bodies insofar as they are subject to the efficacious causal power of the will; perhaps its scope is limited only to bodies insofar as they are "moved" by other bodies,

30. D. Garber argues that something like this is Descartes's position; see "How God Causes Motion: Descartes, Divine Sustenance, and Occasionalism," *Journal of Philosophy* 84 (1987): 567–80, and his essay in this book.

inanimate or animate. The passage occurs in the middle of La Forge's main argument that bodies do not move other bodies and that only God moves bodies. He has not yet considered the mind–body relation (the next paragraph begins: "Let us now turn to what may be the case in particular for the body and the mind of man"). Bodies are moved both by inanimate bodies and by animate bodies (e.g., a baseball thrown by a pitcher). When bodies are moved by inanimate bodies, the story is a straightforward occasionalist one. When an animate body (in voluntary motion) moves another body, however, the bodily motions that occasion God to move the second body are themselves caused by the mind. Thus, even though the second body's causal relationship to the first body is a strictly occasionalist one, a human mind (or, more precisely, a volition) plays a role in the overall occasionalistic picture: had the mind not moved its own body in a certain way, the "first cause" (God) would not have been "determined and obliged" to "apply his force" and move the second body in a certain way. It is in this sense that one must make room for *les esprits* in addition to *les corps* as "particular causes"—occasioning causes—of the motions of bodies moved by God.[31]

Note, furthermore, that in the passage La Forge is referring to an "extension [*l'estendue*]" of the power God has given to the will, and not to that power itself.[32] He is, I believe, referring to an extension of the immediate efficient causal power that the will has over the human body, an extension constituted by the mind's further ability to affect other bodies by means of moving its own body. Again, the occasionalism must kick in at a certain point. The mind has an extended, indirect causal influence over other bodies in that it can move the body to which it is united, which body in turn comes into local contact with another body. This contact occasions God to move the second body.[33] God's role here does not diminish the mind's power to move its body. Rather, it extends that power to allow it indirectly to affect other bodies. And this is the *only* way a mind can move

31. I would extend this explanation to the passage cited above (in section III) in which La Forge, in his "continuous creation" argument for body–body occasionalism, claims that "no creature, *spiritual* or corporeal . . . can change [the position of a body] or that of any of its parts, in the second instant of its creation if the Creator does not do it himself" (*Traité*, 240; emphasis added). That is, La Forge is referring here only to the position of a body insofar as it is moved by an inanimate body or an animate body (and, hence, indirectly by a mind, or "spiritual creature"), *not* to the motion of the human body insofar as it is moved by the mind directly.

32. I would think that if he were using this passage to explain voluntary motions in an occasionalist manner, he would have referred not to an extension of the power that the will has, but to the laws of mind–body union (just as he refers to the laws of motion).

33. Technically, the occasionalism kicks in even sooner than this, since the will has a direct causal power only over the pineal gland.

another body: by extension, by moving its own body and thereby occasioning God to move the other body. This is the import of the last sentence of the passage.

VI

A recognition of the limitations of La Forge's occasionalism, while interesting both for its own sake and for the light it may shed on Descartes's causal doctrines,[34] is also of more general importance for deepening our understanding of the nature of seventeenth-century occasionalism. This is particularly true in at least two respects.

First, my conclusions here should contribute to dispelling the myth—still prevalent in textbooks and even in the scholarly literature[35]—that occasionalism was offered by Cartesians mainly as an ad hoc solution to a perceived "mind-body problem." If mind and body are substances as radically and essentially different as Descartes says they are, how, one may ask, is it possible for them to causally engage one another and interact? How can unextended thinking and thoughtless extension bring about effects in each other (as I show above, La Forge does at least recognize the prima facie force of this question). Occasionalists, the story runs, perceived this difficulty and thus used God to bridge the ontological chasm between mind and body.

This convenient story, however, completely distorts both the doctrine and the arguments behind it. Almost all occasionalists who use God's causal activity to explain mind-body relations also use it to explain body-body relations.[36] Often the *same* kinds of arguments are used to show both that bodies cannot cause motion in other bodies and that minds and bodies

34. La Forge considers himself a faithful and orthodox Cartesian, one who is sometimes merely spelling out Descartes's own doctrines in greater detail, and who is at other times developing and expanding them in ways he believes Descartes would have done had he lived longer; see *Traité*, Préface.

35. For textbook histories, see F. Copleston, *A History of Philosophy* (London, 1958), vol. 4, pp. 176ff., and D. W. Hamlyn, *The Pelican History of Western Philosophy* (London: Penguin, 1989), pp. 145–47. For scholarly examples, see Watson, *The Breakdown of Cartesian Metaphysics*, and D. Radner, *Malebranche: A Study of a Cartesian System* (Assen: Van Gorcum, 1978), pp. 10–12. There are also attempts to correct this pedagogically useful but historically and philosophically false picture; see Lennon, "Philosophical Commentary," in Malebranche, *The Search after Truth*, LO 810ff.

36. Johannes Clauberg may be the exception here in that he appears to argue for occasionalism only with regard to mind-body relations. But Clauberg may not be an occasionalist at all; see note 39 below.

cannot truly interact. This suggests that the real problem does not stem from mind-body dualism per se, but rather from the natural deficiency and impotence of finite beings. In fact, some occasionalists (partial and thoroughgoing) do not even recognize that there is some problem peculiar to the mind-body case. La Forge, for example, explicitly says that "it is not more difficult to conceive how the mind of man, without being extended, can move the body, and how the body, without being a spiritual thing, can act on the mind, than it is to conceive how one body has the power to move itself and to communicate its motion to another body" (*Traité*, 235).[37] Moreover, my examination of La Forge's account reveals that there are certain Cartesian thinkers—and La Forge is not a minor figure—who are occasionalists *only* with respect to body-body relations. La Forge's occasionalism clearly gives lie to the textbook mythology.

Second, it is important in understanding occasionalism to recognize the great variety there is among seventeenth-century occasionalists, even among those who might be considered "mainstream." The occasionalisms of Malebranche, Cordemoy, Clauberg, Geulincx, and La Forge all differ in scope and in argumentation.[38] Malebranche, for example, is as thoroughgoing an occasionalist as one could hope for, as is Cordemoy. Clauberg's alleged occasionalism, on the other hand, appears to be limited to mind-body relations.[39] And then there is the case of Arnauld, who employs occasionalism to explain only one facet of mind-body relations, namely, how bodily motions occasion God to produce sensations in the mind.[40] It may be that a limited employment of occasionalism, such as La Forge's, is the rule rather than the exception among Cartesians. In any case, we should be very careful about any general claims we may be tempted to make about "the occasionalists."

---

37. La Forge is not alone in this regard; see S. Nadler, "Occasionalism and the Mind-Body Problem," *Oxford Studies in the History of Philosophy* 2 (forthcoming).

38. For a discussion of this variety, see Prost, *Essai*, especially chs. 6 and 7, and Battail, *L'avocat philosophe*, pp. 143–44.

39. See Johannes Clauberg, *Disputationes physica*, XII, and *Corporis et animae conjunctio*, in *Opera Omnia philosophica* (Amsterdam, 1691). Clauberg's views on mind-body relations, in fact, appear to be closer to La Forge's than to an occasionalism. See W. Weier, "Der Okkasionalismus des Johannes Clauberg und sein Verhältnis zu Descartes, Geulincx, Malebranche," *Studia Cartesiana* 2 (1981): 43–62.

40. See "Examen d'un écrit qui a pour titre: Traité de l'essence du corps & de l'union de l'Ame avec le corps, contre la philosophie de M. Descartes" (1680), in *Oeuvres de Messire Antoine Arnauld*, 43 vols. (Paris: Sigismond D'Arnay, 1775), vol. 38, pp. 146–48.

Richard A. Watson

Malebranche, Models, and Causation

I. A Framework Problem

In this chapter, I consider a framework problem in the history of philosophy. Framework problems arise in the context of applying the principle of charity in interpretation—always assume that the material you are trying to understand makes sense to the person who wrote it. The historian's job is to find out just what that sense is.

In the case of Malebranche, one must work within a triadic framework, the first arm of which is that the existence of God is accepted as necessary. Second, although we do not fully understand the notions of God's perfections, Malebranche assumes that we do know that omnipotence is of God's essence. And the meaning of omnipotence seems to condense, for Malebranche's metaphysical purposes, to the view that God can do anything within reason. Malebranche does not subscribe to Descartes's voluntarist view that God is the source of the eternal truths, nor to the view that God could make a contradiction true. For Malebranche, even God submits to the principle of noncontradiction. On the basis of archetypal ideas, God creates a contingent world and sustains it in existence through a process of continuous creation, simply by the power of his will. That is, "la puissance de Dieu" is "l'efficace de sa volonté."[1] "Les volontez de Dieu étant efficaces par elles mêmes, il suffit qu'il veüille, pour faire."[2]

God's necessary existence and his omnipotence expressed as the creative force of his will are two arms of the triadic framework of Malebranche's metaphysics. The third arm, which holds them all together, is faith. Now, the framework problem is this: As a historian of philosophy purporting to provide an interpretation of Malebranche, is one required to understand the first two framework principles of his metaphysics, or must one accept their intelligibility on faith? More profoundly, did Malebranche—who had faith—himself understand God's existence and God's essence?

The easier to approach is the concept of God's existence. There is a long tradition in Western philosophy—best known today from Descartes's *Meditations*—that one can have knowledge of existence before knowledge of essence. "What, then, am I?" Descartes asks *after* he is assured that he exists. Obviously a thinking thing.

This knowledge of existence before essence is vacuous until one discovers what it is that exists. Unlike Descartes, Malebranche is uncertain about the true essence of mind, but, like Descartes, he predicates his philosophy on the notion that we are thinking things.

Also following Descartes, Malebranche finds that God necessarily exists. But what, then, is God? The tradition is that God's essence is necessary existence, but this does not advance one's quest for understanding of God's substantive nature. There is little evidence that Malebranche has any more notion about the characteristics of God than he does about those of the human mind, but, again like Descartes, he rests his metaphysics on the notion that God is an omnipotent force or power. And this perfection is crucial to Malebranche's notion of causation. It seems reasonable to say that if there is existence—whether contingent or necessary—something must have caused that existence. Descartes and Malebranche call this cause God.

The framework problem is this: Do we understand this notion of divine causation, and, if so, how? Specifically, this notion is God's omnipotence interpreted as his power to create the world out of nothing. This is an important concept, because if God can do this, God can *cause* anything. That is, creation out of nothing can be translated in the contingent sphere into causation, so to speak, "without cause." If God can create anything out of nothing, then he can make any *B* follow any *A* by fiat. Then a

---

1. Nicolas Malebranche, *Recherche de la vérité*, Éclaircissement XII, OC III, 175.
2. *Recherche*, Éclaircissement XV, OC III, 241.

contingent "cause" need have nothing in it to be understood (or that can be understood) as what explains how a given effect comes from it. Thus, Malebranche says that "[q]uand je vois une boule qui en choque une autre . . . la véritable cause qui meut les corps ne paroît pas à mes yeux . . . les corps ne pouvant se remuer eux-mêmes . . . leur force mouvante n'étant que la volonté de Dieu qui les conserve successivement en différens endroits."[3] He thus does not support Descartes's claim that God makes it so that mind and body interact causally, even though such interaction seems impossible to us. Malebranche accepts the impossibility of mind–body interaction and proposes occasionalism instead. But to understand this occasionalism, one must understand the notion of omnipotence—the notion of creation out of nothing. Do *you*, as an interpreter of Malebranche, understand the notion that "[l]es volontez de Dieu [sont] efficaces par elles mêmes"?[4] I do not, but let us look at what reliance on this principle can do, anyway.

Although some interpreters say that Malebranche's occasionalism is not designed to solve the problem of how mind and body interact causally, it does provide a solution. Briefly, here is the problem: Descartes says that active unextended mind is so utterly different from passive extended matter that we can comprehend neither how a mind could move a body (it cannot push it) nor how a body could impose ideas of itself on a mind (there is nothing to push). For Descartes, causation in the material world is by contact, by mechanical interaction, like the teeth of gears engaging, but minds cannot contact bodies mechanically, and also bodies cannot press against minds to influence them. A mind cannot make an impact on a body, and a body cannot make an impression on a mind. Mind and body cannot interact with each other in any way at all.

But they do appear to interact. So what is going on? Malebranche says that on the occasion of your willing to move, say, your arm, God moves it for you: "il me paroît tres-certain que la volonté des esprits n'est pas capable de mouvoir le plus petit corps qu'il y ait au monde: car il est évident qu'il n'y a point de liaison nécessaire, entre la volonté que nous avons, par exemple, de remüer nôtre bras, & le mouvement de nôtre bras. Il est vrai qu'il se remüe lorsque nous le voulons: & qu'ainsi nous sommes la cause naturelle du mouvement de nôtre bras. Mais les causes *naturelles* ne sont point de véritables causes: ce ne sont que des causes *occasionelles*, qui n'agissent que par la force & l'efficace de la volonté de Dieu."[5] He goes on

3. *Recherche*, Éclaircissement XV, OC III, 208.
4. *Recherche*, Éclaircissement XV, OC III, 241.
5. *Recherche* VI.2.iii: OC II, 315.

to say that although "les hommes veulent remüer leur bras . . . il n'y a que Dieu qui le puisse & qui le sçache remüer."[6]

How is this accomplished? Malebranche says that "[c]ause véritable est une cause entre laquelle & son effet l'esprit apperçoit une liaison nécessaire, c'est ainsi que je l'entens. Or il n'y a que l'être infiniment parfait, entre la volonté duquel & les effects l'esprit apperçoive une liaison nécessaire. Il n'y a donc que Dieu qui soit véritable cause, & qui ait véritablement la puissance de mouvoir les corps."[7] Against Cartesians who claim that God could give men and bodies causal power, Malebranche says "qu'il n'est pas concevable, que Dieu puisse communiquer aux hommes ou aux Anges la puissance qu'il a de remüer les corps; & que ceux qui prétendent, que le pouvoir que nous avons de remüer nos bras, est un véritable puissance, doivent avoüer que Dieu peut aussi donner aux esprits la puissance de créer, d'anéantir, de faire toutes les choses possibles, en un mot qu'il peut les rendre tout-puissans,"[8] which is a reductio.

But do we—does Malebranche—understand this creative willpower of God? How does it work? Does Malebranche provide an ontological model to explain it? No. He says that "Dieu n'a pas besoin d'instrumens pour agir, il suffit qu'il veüille afin qu'une chose soit, parce qu'il y a contradiction, qu'il veüille, & que ce qu'il veut ne soit pas. Sa puissance est donc sa volonté, & communiquer sa puissance c'est communiquer l'efficace de sa volonté."[9] This is all quite logical, of course, that "il y a une liaison nécessaire entre la volonté de Dieu & le mouvement de ce corps: Et par consequent c'est Dieu qui est véritable cause du mouvement de ce corps."[10] But like the proof of God's necessary existence, it is empty tautological wordplay.

Malebranche also argues that, on the occasion of a body striking your body, God causes you to see and feel the appropriate mental ideas and sensations. Whenever we know an idea, "elle est en Dieu, & nous la voyons, parce qu'il lui plaît de nous la découvrir."[11] Malebranche denies "que ma volonté soit la cause véritable . . . des idées de mon esprit."[12] On every occasion of apparent mind-body interaction, then, God exerts his causal power, not to endow actual (but to us unintelligible) causal interaction between mind and body as Descartes asserts, but rather to correlate bodily and mental events as though mind and body were interacting causally.

6. *Recherche* VI.2.iii: OC II, 315.
7. *Recherche* VI.2.iii: OC II, 316.
8. *Recherche* VI.2.iii: OC II, 316.
9. *Recherche* VI.2.iii: OC II, 316.
10. *Recherche* VI.2.iii: OC II, 317.
11. *Recherche* III.2.vi: OC I, 445.
12. *Recherche*, Éclaircissement XV, OC III, 225–26.

Because God can cause anything, it would seem to be a moot point whether God underwrites actual causal interaction between mind and matter as Descartes says, or only apparent interaction as Malebranche says. In either case, the explanation of causation rests on an assumed notion of God's omnipotence. God, the first cause, can do anything: end of explanation.

Besides causal interaction, the other half of the mind-body problem is how minds know bodies. Malebranche says that minds know bodies by way of ideas that God shares with us. God knows all possible ideas because one of his perfections is omniscience. Malebranche is famous for saying that "Dieu ait en lui-même les idées de tous les êtres qu'il a créés," that God is "le lieu des esprits," and thus that "il est certain que l'esprit peut voir ce qu'il y a dans Dieu qui represente les êtres crééz . . . supposé que Dieu veüille bien lui découvrir ce qu'il a dans lui qui les represente."[13] These ideas are in God, but they are neither in his mind nor are they properties of his mind. They are God's "substance [qui] est véritablement représentative de l'ame, parce qu'elle en renferme l'archetype ou le modele éternel. . . . Il voit dans son essence les idées ou les essences de tous les êtres possibles."[14] Ideas are models or archetypes of things that make their objects known by representing "quelque chose qui est hors de l'ame, & qui leur ressemble en quelque façon, comme les idées du Soleil, d'une maison, d'un cheval, d'une riviere, &c."[15] God creates the world "sur ses idées, sur le modele éternel qu'il en découvre dans son essence."[16] But the problem with the notion that ideas represent bodies by resembling them is that God's substance is spiritual, and thus ideas are spiritual, so how could they resemble bodies?

What exactly does God make known to us? We know that there is a material world (only) because this knowledge is revealed by God. And the only knowledge we have about this world is revealed by God when he shares his ideas with us: "comme l'existence des créatures ne dépend point de nos volontez, mais de celle du Créateur; il est encore clair que nous ne pouvons nous assurer de leur existence que par quelque espece de révélation ou naturelle ou surnaturelle."[17]

This purported explanation of knowing rests on an assumed notion of God's omniscience combined with his omnipotence. God, all powerful and all knowing, can make us know anything. Again: end of explanation.

Given dualism—which Descartes and Malebranche think necessary to preserve the soul's independence from material bodies and their corrup-

13. *Recherche* III.2.vi: OC I, 437.
14. *Recherche* IV.11: OC II, 98.
15. *Recherche* III.2.v: OC I, 433.
16. *Recherche* IV.11: OC II, 99.
17. *Recherche* IV.11: OC II, 98.

tion—we have the mind-body problem. Whether or not Malebranche means to solve that problem, he agrees that mind-body interaction is impossible. His occasionalism explains how and why it appears that there is mind-body interaction when there is not. Because we are naturally inclined to believe that mind and body do interact, occasionalism means that God is a deceiver. Malebranche admits it. But in the Cartesian tradition, it is very important that God not be a deceiver. If God were a deceiver, he might deceive us into believing that some ideas are clear and distinct—and thus true—that truly are false.

Malebranche's occasionalism raises an even more difficult problem. Deceived or not, how do we know it's us? We can worry about who we are because Malebranche takes over from Descartes the doctrine of continuous creation. That is, Malebranche denies that there is such a thing as inertia of being in created things. Whatever power or force is required to create something must be sustained to keep the created being in existence. The existence of the world as we know it, the existence of all the things in the world, including you and me, depends on their being continuously created. And, on a common interpretation, this gives rise to a new deception.

It seems to us (in our memories) as though our minds and bodies exist continuously, but God's continuous creation of the world takes place moment by moment. In continuous creation, what remains the same from moment to moment—if anything *does* remain the same—is a pattern or structural order of a concatenation of bodies and minds, but not persisting bodies and minds. God actually creates a new world at each instant.

Note precisely that bodies and minds are not *re*-created each instant; bodies and minds that have expired are not brought back into being; at each instant *new* bodies and minds are created. This might be thought to be acceptable because the new bodies and minds are created according to the same patterns or developmental plans that the now-nonexistent bodies and minds of the past fitted into. That is, unless God is deceiving us about that, too.

So—on this common interpretation—not only does Malebranche's system show how minds and bodies do not interact, although we think they do, it also shows how bodies and minds do not have continuous existence through time, although we think they do. So *I* am not the continuously existing being that I thought I was. At each moment there is a new I that (unless God is deceiving this present I about the past) has the same pattern of memories, thoughts, and characteristics as a sequence of I's in the past. But given that God has deceived me into thinking that minds and bodies interact when they do not, and that I have continuous existence when I do not, how much assurance can I have that the I that I am right now has anything in common with a sequence of now-nonexistent I's that supposedly existed in the past?

An alternative interpretation is that continuous creation means that once minds and bodies are created, God keeps them in existence continuously with his continuing creative force—and not by new creation moment by moment—so I am the I of a moment ago, and am not deceived at least about that. This is the more charitable interpretation, and if one finds creation out of nothing intelligible, then the power of continuous creation—in the sense of keeping something already created in existence—ought to be easy to accept. But the interpretation that continuous creation is repetitive moment-by-moment creation out of nothing, a kind of re-creation, is more common.

In any case, God plays an enormous role here. God saves us from worries that there was no world before this moment. There was, even though it was not exactly this world. And God keeps us from worries that the previous world was different from the present world in pattern or order and concatenation. That is, if we believe in God. And so we move to the third arm of the frame: faith.

II. Occasionalism Is Not Philosophy

God (necessary existence), creation (omnipotence), and faith are theological notions. Leibniz was one of several who tried to make Malebranche understand that theology is not philosophy. More explicitly, Simon Foucher reminded Malebranche that edification explains nothing.[18] The two main problems with God in philosophy are first, that resort to God explains too much, and second, that when we talk of God we do not know what we are talking about.

If we accept the assurance of Scripture that God created the heavens and the earth, we know that they exist, but we notoriously have uncertain knowledge about the essences of the created entities. Descartes says that God gives us innate knowledge of the general nature of mind, matter, and God, but we can generate so many hypotheses about the laws of nature that experimentation is necessary to obtain scientific knowledge both of the psychology of minds and of the physics of bodies. God determines the laws of nature, but leaves it to us to find them out.

18. On Leibniz's and Foucher's cautions to Malebranche, see Richard A. Watson, "The Downfall of Cartesianism," in *The Breakdown of Cartesian Metaphysics* (Atlantic Highlands, N.J.: Humanities Press International, 1987).

The traditional way that philosophers explain how and why things are the way they are is to describe an ontological model that supposedly exhibits the causal powers of things that support the causal interactions among them. The Platonic model involves things striving to attain an ideal state. In the Aristotelian model, forms structure matter, resulting in things that have formal, material, efficient, and final causal powers. Galileo in one way, and Gassendi and Descartes in another way take over the Democritean corpuscular model in which material bodies push each other around by pressure and impact. To explain how bodies act on minds and on each other, these New Philosophers propose underlying mechanical models from which traditional Scholastic causal powers are banned.

Descartes argues that the material world is a plenum—even apparently empty space consists of subtle matter—into which God has introduced a total quantity of motion that is conserved by exchange when bodies interact. There is no empty space, so all movements of bodies are ultimately circular, because if one thing moves, a second thing has to get out of its way, and eventually something has to move into where the first thing was. This is difficult because since space *is* matter, there are no places. Descartes explains how this can be by saying that place is merely relational. The place of a thing is defined by its spatial relations to other things. Things do not move from place to place; instead, they change their spatial relations to one another. But this is a circular argument, for place is defined in terms of spatial relations. It would appear that nothing can move in Descartes's plenum.

Descartes, however, proceeds to describe dynamic mechanical structures or machines made of tiny particles of matter far smaller than anything we can see. These are the basic things in the world and they cause us to perceive as we do. Light, for example, consists of tiny globes that fly through the air and bounce like tennis balls, and, depending on their speed and spin, we see the colors we do.

Malebranche was a Cartesian scientist (even if he denied being a Cartesian philosopher). He saw that mechanisms do not explain sensation because material interactions cannot cause mental sensations. He did not see how causal interactions could take place even among bodies. Cartesian mechanisms are unconnected causally with minds and are apparently even causally disconnected with one another. So the scope of Malebranche's occasionalism extends not only over mind–body interactions but also over body–body interactions, as indicated in the quotations above.

Despite the fact that bodies lack causal efficacy—either on minds or on one another—Malebranche keeps bodies. He even keeps mechanical models because they are instrumentally useful in natural science. But Malebranche breaks with the tradition of explaining real causality in the world with reference to ontological models. Instead, he defers all causal activity to one primary cause. This primary cause, of course, is God.

This in effect substitutes God's willpower for efficient causality in the natural world. But Malebranche himself attacks the notion of such occult or magical powers as that of God's efficacious will. He says of such Scholastic terms as *"formes, . . . vertus, qualitez, facultez,* &c." that they signify nothing, and that they occur in "volumes, dans lesquels il est plus difficile qu'on ne pense de remarquer quelqu'endroit où [les Auteurs] ayent entendu ce qu'ils ont écrit."[19] Yet, Malebranche goes on to say that "[s]i l'on dit que l'union de mon esprit avec mon corps, consiste en ce que Dieu veut, que lorsque je voudrai que mon bras soit mû, les esprits animaux se répandent dans les muscles dont il est composé, pour le remuer en la maniére que je souhaite; j'entens clairement cette explication, & je la reçois."[20]

Which explanation? The physiological explanation is standard, and is understandable in mechanical terms. But God's power of will is an occult force of the highest degree, and it is this power we must understand to understand Malebranche's "explanation." And if Malebranche understands the magic of God's efficacious willpower, then his claim not to comprehend lesser such powers—because God could not delegate them—is specious.

The real problem, as we all know, is that God explains too much. God can do anything. And when God does everything, there is nothing to explain. Or, rather, the explanation of everything is this: God created the heavens and the earth. Nothing more is required. This, then, is what is bad about introducing God into philosophy. Yet Malebranche says that "il est nécessaire . . . pour être Philosophe, de recourir à Dieu, qui est la cause universelle; car c'est sa volonté qui est la force mouvante des corps, & qui fait aussi la communication de leurs mouvemens."[21] But there is no point in trying to explain things philosophically if God just does them by creative fiat. One can still do physics, of course. As a natural scientist, Malebranche worked with mechanical models like all the other New Scientists.

Malebranche's occasionalism seems to result from his abandoning an inexplicable doctrine of Cartesian secondary causes, both between minds and bodies and among bodies. He offers instead the primary cause of everything. He appeals to God's direct causal action. But to do this, one must have faith in God's existence and in God's omnipotence represented by continuous creation out of nothing. One must ground one's metaphysics in theological notions.

19. *Recherche*, Éclaircissement XII, OC III, 179.
20. *Recherche*, Éclaircissement XV, OC III, 226.
21. *Recherche*, Éclaircissement XV, OC III, 214.

Descartes's claim that God makes causal interaction happen, even if we cannot understand how, is inadequate, but at least Descartes retains some dignity for the world of bodies and us. But Malebranche turns the world of bodies into a kind of puppet show, with things behaving as though they were interacting when really they are not.

In short, as Descartes knew and Leibniz said, to resort to God in philosophy is to abandon explanation. Ontological models exhibiting powers of secondary causation are what philosophy is all about. The Aristotelians were on the right track at least about this.

III. Philosophy Is Natural Philosophy

The notion that philosophy is natural philosophy or science has a bad press because of what positivists say about God. But in fact, positivists say nothing about God that has not been said many times—often to high praise—throughout most of Christian tradition, which is that, strictly speaking, we know nothing at all about God. Many theologians agree that we cannot apply empirical, finite, or human categories to God and advocate referring to God negatively only by what he is not. In other words, positive scientific talk of God in empirical naturalistic terms does not make sense.

The trouble stemming from the positivists is that they conclude from this that God talk is total, utterly vacuous nonsense. It is not that God is dead, nor that God does not exist. You cannot even say these things sensibly, because, the positivists conclude, the very notion of God is meaningless.

But this negative view of philosophy as science is unfair to traditional natural philosophers. Of course Democritus, the founder of the mechanistic atomism that inspired the rise of modern science, does not believe in God, but Galileo, Gassendi, Mersenne, Pascal, Descartes, Leibniz, and Newton do.

What gets forgotten by those who reject the notion that philosophy is science is that even Thomas Aquinas stresses the difference between philosophy and theology. Theology has to do with the primary cause, the first cause, God. Natural philosophy has to do with secondary causes, the world. Natural philosophy consists in making ontological models with which to show how things are and to explain why they behave and interact the way that they do. This is what philosophical systems beginning with the Greeks have been designed to do.

Such philosophers as Descartes and Leibniz kept saying that one should not appeal to God in natural philosophy (although they themselves do); by having God play a central role in his occasionalism, Malebranche abandons natural philosophy. My argument is that this leaves him only faith to hold his picture together. Occasionalism rules out any natural philosophy of real secondary causes.

IV. God in Science

Hume analyzes cause into relations of contiguity in space and succession in time. No powers, no forces, no efficient or active agents of causation. Just one thing following another. This strictly empirical, positivist, nonoccult notion of mechanical causation is present in Cartesian mechanism, in which secondary causation is unexplained, and is prefigured in Malebranche's occasionalism, where only God actually moves bodies, particularly where he says that "[q]uand je vois une boule qui en choque une autre . . . la véritable cause qui meut les corps ne parôit pas à mes yeux . . . les corps ne pouvant se remuer eux-mêmes . . . leur force mouvante n'étant que la volonté de Dieu qui les conserve successivement en différens endroits."[22] The Humean analysis of causation has been dominant in science ever since, despite attempts by figures as diverse as Kant, Poincaré, and Einstein to reassert the notion of causal powers in nature.

Berkeley, like Hume, also argues that material corpuscules (supposing they exist) could not cause events of sensory perception, nor could the underlying structures and machines of the mechanical philosophers—being made of passive matter—interact causally even among themselves. Malebranche certainly and Descartes implicitly held the same view. They are usually presented—as I do above—as seeing that a description of a machine and of its movements does not provide any insight into how it causes sensations in our minds. But they also know with respect to body-to-body interactions that you can describe, for example, *what* a watch does, but you cannot see—and thus do not know—why it moves just that way. The reason (they say) is just that God made the world this way (and could easily have made it another way). More profoundly, these observations and descriptions give you no insight whatsoever into what—if anything—in a body acts causally on other bodies. Malebranche says bodies do not, but Berkeley concludes that bodies cannot, have causal powers. Nor, as Hume stresses, can sensory phenomena have causal powers, either.

Why *did* Galileo, Descartes, and other seventeenth-century natural philosophers adopt mechanism? Two main reasons have been suggested. The primary qualities of size, shape, position, and motion are amenable to

22. *Recherche*, Éclaircissement XV, OC III, 208.

quantification. Thus, laws of the motion of material things can be described by mathematical functions that can be used instrumentally to predict and postdict the behavior of bodies. It is also said that the primary qualities of material bodies do not vary as do secondary qualities. But in the wax example, Descartes shows that the sensible representations of primary qualities do vary, and Berkeley uses these facts to assimilate primary to secondary sensible qualities. If the actual non-sensed primary qualities of bodies themselves are unchanging, we certainly do not know this by perceiving them.

It is also sometimes suggested that mechanism is viable because we see that macroscopic bodies are made like machines, and thus it seems likely that the microscopic parts of macroscopic bodies are also organized as small machines. One can read Lucretius to see how this works—water flows because water atoms wiggle, diamonds are hard because their parts are firmly interlaced, and so on.

This analogical argument to the view that underlying little machines explain why the big machines behave as they do seems reasonable at first, but it is either circular or leads to an infinite regress. Unless we see straight off not only how macroscopic bodies interact with one another, but also that they interact causally, then the attribution of causal powers to microscopic bodies is unsupported analogically. But if we do see that macroscopic bodies have causal powers, we do not need microscopic bodies to explain why they behave as they do. On the other hand, if we do need microscopic mechanisms to explain why macroscopic mechanisms behave as they do, then we will need submicroscopic mechanisms to explain the behavior of the microscopic mechanisms themselves, and so on ad infinitum.

Descartes, Malebranche, Berkeley, and Hume all point out that in fact we do not see causes in bodies, we do not see them interact *causally,* we see only how they move with relation to one another. Descartes does not list causal powers among the primary qualities of matter or extension. Like Malebranche, he holds that only God really causes motion. As Geneviève Rodis-Lewis says, concurring with Gouhier: "Descartes fonde . . . l'autonomie de la physique mécaniste: le monde de l'objectivité scientifique est purifié de son revêtement qualitatif et de tout dynamisme interne; l'erreur scolastique est ainsi dénoncée, en même temps qu'expliquée par un projection anthropomorphique remontant à l'enfance."[23] Once God puts matter into motion, bodies interact according to the physical laws God establishes, but bodies in themselves neither initiate motion nor have causal power. The postulation of microscopic mechanisms on this view can be defended not

---

23. Geneviève Rodis-Lewis, *L'anthropologie Cartésienne* (Paris: Presses Universitaires de France, 1990), p. 44.

because they explain why macroscopic bodies behave the way they do, but only for their instrumental value in predicting and postdicting the behavior of macroscopic bodies.

Beyond dismissing occult powers in bodies, Malebranche points out that we cannot see and feel bodies themselves causing us to have ideas and sensations because we see only ideas and feel only sensations. But whether or not ideas and sensations are actually caused by underlying material particles in motion, all the problems of representationalism arise. How do we know that sensations represent bodies correctly or at all?[24] The reality of underlying micromechanisms would seem to be doubly dubitable.

Did the New Philosophers, then, actually mean their mechanical models to be only instrumental calculating devices that are not even intended to be representations of what there is in the world? They themselves are not entirely clear about this. There is a long-standing debate over whether Galileo took his mathematical model only instrumentally as an aid to predicting planetary positions, or whether he took his theory as a realistic description of the way things actually are. It is said that Galileo had to profess instrumentalism to keep from being imprisoned for going against the ontological dogma of the church.

Whatever Galileo and the other New Scientists intended, it can be argued that instrumentalism is implied from the very beginning of modern mechanistic science by the facts that adherence to a radically dualist ontology makes it impossible to understand how minds and bodies can interact causally, and that the elimination of Scholastic powers and forces from physics leading to a notion of the essence of matter as passive makes it difficult to comprehend how even bodies can interact causally. Among the New Scientists, only Leibniz retained entitive forces and powers, and even he did not claim to perceive them in bodies.

All the New Scientists proposed mechanical models that were justified at least because of their powerful instrumental use in prediction and postdiction. It may seem reasonable to think that bodies interact causally, but our attribution of causal powers to underlying mechanisms—as proposed by both Descartes and Locke—is not based on analogy to such powers observed in our experience of macroscopic bodies. We may experience (or think we do) causal power in our own willed actions, but it is, as Descartes says, a childish anthropomorphic error to project such power into material bodies. The spurious nature of causality in matter is recognized by Descartes, it is one source of Malebranche's occasionalism, it is the ground of Berkeley's immaterialism, and its full exposure is the basis of Hume's analysis of causation as mere sequence.

24. *Recherche* IV.11: OC II, 96–99.

What I am saying is that Hume's view of causation is not new. Anti-Aristotelians like Descartes deny that bodies have causal powers. Malebranche sees this as a serious problem. The mechanical models—bereft of causal powers—do not in fact support secondary causation as the mechanical philosophers claim they do. Malebranche, like Berkeley after him, thus throws out secondary causation to rely entirely on primary divine causation, that is, creation. But then Hume finds the notion of creation as groundless as the notion of causation.

Nevertheless, God has not been eliminated. Descartes says that we are made in the image of God as witnessed by our possession of an infinite power of will. This power of willing is cited by Locke and many others as the only experience we have of an active force, of a causal power. It is a power like God's. I want my arm to rise in the air. I exercise my willpower. My arm rises in the air. Real causal power. Malebranche, also, sees willing as the only motive power, but he seats it all in God.

Does the idea of God's omnipotent willpower derive from our imaginatively magnifying to infinity this causal willpower we seem to possess? It is clearly the case that pagan gods are projections into things of our own desires and feelings and intentions and powers of acting. Christians got rid of these pagan gods, but their God retains anthropomorphic force and power. So be it. Even if this notion of willpower were not magic—as it is—is this appeal to *primary* power adequate for science? Given that God creates the world the way we raise our arms, or, more often used as an example, the way we imagine things, does this give us a concept of *secondary* causation? Obviously it does not. This, again, shows how importing God and his primary creative power into natural philosophy explains nothing. One cannot make sense of God as a secondary power. God's causation—if it is intelligible to us at all—is primary creation, which at best can be translated into a notion of secondary causation "without cause" as I do above. And this leads inexorably to an instrumental interpretation of mechanical models.[25]

V. God Banished from Science

As indicated in the quotation from Rodis-Lewis above, one thing Descartes and the founders of modern science mean to do when attacking Aristotle is

---

25. On the demand for ontological models of explanation, see Richard A. Watson, "Foucher's Mistake and Malebranche's Break: Ideas, Intelligible Extension, and the End of Ontology," in *Nicolas Malebranche: His Philosophical Critics and Successors*, ed. Stuart Brown (Assen/Maastricht: Van Gorcum, 1991), pp. 22–34.

to banish the remnants of animistic powers, forces, and occult natures from the material world. Occult powers explain nothing. It is not a scientific explanation, as Molière points out, to say that opium puts you to sleep because it has a dormitive power. And it does not help to say that God put that power in opium, no more than it does to say that mind and matter interact because God endows them with the power to do so.

But if there are no powers in things, how can they do the things they do? Malebranche says God does it. But as I argue above, what Malebranche really manages to do by this move is to show that God has no role in philosophy. If you try to explain things by appealing to God's creative power, either you have no explanation at all because God just creates everything, or you get an ad hoc system like occasionalism. On the other hand, Malebranche's occasionalism makes quite clear the important fact that in the natural world all we can observe in the name of causation are regular sequences of B's following A's. Knowledge of Malebranche's puppet dance—without the strings—*does* turn out to be enough for science if you just ask *what* and *how,* and not *why.*

If we start postulating causal powers in things, we revert to the pantheistic world of spirits or the Aristotelian world of occult forces. We talk of the natures of things, their inner essences that make them behave as they do. We talk of dormitive powers in opium.

Nevertheless, some people still postulate powers in things. That some of these people no longer believe in God makes it even more imperative, apparently, that there be causal natures in things. A contemporary proponent of the search is Rom Harré, who says the scientist's task is to find "the real essence of a thing . . . *whatever* is responsible for its causal powers."[26] That is, he says scientific explanations should be of the form: "Under conditions $C,$ A will manifest sensible quality or characteristic B in virtue of its being of nature N."[27] Harré says further that "[t]he ultimate entities are causally responsible for the states of the world without anything being causally responsible for them."[28] So these ultimate entities cause but are not caused. This certainly sounds like God, but, if so, Harré's powers are not those of secondary causation.

I have taken these Harré quotations from the two-volume work *Causality and Scientific Explanation* by William A. Wallace, who himself concludes:

> I have . . . urged an expansion of causal thinking far beyond the narrow domain of Humean causation, to include what contemporary

26. Rom Harré, *The Principles of Scientific Thinking* (Chicago: University of Chicago Press, 1970), p. 299; emphasis added.
27. Ibid., p. 187.
28. Ibid., p. 297.

thinkers have spoken of as "powers," "inner determiners," and other real "explanatory factors" that can account for the phenomena being studied by today's scientists . . . the manifold of ontological anteced-ents that can truly explain natural phenomena.[29]

Wallace, like Harré, insists that the powers are there, and that they *truly* explain, but he has no idea what they are nor how they do what they do. In the examples Wallace gives throughout his two volumes, these powers are defined generally as something that causes the effects whose cause is to be explained.

Now what *is* this something? *Who* is this something? The only possible candidate is God.

Throughout Malebranche, Original Sin and the Fall of Man are evoked to explain why sensations are confused and our ideas are not pure. One might tolerate this as a charming fairy tale interwoven in the text, but the fact is that it is part of a theological doctrine integral to the development of occasionalism. That is, in the center of this doctrine is God, who plays the crucial role in occasionalism. Occasionalism without God is nonsense. You must take God seriously to take occasionalism seriously. Otherwise you have a mysterious unknown power causing the parallelism, or you have parallelism by chance, or—and I think this is what actually followed—you have Hume's analysis of causation. Because if you cannot see causation in bodies bumping one another (and Malebranche says you cannot), and if you are not a dogmatic believer in God so that you can turn to God as the cause for everything, including the parallelism, you simply have no way empirically to get any notion of causal power.

Malebranche in the tradition of the New Philosophers ruled out Scholas-tic occult forces, but he was not worried because he had God. He felt so secure that he could deny the standard argument by analogy from human will to powers in things—that is, the anthropomorphizing of things as though they had willpower as we supposedly do. But in fact, Malebranche said, we do not have any willpower. We will, but there is no power in it. Our willing is merely the occasion for God to exert his power. We do not in fact have willpower at all. But when we will that our arms rise, our arms rise. This is either magic, or God does it. Malebranche says God does it. So I ask you as an interpreter of Malebranche, "Do you comprehend the concept of God having the power to create something out of nothing?" If you do not, then for you occasionalism literally does not make sense.

But suppose we go ahead and postulate God as creator of the world and

---

29. William A. Wallace, *Causality and Scientific Explanation*, vol. 2, *Classical and Contemporary Science* (Ann Arbor: University of Michigan Press, 1974), p. 326.

of its ways. A major problem with God as creator is that the statement that something comes from nothing is contradictory. This notion of God's creative force is denied by Malebranche's assertion that God is subject to the principle of noncontradiction, although this stricture does not apply to God as Descartes conceives him.

The problem with the Malebranchian framework—God, creation, and faith—is that even if one could grasp in some sense that God and existence are the same (the essence of God is existence), his perfections seem to be unintelligible or only negatively characterizable, and the concept of creation contradictory. Malebranche himself just takes it for granted that we know that God exists and that we understand God's power to create something out of nothing. He does not explicate the two substantive framework principles of his metaphysics—God and creation. But where he uses faith to hold the other two together, I tend toward Humean skepticism, and find that Malebranche's framework collapses.

In conclusion, the framework problem concerning Malebranche's occasionalism arises because God's necessary existence and his efficacious will-power are generated as empty tautologies. God and creation are unintelligible and clearly unexplanatory. They are opaque notions, not just in my interpretation as a historian trying to understand, but also for Malebranche himself. Malebranche finds faith in God crucial for holding his metaphysics together, and obviously takes this as a strong recommendation for religion. Ironically, against all his intentions, by stressing that mechanical models do not contain secondary causation—that bodies do not interact causally—Malebranche also lays the ground for instrumentalism and the highly successful New Science, void of occult forces, powers, and God.

Mark A. Kulstad

Causation and Preestablished Harmony in the Early Development of Leibniz's Philosophy

Leibniz's denial of genuine causal interaction among created substances and his assertion of concomitance or preestablished harmony are familiar doctrines. They are clearly present in his writings by the latter half of the 1680s, notably in the *Discourse on Metaphysics* and the correspondence with Arnauld. What is far less familiar is the history of Leibniz's coming to hold these doctrines, a potentially important and interesting story given the context of the lively seventeenth-century discussion of causation and the mind-body problem.

Many of course have claimed that the *Discourse on Metaphysics* contains the first statement of Leibniz's mature philosophy. But agreement on this point does not always bring with it agreement on what precisely is supposed to distinguish this work, in a significant way, from Leibniz's earlier writings. One striking hypothesis, having some relation to present concerns, is that the critical new doctrine in this work is Leibniz's assertion that each substance expresses the whole universe.[1] G.H.R. Parkinson has offered a nicely balanced critique of this position, leaving part of the thesis intact, but pointing out what must be seen as clear anticipations of the doctrine of expression in Leibniz's earlier writings.[2] A counterhypothesis might be this: perhaps it is more a matter of the emergence of the preestablished harmony in Leibniz's thought at the time of the *Discourse* that marks a significant break from the earlier writings. After all, some scholars[3] have taken the intriguing first lines of the *New System*[4] of 1695 to indicate that Leibniz himself dates the maturation of his "system" to the time of the *Discourse on Metaphysics*. And in the 1695 work, Leibniz suggests strongly that it was the discovery of the preestablished harmony as a solution to the problem of mind-body union that provided the final step in bringing his new system to completion.[5] Presumably the final step has the same date as the maturation.[6]

Expanding on this point, let us take as one extreme in the possible histories of Leibniz's development in connection with the preestablished harmony and the denial of intersubstantial causation[7] that neither of these

1. Lucas and Grint make this claim in the Introduction to their *Leibniz: Discourse on Metaphysics*, trans. Peter G. Lucas and Leslie Grint (Manchester: Manchester University Press, 1953), p. xiv. They cite Paul Köhler, *Der Begriff der Repräsentation bei Leibniz* (Berne, 1913), as having presented an earlier form of the thesis. The connection between this expression thesis and preestablished harmony is that Leibniz often links the two, at times appearing to claim that not only does the latter entail the former but also the former entails the latter. There is a fine discussion of this in R. C. Sleigh, Jr., *Leibniz and Arnauld: A Commentary on Their Correspondence* (New Haven, Conn.: Yale University Press, 1990), pp. 170–77.

2. The critique appears in Parkinson's Introduction to *The Leibniz-Arnauld Correspondence*, LA xlvi–xlviii.

3. Including Lucas and Grint; see their Introduction to the *Discourse*, p. xiii.

4. "A New System of the Nature and the Communication of Substances, as well as the Union between the Soul and the Body" (G IV, 477; L 453).

5. The key paragraphs begin with the well-known statement "Having established these things, I thought I had reached port. But when I began to think about the union of the soul with the body, it was like casting me back into the open sea" (G IV, 483; L 457).

6. At least one commentator seems to claim explicitly that we encounter the preestablished harmony for the first time in 1686, in studies preliminary to the *Discourse on Metaphysics*. This is Herman Jan de Vleeschauwer in the article "Occasionalisme et Harmonie Préétablie—Geulincx et Leibniz," *Studia Leibnitiana Suppl.* 14 (1975), p. 285. Unfortunately, he provides no further information, despite the fact that his key phrase, "Vorarbeiten du Discours de métaphysique (1686), où nous rencontrons pour la première fois l'harmonie préétablie," is both vague and ambiguous. One would want to know just which preliminary study he has in mind. Also, it is possible—but I think unlikely given the context—that the intended disambiguation of the date, 1686, is that it applies only to the *Discourse* and not to the *Vorarbeiten*, or preliminary studies (in which case the original assertion of this note would be compromised).

7. To avoid the constant repetition of an overly long statement, I occasionally use this

two doctrines is firmly established in Leibniz's mind until the time of the *Discourse on Metaphysics*. With this as a convenient initial hypothesis, we will examine and evaluate assertions of various commentators on the history of Leibniz's development in this area, ending with some independent observations.

The major theses I wish to defend are these: (1) the assertion of Belaval and the suggestion of Robinet that Leibniz had adopted the preestablished harmony by about 1679 should be rejected on the grounds of inadequate support; (2) the use of material from "Primary Truths" to argue that Leibniz accepted the preestablished harmony and the denial of causal interaction among creatures prior to the *Discourse* is illegitimate; (3) Leibniz came to deny causal interaction between the realm of mind or ideas and the realm of bodies before the writing of the *Discourse*, more specifically, by 1679; (4) there is evidence from the years before 1679 of Leibniz's prior *acceptance* of the action of mind on body and, albeit from a different passage, of the action of body on mind; nonetheless, (5) Kabitz's suggestion that Leibniz was, in 1667, a dualistic interactionist at least partially under the influence of Descartes is unfounded or at least misleading; (6) claims about a possible strong dependence on the occasionalism of Malebranche and Geulincx during Leibniz's Paris period[8] turn out to be weaker than they might at first have seemed; even so, (7) there is some evidence that Leibniz at least briefly adopted a basically occasionalist position a few years after the Paris period; and finally, (8) there are reasons to believe that Spinoza may have had a significant influence, at an important stage, on Leibniz's development of his views on mind–body causation and also other elements of the later doctrine of preestablished harmony.

The defense of these theses, along with the review of the literature that precedes this, hardly constitutes a complete history of Leibniz's development with respect to the denial of intersubstantial causation and the assertion of preestablished harmony. Indeed, I am all too aware of the limitations of this survey. But it may serve nonetheless to spur further

---

abbreviated formulation of Leibniz's position. Strictly, of course, Leibniz allows for the causal action of infinite substance on finite substances, that is, for at least one kind of intersubstantial causation. Another qualification: although I often emphasize the denial of intersubstantial causation, the denial of mind–body causation is obviously of central concern for the present investigation also, whether or not this turns out to be inter*substantial* causation. As it happens, some of the commentators discussed in these pages in fact claim to find a dualism of mental and bodily substances in the writings of the early Leibniz. But, as we shall see, there are reasons for being cautious about such findings.

8. Leibniz spent the years from 1672 to 1676 primarily in Paris, originally sent on a diplomatic mission from the court of the Bishop Elector of Mainz.

thinking and improved understanding of the emergence of these two central doctrines in the thought of the author of the system of preestablished harmony.[9]

The divisions of my essay are as follows: in section I, I set out some terminology and dispense quickly with an intriguing but in the end untenable hypothesis about Leibniz's development with respect to our topic in the period leading up to the *Discourse*. In section II, I present some of the more important views of commentators on Leibniz's development before 1686 concerning the question of the interaction of finite substances and preestablished harmony, with particular attention to Leibniz's relation to occasionalism. In section III, I evaluate these views, basing my critique largely on interpretations of important Leibnizian passages, and employing the evaluation as the vehicle to the defense of many of the theses above. In section IV, I use the work of the preceding sections and some new material as a base for two independent conclusions about Leibniz and occasionalism and Leibniz's relation to Spinoza. In section V, I close with some hypotheses, in the spirit of suggestions for future work rather than as defended theses, on aspects of Leibniz's development that are relevant to causation and preestablished harmony but that are not specifically addressed earlier in the chapter.

I

Before we begin, some rough-and-ready terminological clarifications are in order, along with some information on what will and will not be assumed in the pages that follow. By *spontaneity* I mean the view that created substances can be real causes, or, more specifically, that each state of a created substance arises causally from its preceding state.[10] (Thus Leibniz can allow for causation—intrasubstantial—in creatures while denying them intersubstantial causation.) By *parallelism* I mean the thesis that the states of each creature correspond or agree perfectly[11] with the states of every other

---

9. An example of Leibniz using this phrase to refer to himself occurs in the title of the "Remark of the Author of the System of Pre-established Harmony on a passage from the *Mémoires de Trévoux* of March 1704," published in 1708 (G VI, 595–96; AG 196–97).

10. Robert Sleigh offers valuable detail and greater precision in discussing this concept. See, for instance, his remarks in "Leibniz on Malebranche on Causality," in *Central Themes in Early Modern Philosophy: Essays Presented to Jonathan Bennett*, ed. J. A. Cover and Mark Kulstad (Indianapolis, Ind.: Hackett, 1990), pp. 162 and 188, n. 3. A fascinating discussion relating to spontaneity and miracles occurs in Sleigh's book, *Leibniz and Arnauld*, pp. 133–34.

11. These terms are notoriously vague. Here again I direct my reader to R. C. Sleigh, Jr., for greater specificity on these difficult concepts: *Leibniz and Arnauld*, pp. 177–78.

creature at any given moment. And by *concomitance* or *preestablished harmony* I mean the doctrine that God created finite substances in such a way that they do not causally interact but nonetheless exhibit parallelism in virtue of their own spontaneity.

For the purposes of this essay, I do not assume either that the expression thesis—that each substance expresses the universe—entails preestablished harmony or that preestablished harmony entails the expression thesis.[12] This allows us to avoid some of the entanglements that can easily plague discussions of either of these doctrines because of the easy way that Leibniz, in his writings after 1685, passes from the one to the other. Two points about our central topics should be noted explicitly before we end this treatment of preliminaries: (1) granting our terminology, the preestablished harmony entails the denial of causal interaction among created substances, while the converse does not hold; and (2) in temporal terms, the foregoing implies that Leibniz could not consistently have adopted the preestablished harmony before denying intersubstantial causation among creatures, although he could consistently have endorsed such a denial before accepting the preestablished harmony.

Before beginning the survey of commentators, let us take a moment to dispense with a possibly tempting hypothesis in the spirit of Louis Couturat. The famous little paper "First Truths" contains both the denial, strictly speaking, of interaction among created substances and the assertion of preestablished harmony (unlabeled in the *Discourse* and termed the 'hypothesis of concomitance' in both "First Truths" and the correspondence with Arnauld). Especially given Loemker's approximate dating of "ca. 1680–84" for "First Truths,"[13] many will be attracted by the idea that not only do the statements of the "First Truths" antedate those of the *Discourse* (and hence contradict the hypothesis with which we began), but that they also may provide the answer to the question of how these views on the denial of intersubstantial causation among creatures and the preestablished harmony might have arisen in Leibniz's thought: he came to believe that they followed from his theory of truth—that the predicate is always contained in the subject of a true proposition—and adopted them as a result of this.

Without prejudging the issue of the role of Leibniz's theories of truth and

---

12. Here again Sleigh has covered the territory. He has addressed, to be sure with considerable caution, the question of Leibniz's views on the logical relations of these two doctrines. His conclusion: Leibniz holds that the preestablished harmony entails the expression thesis, but not that the expression thesis entails the preestablished harmony (*Leibniz and Arnauld*, p. 177—he indicates that he is less certain about the second point and discusses potentially opposing evidence).

13. L 267.

complete concepts in the development of his views on interaction and preestablished harmony, let me call into question a critical element of the idea just presented. The "First Truths," it now appears, does *not* antedate the *Discourse*, but rather can be assigned, by the method of watermark, to 1689.[14] This would obviously rule out "First Truths" as a counterexample to the thesis that our two theses first appeared in the *Discourse on Metaphysics*.

II

Is, then, the *Discourse* the first writing in which the denial of interaction and the assertion of preestablished harmony appear? As notable a figure as Yvon Belaval does not think so.

> For real causality the theory of expression substitutes . . . ideal causality. This leads to the "concomitance" or "pre-established harmony," which will not be named until 1686, *but which Leibniz has already introduced into his system. He formulates it in 1678*, when he comments on the *Ethics* of Spinoza: "For the series of ideas is distinct from the series of bodies, and they only mutually correspond to one another" (Grua, 282); *in the year following* [1679] he confides to Malebranche that for a long time he has not believed in the action of bodies on minds, and to Weigel, [that he does not believe in the action] of minds on bodies. (Grua, 259)[15]

Another renowned French Leibniz scholar, André Robinet, seems to adopt a similar position in his *Malebranche et Leibniz: Relations personnelles*.[16] Although he is not perfectly explicit, it is reasonably clear that he too ascribes the preestablished harmony to Leibniz in the late 1670s. He too finds evidence in the correspondence with Malebranche—albeit in a different letter from the one Belaval refers to.[17] We will look at the relevant text

14. *Vorausedition*, Faszikel 8, 1989, p. 1998.

15. Yvon Belaval, *Leibniz. Initiation à sa philosophie*, 4th ed. (Paris: J. Vrin, 1975), pp. 133–34 (emphasis added). Parkinson also cites the passage on Spinoza, but without the claim that it is a formulation of the preestablished harmony. Instead, he focuses on the passage as a denial of interaction between perceivers and what is perceived (see LA xlviii).

16. ML 85.

17. Although Belaval gives no specific citation, the phrase he offers, plus the reference to the year and the mention of Malebranche, points clearly to Leibniz's letter to Malebranche of 22 June 1679—more specifically, to the first paragraph of the letter printed in G I, 330.

of that letter when, in section III, we turn to a (negative) evaluation of Belaval's and Robinet's claims to find the preestablished harmony in these relatively early passages.

Just as some commentators point to Leibniz's connections with the leading occasionalist of the day, Malebranche, in discussing the development of Leibniz's views on causation and the preestablished harmony, so do others point to lesser occasionalists in this regard. I have in mind a proposed connection between Leibniz and Arnold Geulincx. The basic idea is that Leibniz borrowed (plagiarism is charged at one point) some ideas and/or images from the occasionalist Geulincx, with some features of their possible relationship pointing toward borrowing around 1676.

As it turns out, there was a heated debate, a little more than a century ago, on the question of Leibniz's connection to Geulincx. Here is a brief summary, drawn from material in an interesting article by Herman Jan de Vleeschauwer, "Occasionalisme et Harmonie Préétablie—Geulincx et Leibniz."[18]

Edmund Pfleiderer formally accused Leibniz of plagiarizing the clocks analogy from Geulincx, the analogy that after 1696 came to be perhaps the most famous image associated with Leibniz's doctrine of the preestablished harmony. On Pfleiderer's view, Leibniz remained strangely silent about Geulincx during his life[19] and intentionally falsified his statements of the doctrine of occasionalism to safeguard the originality and superiority of the view that he, Leibniz, championed.[20]

German interpreters rose to the defense of Leibniz. Rudolf Christoph Eucken and others pointed out that the example of the clocks had been fairly widely used, being found, for instance, in La Forge and Cordemoy also, so that the accusation of plagiarism from Geulincx was not really legitimate: the example was common property, so to speak.[21]

Pfleiderer responded by dropping the charge of plagiarism but still insisted that Leibniz had borrowed from Geulincx.[22]

Edward Zeller, speaking before the Prussian Academy in 1884, "absolutely denied *any* kind of relation between Leibniz and Geulincx and passionately objected to any dependence, be it historical or material, of Leibniz on the occasionalism of Geulincx."[23]

Obviously, the truth of this final position would render pointless any further investigation of Geulincx in trying to understand the development

18. *Studia Leibnitiana Suppl.* 14 (1975), pp. 279–92.
19. Ibid., pp. 279–80.
20. Ibid., p. 285.
21. Ibid., p. 280.
22. Ibid.
23. Ibid.

of Leibniz's views on causation and the preestablished harmony. But de Vleeschauwer, in a detailed reexamination of the issue, does not come down on Zeller's side. Without entirely supporting Pfleiderer either, he claims it is quite likely that Leibniz knew Geulincx's work and seems to leave open, without insisting on, the possibility of some borrowing by Leibniz.

In turning to a few of the details of de Vleeschauwer's position, we begin with what he says about Leibniz's Paris period.

> One can ask oneself how . . . the name of Geulincx could have remained unknown to [Leibniz], Geulincx who should have interested him greatly as the initiator of the occasionalism so clearly related to his own problematic of the universal order and as the initiator of the solution that had interested him so much during his stay in Paris.[24]

Even stronger is the following statement:

> Indeed, one cannot conceive how Leibniz could have been unaware of this independent Cartesian [Geulincx], and this precursor of the French occasionalists whom he had encountered in Paris.[25]

De Vleeschauwer adds reasons for thinking that Leibniz, during his visit with Spinoza in Holland in 1676, just after the Paris period, would almost certainly have garnered information and opinions about Geulincx's *Ethica*, published posthumously only a year before. While admitting that the case remains circumstantial, de Vleeschauwer insists that the body of evidence makes it "very highly probable" that Leibniz knew Geulincx's *Ethica*.[26] He grants, however, turning to Leibniz's later characterizations of occasionalism, that it is "scarcely believable" that "Leibniz had the theory of Geulincx in mind" in describing occasionalism.[27] The discrepancies are simply too significant.

In sum, this review of the debate comes down firmly on the side of Leibniz's having knowledge of the work of Geulincx and leaves open the possibility of some borrowing on Leibniz's part, while parting company with Pfleiderer's original charges of plagiarism and intentional falsification. But it raises as many questions as it puts to rest about Leibniz's relation to occasionalism in the Paris and very early post-Paris periods and about how

---

24. Ibid., p. 281.
25. Ibid., p. 280.
26. Ibid., p. 291.
27. Ibid., p. 286.

this might have affected the development of Leibniz's views on causation and preestablished harmony. We will consider such questions again when we return to de Vleeschauwer in section III.

There are two important topics we have not yet touched on in this brief survey of views on Leibniz's early development on causation and the preestablished harmony. The topics are Leibniz as interactionist and Leibniz as dualist. We turn to these now in considering remarks of Willy Kabitz.

Kabitz, in his influential book *Die Philosophie des jungen Leibniz*, considers the question of interaction, and also dualism, in a section devoted to the relation of mind and body. He begins by saying,

> In the "New Method" (1667) we encounter a first passage which intimates a dependency on Descartes in this connection [that of the relation of mind and body]. According to this, *mind can act on body*.[28]

After continuing his paraphrase of the full passage, he comments:

> But this is essentially Descartes's position also: mind and body are really distinct substances, which are united by God and can be subsequently divided; their unity cannot be abstractly understood, it is therefore a miracle; nevertheless both substances act upon one another.[29]

Kabitz's position, surprising though it is, seems clear, namely, that at this point in his early years, in 1667, Leibniz was an interactionistic dualist, accepting the same basic position as Descartes, one possibly dependent on Descartes. According to this view, mind and body are two distinct substances, and, among other things, they mutually interact. Perhaps, despite what his words indicate, Kabitz does not really mean this. But at a minimum he ascribes to Leibniz the view that mind can act on body, and this in itself is important.

III

Having concluded the presentation of some important views of commentators relevant to the development of Leibniz's positions on causal interaction

---

28. Willy Kabitz, *Die Philosophie des jungen Leibniz* (Heidelberg: Carl Winter, 1909), p. 84 (emphasis added). The work referred to is the "New Method for Learning and Teaching Jurisprudence" of 1667. The passage, abbreviated, is this: "This quality [causality] . . . exists in the cause of the world, or God . . . , and finally in our soul as the cause of the motion of body, although we cannot understand the manner of the causing" (A vi. I, 286–87). (In references to A, the two roman numerals refer, respectively, to series and volume.)

29. Ibid.

and preestablished harmony, we turn now to an evaluation of their details. The order of presentation is altered, so as to work through the topics in something like the temporal order in which they become relevant in Leibniz's philosophical development. We begin, then, with Kabitz's view of Leibniz as a very young man, in the year 1667.

Without attempting a full documentation, which would in any case take us beyond the bounds of the present project, let me propose that Kabitz, if he is really serious about finding not only a possible Cartesian influence but also a full-blown interactionist dualism in the "New Method," is almost certainly mistaken. For Kabitz, the crucial phrase from that work is that our soul is "the cause of motion of the body." This is quite similar to another view of almost exactly the same period, namely, that of "On Transubstantiation," where it is combined with another proposition to yield a conclusion flatly contradictory to Cartesian dualism.

The similar view of "On Transubstantiation" is that "[n]o body has a principle of motion within itself apart from a concurrent mind."[30] From this premise, combined with the view that all substance has a principle of action within itself, Leibniz draws the anti-Cartesian conclusion that "no body is to be taken as substance, apart from a concurrent mind."[31]

My point is simple (although of course not definitive): there is nothing obvious about the passage that Kabitz quotes from the "New Method" that rules out its being a part of a position that is as antithetical to Cartesian dualism as the position of "On Transubstantiation" is. No dualism, with mind and body being "really distinct substances,"[32] is implied. On the contrary, if we take a clue from "On Transubstantiation," something more like a traditional, rather than a Cartesian, concept of substance may well be at work. As we have seen, Leibniz says in the latter work that body taken apart from mind is not itself a substance; the principle of motion in body is mind. When we compare this with the traditional idea of an individual person being a substance consisting of matter and form, with the matter not constituting a substance by itself and the form being that by which we

30. "De Transsubstantiatione," A vi. I, 508; L 116.
31. Ibid. A qualification is needed. Although Leibniz clearly denies here that a body alone is a substance, and this clearly contradicts, verbally, Descartes's position, there is a strict contradiction only if Leibniz denies precisely the proposition that Descartes meant to assert by his words. There is good reason to doubt that this condition is met. The concept of substance involved in the proposition at issue seems quite different for the two philosophers. In particular, the principle that it is essential to a substance that it have a principle of action within itself seems to be one that Leibniz accepts but Descartes denies. While this point weakens the specific argument given above, it is not clear that it opens the way for an easy defense of Kabitz's view that Leibniz's position on mind and body is "essentially the same position" as that of Descartes. The disagreement about the nature of substance seems, rather, to provide a distinct line of reasoning for concluding that their positions are different.
32. Kabitz, Die Philosophie des jungen Leibniz, p. 84.

move ourselves, and then consider the words of the "New Method," it is quite possible to read in something far from Descartes's position. Christia Mercer has recently done interesting work on an Aristotelian conception of substance to be found in Leibniz's early writings.[33] This is the sort of thing that should be looked at very carefully before any conclusions of a Cartesian interactionistic dualism are read into the early works of Leibniz.

In short, I doubt very much that the passage Kabitz brings forward can support the claim of Leibniz's view on the relation of mind and body being essentially the same as that of Descartes. A lesser point, but one that should not be overlooked entirely, is that the passage in question affirms only the mind's causal action on the body. Kabitz's assertion that mind and body act on *each other*—that *inter*action obtains between mind and body—involves an addition on his part to what the text actually says.

Having made these negative points, I conclude with something more positive. Kabitz provides a real service in locating a clear early text in which Leibniz accepts, apparently without qualification, the causal action of mind on body. When we find that G.H.R. Parkinson highlights another early text, this time from 1676, apparently endorsing the causal action of body on a perceiver, or mind,[34] we have some evidence of mind–body causation in the opposite direction (albeit from a different date).[35] What we do not have from either of these texts is evidence of an essentially Cartesian position on mind and body in the early Leibniz.

The preceding few sentences carry us from the very early years of Leibniz's philosophizing into the Paris period. Let us continue this direction by turning to de Vleeschauwer's claim that occasionalism was a doctrine "that had interested [Leibniz] so much during his stay in Paris."[36]

To be sure, there certainly is some initial reason to think this. We know

33. Admittedly emphasizing also Leibniz's attempts to reconcile this with positions of the moderns.

34. A vi. III, 510; L 252. The quotation is, "Sense is a kind of reaction." Parkinson, writing in the Introduction to *The Leibniz-Arnauld Correspondence*, LA xlviii, takes this passage as indicative of, or at least suggestive of, perceivers being acted upon by objects perceived. (Evidently, he is thinking of bodies here in talking about objects perceived—see his subsequent statement in the Introduction.)

35. Note that the assertion of mind-body causation does not necessarily imply anything about Leibniz's position on intersubstantial causation. To see this, consider a position that interprets a human body and mind as the matter and form, respectively, of a single substance, a human being. If neither matter nor form is itself a substance in its own right, then the mind-body causation involved is intrasubstantial, not intersubstantial. (To be sure, if one of these items, say, the mind, *is* a substance in its own right, then in some sense more than mere intrasubstantial causation would be present.)

36. De Vleeschauwer, "Occasionalisme et Harmonie Préétablie," p. 281; occasionalism is not actually mentioned explicitly in de Vleeschauwer's passage, but it seems clear that it is what he is referring to.

that Leibniz met and talked privately with Malebranche, the latter conversation probably occurring, according to Robinet, at the beginning of 1675.[37] And Belaval notes, with the point being confirmed by Müller and Krönert,[38] that Leibniz met Cordemoy at some unspecified point during Leibniz's Paris period. There may have been other relevant personal contacts and readings. But the question remains: Do we really know that Leibniz was well acquainted with and quite interested in the position of occasionalism during his stay in Paris?

De Vleeschauwer himself merely offers the point without support— something a bit unusual in his generally well documented paper. Perhaps he takes the point as obvious. But I would like to be better acquainted with the evidence. For one thing, it may simply be assumed that since Leibniz was acquainted with Malebranche in Paris, and certainly had significant philosophical interaction with him, overlooking occasionalism would have been an impossibility for Leibniz.[39] Let me give just one piece of evidence that calls this into question. Robinet states repeatedly in his book, *Malebranche et Leibniz: Relations personnelles*, that Leibniz at first viewed Malebranche as just one among several Cartesians and only after leaving Paris came to appreciate the originality of the Oratorian.[40] A vivid example of what he has in mind, and the one most relevant for present purposes, is given in a note near the end of Robinet's chapter describing the interactions of Leibniz and Malebranche during the period between 1672 and 1676:

> The reading of the three first books of the *Recherche de la Vérité*, even if Leibniz had performed it with care, could not have permitted him to grasp the originality of Malebranche: "In none of the three first books of the *Recherche* does Malebranche consider occasional causes for themselves, that is, in posing the question of causality; *he does not even employ the term 'occasional cause'*. According to the apt remark of Delbos, 'As a result of this readers of the first volume, containing the first three books, *could very well not have perceived the least bit of Malebranche's world of occasionalism'*." This is what happened to Huet, Foucher, and Leibniz.[41]

37. ML 37.

38. *Leben und Werk von Gottfried Wilhelm Leibniz: Eine Chronik*, ed. Kurt Müller and Gisela Krönert (Frankfurt am Main: Vittorio Klostermann, 1969), p.44.

39. De Vleeschauwer at least suggests that this is how he sees things in a remark about La Forge, Cordemoy, and Malebranche ("Occasionalisme et Harmonie Préétablie," p. 280).

40. See, for example, ML 77. Note 1 of ML 40 indicates that what Robinet has in mind by Malebranche's "originality" is his occasionalism.

41. ML 40, n. 1 (emphasis added). Robinet is quoting from Gouhier, "Philosophie Chrétienne et Theologie," *Revue Philosophique* (March–April 1938): 110. Richard Watson has kindly

My guess is that not many will share my suspicion, based admittedly on an imperfect knowledge of the intellectual life of Paris in the mid-1670s. The suspicion is that Leibniz, contra de Vleeschauwer,[42] was very little gripped by occasionalism in the Paris years. To be sure, I cannot claim the detailed knowledge of the Academy edition volume covering Leibniz's philosophical writings of the Paris years that would be required,[43] not to demonstrate this (because proving a negative in such cases is difficult if not impossible), but rather to raise the suspicion to something better founded. But I can say that a general review provides preliminary support for the speculation. To mention just a minor point: it should be surprising for someone of de Vleeschauwer's convictions to learn that the index of this volume appears to provide no entry for the term *'causa'*, which references a passage discussing occasional causes (despite a very large number of entries for this term); nor is there any entry of this type for the term *'occasio'* (with many fewer entries—four, to be exact).

This brings us to the post-Paris era, and here, in my view, is where significant things start happening in our present area of investigation. Remember that Belaval and Robinet point to the years 1678 and 1679 as important for the foundation of the preestablished harmony. And de Vleeschauwer thinks that the 1676 visit to Holland was surely significant for Leibniz's appreciation of occasionalism, particularly in the form Geulincx gave it. Even if one is not in agreement with the whole story of any one of these three, this confluence of views among them about the importance of the early post-Paris period with respect to Leibniz's development of the doctrine of preestablished harmony merits our attention.

I will not say more here about Geulincx than I have said already, but I

provided me with more information about the case of Foucher and has helped me improve my limited knowledge of the intellectual scene in Paris during Leibniz's years there; see his *Breakdown of Cartesian Metaphysics* (Atlantic Highlands, N.J.: Humanities Press International, 1987).

42. De Vleeschauwer gives us a hint about the basis of his position with an interesting statement: "Indeed, one cannot conceive how Leibniz could have been unaware of this independent Cartesian [Geulincx] and this precursor of the French occasionalists that he had met in Paris, La Forge, Cordemoy, Malebranche" ("Occasionalisme et Harmonie Préétablie," p. 280). The suggestion, though not the implication, is that de Vleeschauwer thinks Leibniz knew these three in Paris *as* occasionalists. We have now seen that there is good reason to doubt this in the case of Malebranche. Does de Vleeschauwer have better evidence in the case of the others? La Forge was arguably not an occasionalist, so his case is probably not relevant to present discussions. Cordemoy's relations with Leibniz seem poorly known (see note 38 above; but see also item 4174 in *Leibniz-Bibliographie: Die Literatur über Leibniz bis 1980*, initiated by Kurt Müller, edited by Albert Heinekamp [Frankfurt am Main: Vittorio Klostermann, 1984]. p. 399, for two items of possible interest—apparently the only ones this comprehensive work has to offer on the subject).

43. A vi. III.

will say more about Robinet and Belaval. Robinet seems to draw a question-able conclusion, admittedly from a fascinating passage. He quotes from a letter by Leibniz to Malebranche of 13/23 January 1679, saying that Male-branche has revealed weaknesses in Descartes's metaphysics but has "gone only halfway."[44] Robinet's next sentence suggests his interpretation of this: Leibniz believes, at this date, that Malebranche's occasionalism gets only halfway to the doctrine of preestablished harmony; but to believe this, Leibniz must already hold the preestablished harmony at this date, that is, in January of 1679.

Even if one does not accept this suggestion as being what Robinet intends in his statement, the implication remains. For what he says in that next sentence, having just quoted from the letter of 13/23 January 1679, is that "from this moment forward Leibniz will situate his pre-established har-mony in the line of occasionalism." One cannot place one's doctrine in relation to another view at a particular time without already holding the doctrine at that time. So Robinet is, by implication, ascribing the preestab-lished harmony to Leibniz from 1679 forward.

What is the statement from the correspondence to Malebranche that apparently generates this important conclusion? I here quote the full state-ment, adding emphasis to the short portion that Robinet quotes.

> As for his [Descartes's] metaphysics, you yourself have shown its imperfection, and I am entirely of your opinion concerning the impossibility of conceiving that a substance which has nothing but extension, without thought, can act upon a substance which has nothing but thought, without extension. But *I believe that you have gone only halfway* and that still other consequences can be drawn than those which you have made. In my opinion it follows that matter is something different from mere extension, and I believe, besides, that this can be demonstrated.[45]

---

44. Robinet, in his full statement, says that Leibniz eventually comes to view Malebranche as

> an occasionalist and a religious Cartesian. If he [Leibniz] is in agreement in recognizing that in metaphysics the Oratorian has made significant progress over Cartesianism, . . . he judges that this is insufficient: "I believe that you have gone only halfway." From this point of view, he [Leibniz] will situate his pre-established harmony from this moment forward [désormais] in the line of occasionalism: but it remains evident that one is dealing more with a transformation than with a simple advance. (ML 85)

The short quotation from Leibniz is, as is indicated by the above, not referenced in Robinet's statement. But Robinet is here introducing the selections of chapter 2 of his book, where this pronouncement of Leibniz occurs—as we have noted, in the letter to Malebranche of 13/23 January 1679 (ML 104).

45. ML 104; L 209.

I think it will be agreed, since this passage does not refer explicitly to the preestablished harmony—or, for that matter, to occasionalism—that some interpretation is required to extract from it a commitment to the preestablished harmony at this point in Leibniz's development. I have already offered a suggestion as to what that interpretation might be. It is that Leibniz, in writing here that Malebranche has gone "only halfway," is allowing that Malebranche's occasionalism constitutes a significant advance over Descartes, while insisting that one needs to go significantly further, that is, all the way to the preestablished harmony.[46]

But this reading, supportive though it would be of Robinet's implication, does not really fit the passage in a natural way. Even the beginning of the statement, which can be read as fitting well with the suggested reading, turns out to be problematic when viewed in the context of the whole passage. Here is how that fit might look, and here is what is wrong with it. Leibniz joins Malebranche, at the beginning of the passage above, in condemning Cartesian interactionism. But since he knows Malebranche responds to the resulting unexplained parallelism between mind and body by postulating the occasionalist doctrine that Leibniz views as flawed, he says that Malebranche has gone only halfway: he has gotten to the denial of interaction, but he needs to continue, not toward occasionalism, but instead all the way to the correct theory, namely, the preestablished harmony.

The problem with this is that it assumes that the denial of Cartesian interactionism with which the statement begins leaves a problematic situation that Leibniz feels must be resolved—and better by the preestablished harmony than by occasionalism. But the latter half of the passage shows that this assumption cannot go uncontested. The denial implies a problematic situation for Leibniz only if he views *our* body as being of the sort described in the denial of a body acting on mind, namely, as a substance having nothing but extension. But Leibniz does not accept this, as his words later in the passage indicate: "matter is something different from mere extension."[47]

Louis Loeb has examined this passage independently of Robinet's (and the present) treatment. He notes, as we have, that the passage cannot be taken as a simple denial of body acting on mind, but only as a denial of substance containing nothing but extension acting on mind. But he goes further, first speculating that the passage "results from a temptation to

46. Remember that Robinet says, in the very next sentence after quoting Leibniz's remark about Malebranche's going "only halfway," that Leibniz "will situate his pre-established harmony from this moment forward in the line of occasionalism" (ML 85).

47. Malebranche would have been aware of this nonacceptance, since Leibniz had already written him during the Paris period on this topic in some detail (A ii. I, 254–55).

allow for interaction between minds and extended matter [with the extended matter being explained in such a way as to differentiate it clearly from mere extended matter],"[48] and then concluding his discussion of the passage—in what appears to be exact opposition to Robinet—with this statement: "The point is that the preestablished harmony and the denial of interaction were still waiting in the wings [at the time of this letter to Malebranche]."[49]

Once these points are made (even if the more speculative of them are set aside), Robinet's suggested interpretation of "halfway" becomes contentious, and other interpretations present themselves. One of the clearest can be drawn quite directly from the materials explicitly in the passage from the letter to Malebranche. On this interpretation, going halfway is getting to the conclusion that a substance that has nothing but extension cannot act on a substance that has nothing but thought, without extension. Going all the way is concluding that "matter is something different from mere extension." Nothing so grand as the entire systems of occasionalism and preestablished harmony need be intended.

When we turn to Belaval, the texts become more compelling, but puzzling issues remain. In making his striking assertion that Leibniz already maintained the doctrine of the preestablished harmony in the years 1678–79, Belaval refers to three interesting texts in support. He does not quote them all, but we list them all here:

1. "The series of ideas is distinct from the series of bodies, and they only correspond mutually."[50]
2. "I approve most heartily these two propositions which you

48. Louis Loeb, *From Descartes to Hume: Continental Metaphysics and the Development of Modern Philosophy* (Ithaca, N.Y.: Cornell University Press, 1981), p. 310 (emphasis added). Loeb has some very interesting things to say, relevant to the present investigation, in the section from which these quotations have been taken; indeed, this chapter originally contained a section on Loeb's work. Considerations of length and problems with dating (e.g., in connection with "First Truths" and Loeb's general statements about the period before 1687—which were problematic relative to the present investigation, with its consideration of the *contrast* of the *Discourse* and pre-*Discourse* writings) led to its omission here. But one of Loeb's theses—that Leibniz's preestablished harmony arose originally out of problems he saw with the mind-body relation (more specifically, a dualistic mind-body relation), but that later the preestablished harmony lost this underpinning with Leibniz's rejection of extended or material substances (p. 316)—is a fascinating one that I recommend to the reader. (Given the remarks above, it is no doubt clear that I would want to investigate further the details of the claimed dualism of the earlier writings.)

49. Ibid., p. 311.

50. Grua, 282: comments on the *Ethics* of Spinoza. Grua dates these comments as "after February 1678" (Grua, 277). The Academy editors give a preliminary dating range, based at least in part on watermarks, of 1678 to 1682 (*Vorausedition*, Faszikel 3, p. 533). Notice that this slightly weakens Belaval's case for the specific years 1678 and 1679.

advance: that we see all things in God and that strictly speaking, bodies do not act upon us. I have always been convinced of this for important reasons which seem to me indisputable and which rest on certain axioms which I do not as yet see used anywhere, though they could be most serviceable in proving some other theses no less important than those I have just mentioned."[51]

3. "For I judge that it is not so much that our mind acts on things as that God acts on things according to his will."[52]

Belaval's gloss on these is that the first is a formulation of the preestablished harmony and that the second and third together constitute a "thesis of parallelism," by which he seems to mean, again, the preestablished harmony.

It is clear that these are important messages. It is not nearly so clear that they say what Belaval seems to think they do. The second and third together constitute a denial of mind-body interaction. This is quite important. But it is hardly all there is to the preestablished harmony. The first seems to be directed squarely against Spinoza's *Ethics* III P. 2, Schol., which says basically that the series of ideas and the series of bodies are one and the same, although expressed in two ways. Leibniz definitely objects to that, and he indicates this clearly in the quotation, saying that the two series are distinct, not one. But what Leibniz retains from Spinoza, Belaval seems to imply, are the ideas that (i) the series mutually correspond, that is, one assumes, they correspond in every detail, and (ii) they *only* correspond, that is, that they do *not* causally interact. Now this may well constitute progress toward the preestablished harmony, in part simply because something has been added beside the denial of causal interaction, but also because we may be able to assume that Leibniz accepted Spinoza's idea that each series operated in accordance with its own laws, laws of bodies on the one hand, and laws of minds, or ideas, on the other, with neither interfering with the other.[53] Without any clear assertion of the key doctrine of spontaneity, however, the passage can hardly be considered a full statement of the preestablished harmony.

Let us consider now the passage from the letter to Malebranche that Belaval refers to ([2] above). Its denial of body acting causally on mind seems more decisive than the one in the earlier letter to Malebranche (the

51. Letter to Malebranche, June 22/July 2, 1679; G I, 330; translation from L 210. Belaval refers to only a brief part of this, the part on bodies not acting on us. For reasons that will become clear, I quote some of the surrounding material also.

52. "*Arbitror enim non tam mentem nostram in res agere quam Deum ad ejus voluntatem.*" Letter to E. Weigel, A ii. I, 487, September 1679.

53. We shall have more to say about these two points below.

one cited by Robinet), although it may still be possible to read it in a way that is weaker than the original impression. The two really striking things, which Belaval does not comment on, are that Leibniz says he has *always* been convinced of the denial of body acting on mind,[54] and that he also agrees with Malebranche on vision in God. It is hard to know what to make of these points, but in my mind they awaken a sense of incredulity. The specter of Leibniz having "given a good sense"[55] to the two formulations— one quite different from what the original author intended—looms, if not large, then at least as a disturbing possibility.

Still, I do not in the end oppose the limited view that by about 1679 Leibniz denied interaction between mind and body. The comment on Spinoza is, to me, persuasive, and despite some qualms I think that Belaval's passage from the letter to Malebranche constitutes fairly strong evidence. But we do not have to leave it at that. Other texts, not adduced by the commentators discussed, are in the offing. Here is one from 1679:

> . . . but you would even wonder at the blindness of those who imagine that some motions and divisions of matter could destroy the indivisible substances which give all action and even all existence to matter, and *which do not receive impressions except from God.*[56]

Notice that this passage is also from 1679—and the argument for the Academy editors' dating seems strong.[57]

IV

I will limit myself to two points in this penultimate section, stating them briefly here at the outset, and then adding some flesh to the bones in the

54. The passage (A vi. III, 510; L 252) pointed out by G.H.R. Parkinson and discussed earlier in this chapter provides a putative counterexample; see the Introduction to *The Leibniz-Arnauld Correspondence*, LA xlviii. (To be sure, one could argue that the passage I am now considering is evidence against Parkinson's interpretation of his passage.)

55. Keep in mind that Leibniz was able to give a good sense to the phrase "we see all in God" in his late writings, even though it is clear that he then rejected the theory Malebranche associated with those words (see A vi. VI, 558).

56. *Vorausedition*, Faszikel 1, p. 41 (emphasis added); "Dialogue entre Theophile et Polidore," preliminary dating: second half of 1679. Robert Sleigh has mentioned some possible problems associated with the term 'impression' that could affect the strength of this passage.

57. Parkinson mentions another idea that appears in Leibniz's logical writings of this same year, 1679—the theory of truth (Introduction to *The Leibniz-Arnauld Correspondence*, LA xl— he cites C 51, 68). Logicists may wish to make something of the possible coappearance of these views. I have no special evidence to offer indicating that they are connected.

sequel. The first is that there are passages in Leibniz's early writings suggesting that he leaned toward, or perhaps even adopted, occasionalism at some stages. The second is that Spinoza deserves a perhaps more prominent place than he has been given among those having an influence on Leibniz's developing thinking on interaction and concomitance.

With regard to Leibniz as an occasionalist, I offer two quotations, one of which we touched on briefly before. It is from a letter to E. Weigel in September of 1679. Leibniz says,

> I judge that it is not so much that our mind acts on things as that God [acts on things] according to his will.[58]

We saw this earlier in Belaval's hands, as evidence that Leibniz rejected the mind's action on body. But that use takes into account only half of what this passage has to offer. If we ask in response to the first half of Leibniz's statement, why then *does* our arm go up when we will to raise it,

---

58. A ii. I, 487. I have consulted with a specialist on Latin from the Renaissance onward in connection with the translation of this passage. She agrees generally with my way of handling it, except for the case of the phrase '*in res agere*', which I have translated as "acts on things" and have carried over into the clause on God. She finds this phrase puzzling and has tried unsuccessfully to find justification of my way of handling it (which derives from Belaval and, ultimately, Grua—*Textes inédits*, 259). She suggests, while remaining unsure about the phrase, an approach in which '*agere*' is emphasized as an intransitive verb standing basically alone, so that the key idea becomes this: it is not so much that our mind acts as that God acts according to his will. This leaves '*in res*' still to be explained. She mentions that '*in*' can sometimes take the accusative when used in the sense of "in respect to." So perhaps something like the following is intended: "it is not so much that our mind acts, in respect to [human?] affairs, as that . . ." (I express my debt to Helen Eaker, longtime instructor at Rice University, for her generous assistance in this matter.)

This alternative reading is quite consistent, although in a different way from before, with the point we are suggesting about Leibniz and occasionalism. It suggests, although it stops short of strictly asserting (because of the '*tam . . . quam*'), that it is not our minds that act but rather God who acts, which in turn suggests that real causal power exists not in our minds but rather in God. This is good occasionalism, and is opposed to Leibniz's later views.

It turns out that there is a similar but less difficult passage that adds to the suggestion of occasionalism in the late 1670s. Here I am indebted to Robert Sleigh, whose rich book has time and again proved to have important things to say about issues I thought I was exploring in a new way. The passage, the import of which I have only recently come to recognize, is this: "Properly and accurately speaking, the correct thing to say is not so much that God concurs in an action, but rather that he produces it" (Sleigh, *Leibniz and Arnauld*, p. 184, quoting and translating from Grua, *Textes inédits*, p. 275). The text was written in 1677 and is taken from Leibniz's description of a conversation with Nicholas Steno. The sequel (which Sleigh presents) is relevant to and supportive of an occasionalist reading. The possible disconfirmation, discussed by Sleigh, is that one could take the position as Steno's rather than as Leibniz's. Sleigh doubts this, and introduces the full passage as "apparent evidence of occasionalism" (*Leibniz and Arnauld*, p. 183). I agree.

the answer of this passage—the second half of the information it has to offer—seems pretty clearly to be that *God* causes it to rise. It is not so much we who act on things—*nor things which act themselves in virtue of their own spontaneity*—but rather it is *God* who acts on things.

Notice that an adherent of the preestablished harmony (including the post-*Discourse* Leibniz) would be likely to reject this doctrine, saying rather that in such a case the "things" act independently, according to their own laws and their own spontaneity—that God no more acts on them (beyond universal conservation) than he acts on minds as they progress from one perceptual state to another. From this perspective, the passage seems to offer an occasionalist view on what happens in cases when our mind seems to act on things. The evidence is hardly ironclad, but nonetheless suggestive.

The second passage is from the short work "The Origin of Souls and Minds":

> For there is in all things a certain sense and natural appetite which takes away nothing from the laws of mechanism; for this [appetite, I assume] is not so much a cause as an occasion of acting for God. . . . In God alone is there understanding, willing, and power. In us there is intellect and will, but no power.[59]

This is a rare passage[60] in that we find Leibniz using the language of occasionalism: "not so much a cause as an occasion of acting for God." The occasionalist tone is intensified if one takes strictly the point about there being "no power" in us, so that it indicates not only that we possess no *inter*substantial causal power but also no *intra*substantial causal power. This is flatly inconsistent with Leibniz's later theory of spontaneously acting simple substances and fully consistent with the occasionalist denial of true causation in creatures.[61]

---

59. *Vorausedition*, Faszikel 2, p. 292.

60. But not unique. Robert Sleigh has pointed out that early versions of one of the sections of the *Discourse on Metaphysics* contain what he calls the "language of occasional causes" (*Leibniz and Arnauld*, p. 151—Sleigh does not commit himself explicitly, but the context suggests his meaning to be that although the term 'occasional causes' was used in the draft, Leibniz did not strictly accept occasionalism at that juncture).

61. To be sure, one might find suggestions of a different interpretation of this passage in Leibniz's statement that appetite (or possibly sense and appetite taken together) "takes away nothing from the laws of mechanism." Since these laws are normally restricted to the realm of bodies, this could be read as simply the familiar later view of Leibniz's more popular works that minds do not affect bodies (and hence do not lead to violations of the laws of bodies, i.e.,

The passage from the letter to Weigel and the one just quoted seem to me to be powerful and intriguing statements. Other features of the Weigel letter and the present short work are supportive of an occasionalist reading. The content of the two and the fact that both may have been written in the same year, 1679 (the second is undated but involves interesting—yet very inconclusive—watermark evidence),[62] lends some support to the view that for a brief time shortly after the Paris period Leibniz held or at least experimented with an occasionalist position.[63]

With respect to Spinoza, some points have been made already. Let me add a few more. First, Robinet gives us reason to think that the hold Spinoza exerted on Leibniz was quite considerable in the period up to and including the German's visit to The Hague in 1676 and that this hold was much greater than that exerted by Malebranche in the same period. Robinet catalogs instances of serious opposition between the points of view of Leibniz and Malebranche,[64] and says that while Leibniz, at this stage, views Malebranche as just one among an assemblage of Cartesians, he is attracted to Spinoza as a new, seductive, and powerful philosopher, one whom he calls "a man of profound meditation."[65] Robinet goes so far as to say that "faced with the thought of Spinoza, the spirit of Leibniz affirms itself, it passes from the infancy of intuitions to the adulthood of original theses, which remain to be organized."[66] It is only after the "temptation" of Spinoza has passed, Robinet tells us, when Leibniz is settled in Hannover

---

the laws of mechanism)—with no implication that minds are lacking in real causal power in the matter of intrasubstantial causation. I grant the possibility of this reading. But since we are dealing here with only a suggestion—the reading is not, as it were, forced—I think the possibility is clearly outweighed by the other features of the passage given above, one of which seems to be nothing short of an explicit denial of the existence of any real causal power in us.

62. The work is accompanied by the Academy editors' comment that watermark evidence points to the years 1679 *and* 1692. Daniel Garber has kindly helped me to interpret this, and, if I have understood him correctly, it means that sheets of paper with the same watermark as that of the present work contain writings of Leibniz known to date from these two years. To put this another way, we know that Leibniz was using paper with this watermark in the years 1679 and 1692. Obviously, this means that the work "The Origin of Souls and Minds" *could* have been written in 1679. But it could have been written much later also.

63. Robinet singles out this very year, 1679, as the year in which Leibniz "discovers the originality" of Malebranche (ML 77).

64. ML 39.

65. ML 40, quoting from Georges Friedmann, *Leibniz et Spinoza* (Paris: Gallimard, 1946), p. 79.

66. ML 40.

after the Paris period, that he will be better able to see the value of Malebranche's work.[67]

Second, with respect to the Leibnizian comment on Spinoza that we encountered earlier ("the series of ideas is distinct from the series of bodies, and they only correspond mutually"), the idea of a mutual correspondence between the realm of mind and body is potentially significant, more significant than might at first be realized. In Descartes and Malebranche there is *not* a perfect correspondence between the events of the mind and those of the body: for both of these philosophers there are acts of pure intellect that lack bodily correlates.[68] Spinoza obviously does not follow Descartes in this. Neither does Leibniz.[69] For them every act of the mind, no matter how refined, has a correlate in the realm of bodies.

Third, a very important feature of Spinoza's position is that the series of bodies and the series of ideas each operate in a law-governed, necessary way, but without the slightest interference between the two realms. Leibniz's language is less shocking—he insists that his position is not necessitarian—but the parallel determinism of the natural realms of mind and body, without mutual interaction, is nonetheless similar to Spinoza's in many respects. To put the point in terms of mind and body: for both Leibniz and Spinoza, bodies operate by the laws of body, minds operate by the laws of mind or ideas, there is no interaction between minds and bodies, and yet nonetheless they correspond perfectly. There is no one at work adjusting the series of ideas and the series of bodies to make them correspond.[70]

67. Ibid.

68. Daisie Radner confirms this in the course of discussing Malebranche on the operations of the understanding: "Like Descartes, he [Malebranche] includes sensation, imagination and 'pure intellection' (thinking without the aid of corporeal images in the brain) among the operations of the understanding" (*Malebranche: A Study of a Cartesian System* [Assen/Amsterdam: Van Gorcum, 1978], p. 9).

69. In Spinoza's case the identity thesis mentioned in the next note probably makes further explanation superfluous. In the case of Leibniz, a quotation from the later years of the philosopher's life will indicate the distance from Descartes's position: ". . . we cannot have abstract thoughts which have no need of something sensible, even if it be merely symbols such as the shapes of letters, or sounds. . . . If sensible traces were not required, the pre-established harmony between body and soul . . . would not obtain" (NE, I. i. 5; A vi. VI, 77).

70. To be sure, Spinoza's position that a body and its corresponding idea are one and the same, though expressed in two ways, rules out the need for such adjustment from the beginning, whereas Leibniz's insistence on the distinctness of the series of bodies and the series of ideas initially leaves an opening for continual adjustment as the explanation of correspondence or parallelism. Despite this difference, the commonality just indicated remains, that neither explains the correspondence by continual adjustment, but rather by the parallel and

Given the prior states of bodies and ideas/minds, and given these mental and physical laws, the correspondence for both philosophers is, as it were, preestablished.[71]

I think these are significant points about Spinoza, Leibniz, and the resemblances of their philosophies on the matter of causation and preestablished harmony.[72] And whereas some resemblances in the history of philosophy demonstrably do not involve the influencing of one philosopher by another, this is a case in which influence is a distinct possibility. For there can be little or no question that (i) Leibniz knew about Spinoza's positions, (ii) he was gripped by them, and (iii) shortly after coming into significant contact with them, he put into writing positions of his own, with a clear relation to Spinoza's writings, that at one and the same time revealed the extent of his possible debt and also suggested where the paths of the two philosophers might divide. Let us then conclude this section by pondering the possibility of Spinoza as a significant figure—conceivably even the most significant figure—in the development of Leibniz's preestablished harmony.

V

In the course of the preceding sections, we have included—albeit not point by point—defenses of the eight theses with which we began. The critical reader will no doubt note that these theses leave much still unanswered about the development of Leibniz's views on causation among finite substances and the preestablished harmony. Notably, they provide only nega-

---

constant operation of laws of body, on the one hand, and laws of ideas, or mind, on the other.

71. This statement leaves room for significant differences between the two thinkers: notably that for Leibniz a single mind and its laws would be, or be close to being, a closed deterministic system, while for Spinoza the only closed deterministic system would seem to be the entire infinite system of minds, ideas, and their laws (and probably also the infinite modes of the attribute of thought).

72. There are of course significant points of dissimilarity as well. Some we have mentioned already, while others will be apparent to most readers. The similarities must not be exaggerated. Our main point at the moment is that the similarities that exist are not inconsequential, and that they take on added significance when one compares the possible roles of Spinoza and Malebranche in Leibniz's thinking about causation and parallelism at this point in the latter's development.

tive answers about the date of Leibniz's first formulation of the preestablished harmony.

Partially to address this situation, and partially to provide material for future work in this area, I conclude with a series of historical hypotheses or conjectures on Leibniz's development with respect to our two doctrines. I will not attempt to defend these. In this respect the present hypotheses are to be distinguished sharply from the theses defended earlier. The spirit in which they are offered is, rather, analogous to that of a scientist offering hypotheses in experimental work: the hypotheses are perhaps prompted, but hardly justified or established, by earlier work, and they are formulated to provide focus for future work. I present the hypotheses in temporal order, attempting to skip over topics already addressed in the theses above, but occasionally touching on them as I sometimes expand the reach, in these hypotheses, of narrower theses already defended.

I hypothesize then the following: (a) that in Leibniz's early years he accepted causal interaction among created substances, and did not finally reject this until the late 1670s at the earliest;[73] (b) that Leibniz was never a Cartesian dualist, in the sense of accepting mind and body as distinct substances, with mind consisting of nothing but thought and body consisting of nothing but extension; (c) that Leibniz accepted (nondualistic) mind-body interaction in the same period indicated before (basically from the university years up until the late 1670s), not as an occasional position, but as a fundamental assumption or belief; (d) that sometime in the period from 1678 to 1686 Leibniz moved beyond denying mind-body interaction and denied the causal interaction of all created substances; (e) that in the same period, from 1678 to 1686, Leibniz adopted the thesis of spontaneity for all created substances; and (f) that it was only at about the time of the writing of the *Discourse on Metaphysics* that Leibniz finally came to adopt the preestablished harmony.[74]

---

73. Keep in mind that for a nondualist this is quite a different thing from accepting or rejecting mind-body interaction.

74. Although this is a section containing hypotheses, and not defenses of hypotheses, I should not fail to mention again the exceptional brief work by G.H.R. Parkinson—the Introduction to *The Leibniz-Arnauld Correspondence*—focusing this time on the thesis he propounds there about the preestablished harmony. He says, "It seems, then, that by 1678 Leibniz had all the materials for what he later called the hypothesis of concomitance, at any rate as far as it concerns minds" (LA xlviii). Of course, it is possible that he means nothing here inconsistent with hypothesis (f): one may have all the materials for a doctrine without putting them together and propounding them as a doctrine; in any case the limitation to minds could be significant. But I have not placed great weight on this statement of Parkinson's

primarily because, as far as I can tell, he makes no mention at all of spontaneity—an essential element of preestablished harmony as I have defined it—in the section involving this statement. And without spontaneity, Leibniz would *not* have had all the materials for the doctrine of preestablished harmony in 1678. My suspicion, based in part on what Parkinson says at the bottom of LA xlvi, is that what Parkinson has in mind by the preestablished harmony does not include spontaneity as an essential element (although it would allow for this), but rather includes the expression of the world combined with these other elements: "that no created substance acts on any other, and that to speak of cause-effect relations between substances, and also of the union of mind and body, is to speak of the ways in which substances express one another, and ultimately of the way in which they express God." In sum, I do not necessarily view Parkinson as someone who, in the statement quoted above, has already launched an attack on hypothesis (f).

Margaret D. Wilson

Compossibility and Law

The notion of compossibility performs two related functions in Leibniz's philosophy. It helps to explain why not all possibles (possible substances) are actual: not all possibles are *com*possible, or such that they can exist *together*. And it underlies the partitioning of possibles into different *possible worlds*: a possible world is just a set of compossible possibles (and, it seems, there are infinitely many of these worlds).

But what is the basis of compossibility? Generally Leibniz regards a possible as that the concept of which is free from self-contradiction. To illustrate *im*possibility in a concept Leibniz cites the example of "the most rapid motion": he argues that this description cannot be satisfied because its ascription sustains contradictory conclusions.[1] But the concept of possibility at issue in this case is, more specifically, that of "logical" or "meta-

---

1. "Meditations on Knowledge, Truth, and Ideas," G IV, 424 (L 293).

physical" possibility: Leibniz uses the terms 'possibility' and 'impossibility' in other senses as well. For instance, an event may be (merely) "physically" impossible (in a given world) if it simply fails to conform to the general laws of nature in that world.[2] Thus there is room for legitimate doubt about how, precisely, the term 'incompossible' should be understood.

Two alternative interpretations of incompossibility prevail in the recent literature. Most critics think that the notion must, indeed, be understood as implying a logical relation among possible substances, or substance concepts: two such possibles are incompossible just in case the assumption that both are actualized gives rise to self-contradiction.[3] Some, however, have held that Leibniz's concept of compossibility has to do not with logical relations but with orderliness and lawfulness of relations among substances: two substances are compossible if and only if they relate to each other in suitable ways under possible laws of nature. (On this reading the notion of compossibility seems more closely tied to the Leibnizian conception of "physical" possibility.) Ian Hacking is a recent proponent of this interpretation, and Gregory Brown has expressed at least a leaning toward it.[4] They both cite Bertrand Russell as the originator of this understanding of compossibility: thus Brown often alludes to "the Russell-Hacking interpretation."[5] Fred D'Agostino has characterized these respectively as the "analytic" and "synthetic" interpretations of the compossibility relation.[6] I

2. Additionally, an event can be "morally" impossible if it violates the principle that a rational being always chooses the apparent best. But this does not seem to be a notion that even potentially excludes any collections of substances as compossible; and I therefore set aside the notion of moral possibility in what follows. For fuller discussion of Leibniz's distinctions among senses of 'possibility' see my dissertation, *Leibniz's Doctrine of Necessary Truth* (Harvard University, 1965; published by Garland, Harvard Dissertation Series, 1989).

3. See, for instance, Benson Mates, *The Philosophy of Leibniz: Metaphysics and Language* (New York: Oxford University Press, 1986), p. 75; Nicholas Rescher, *Leibniz's Metaphysics of Nature* (Dordrecht: D. Reidel, 1981), p. 57; Jaakko Hintikka, "Leibniz on Plenitude, Relations, and the 'Reign of Law,' " in *Leibniz: Critical and Interpretive Essays*, ed. Harry G. Frankfurt (Garden City, N.Y.: Doubleday, Anchor, 1971), pp. 158–59.

4. Hacking, "A Leibnizian Theory of Truth," in *Leibniz: Critical and Interpretive Essays*, ed., Michael Hooker (Minneapolis: University of Minnesota Press, 1982); and Brown, "Compossibility, Harmony, and Perfection in Leibniz," *Philosophical Review* 96 (1987): 173–203. Hacking says straightforwardly, "It is not logical inconsistency that prevents compossibility"; and Brown says that he is very strongly inclined to agree with Hacking's interpretation. (In the end, though, it is not entirely clear to me that Brown does agree with Hacking on the principal issue of whether incompossibility is a matter of logical inconsistency.)

5. Fred D'Agostino, who opposes the type of interpretation defended by Hacking, also cites Russell as an exponent of it. See his "Compossibility and Relational Predicates," in *Leibniz: Metaphysics and Philosophy of Science*, ed. R. S. Woolhouse (Oxford: Oxford University Press, 1981), pp. 89–103 (originally published in *Philosophical Quarterly* 26 [1976]).

6. Ibid.

personally would prefer some other characterization of the distinction (such as "logical" vs. "lawful"); but because I want to draw on passages from D'Agostino shortly, it will be convenient to accept his terminology.

The analytic understanding of compossibility is widely regarded—even by some of its proponents—as ascribing to Leibniz a position apparently inconsistent with one or two other tenets of his philosophy. The synthetic interpretation, on the other hand, has been held untenable on the grounds that it deprives incompossibility of an essential part of its role in Leibniz's system. I believe that the negative arguments are in *both* cases inconclusive: my first step in what follows is to explain why (section I).

I go on to argue (section II) that there are simple reasons for regarding the analytic understanding of (in)compossibility as *basically* correct. But, as I explain in section III, there are also some textual grounds for thinking that lawfulness (and hence "synthetic" features) must come into the picture somehow.

I go on to suggest two paths for accommodating the notion of lawfulness within an analytic understanding of (in)compossibility. The first is one that, oddly enough, I derive from Russell. But on my reading of Russell he is not so much rejecting the analytic view as refining it. That is, he introduces the notion of lawfulness into the interpretation of Leibnizian compossibility in such a way that the coinstantiation of incompossibles would still result in logical contradiction. (Thus I deny that there is such a thing as "the Russell-Hacking interpretation.") Russell's reading, however, relies on a notion of what could (logically) count as a "sufficient reason" for God's creative act that may be problematic.

The second approach I will sketch is in some ways simpler than Russell's. It allows us to recognize the relevance of lawfulness in interpreting compossibility, without relying on the potentially awkward restrictions on sufficient reason that Russell's proposal seems to require.

In conclusion (section IV) I acknowledge that my efforts to account for incompossibility in analytic or logical terms are very much bound up with highly idiosyncratic Leibnizian metaphysical assumptions. That is, I do not pretend to offer an intuitively satisfying sense of the notion, but only a viewpoint on certain interpretive issues.

I

A prominent argument *against* the "synthetic" line of interpretation rests on a particular understanding of the role of incompossibility in Leibniz's system. According to this argument, incompossibility must be interpreted logically to serve the purpose of separating Leibniz's system from Spino-zistic necessitarianism. Fred D'Agostino, for instance, notes the importance for Leibniz of the view that not all possibles are actual:

> . . . for Leibniz, not all possible individual substances are actually realized in the world. . . . It is important for Leibniz to make this claim, because, without it, his system collapses into Spinozistic necessitarianism of a kind he wished to avoid.[7]

D'Agostino goes on to cite a remark recorded by Leibniz the day after his meeting with Spinoza in 1676:

> If all possibles existed, no reason for existing would be needed, and possibility alone would suffice. Therefore there would be no God except in so far as he is possible. But such a God as the pious hold to would not be possible if the opinion of those is true who believe that all possibles exist.[8]

D'Agostino thinks this passage implies that Leibniz's opposition to "Spi-nozistic necessitarianism" hinges on the claim that not all possible sub-stances are compossible.[9] He thus maintains that a viable notion of incom-possibility is essential to Leibniz's defense against Spinozism.[10] He then argues that only an analytic notion will really do for this purpose. On a reading that finds the source of compossibility—and hence of partitioning into possible worlds—in lawful relations,

> God's role as Creator logically presupposes his role as Law-Maker. Any argument of this form against necessitarian atheism is thus surely a very weak and nearly circular one. This difficulty seems intrinsic moreover to any synthetic solution to the incompossibility problem, and thus suggests that we must seek an analytic solution.[11]

7. Ibid., p. 90.
8. C 530 (L 169). In the preceding paragraph of this note, Leibniz claims that the fact that minds *have no volume* rules out their incompossibility or incompatibility "with all other things," or their "imped[ing] the course of things," and thus helps establish their immortality. This crude conception appears to have the implication that all minds are compossible (compatible). Clearly, it is not consistent with a theory of incompossibility within the context of Leibniz's later position, which holds that all possible substances are unextended. (The passage in question is among those cited by Ian Hacking in the essay I briefly discuss below.)
9. Compossibility is, indeed, a topic of the previous paragraph (see note 8).
10. D'Agostino, "Compossibility and Relational Predicates," pp. 90, 92.
11. Ibid., pp. 94–95. See also Rescher, *Leibniz's Metaphysics of Nature*.

I take it D'Agostino's point is that if God is brought in as the ground of incompossibility—as the partitioner of possibles into worlds according to laws—then one cannot very well argue from the plurality of incompossible possibles to the need for a divine chooser among them. As the passage indicates, this is his main ground for rejecting the synthetic type of reading. But I think it is not a cogent one, for the following reason.

It is one thing to say that Leibniz needs to postulate unactualized possibles—and the concomitant requirement of "a reason for existing"—to avoid Spinozistic necessitarianism. It is quite another to say that he needs these assumptions to ground an independent "argument" for a wise Creator.[12] Leibniz does, to be sure, regard the "harmony" of the actual world as the basis of an argument for the existence of a wise and beneficent Creator.[13] But *this* argument—and the general opposition to Spinozism—requires only the assumption of (possibly?) unactualized possibles: it does not rely on any particular interpretation of incompossibility. To the question, "Why did God not actualize *all* the possibles?" a sufficient answer would be: "Because not all possibles are compossible in the sense of relating to each other under suitable laws of nature." Thus a God-independent conception of incompossibility is not an essential component of the rejection of Spinozism.[14]

Further, the doctrine of incompossibility—on any interpretation—is not *sufficient* to defeat Spinozism if (as I suppose) this requires establishing a wise Creator. Leibniz does, after all, speak of the incompossible possibles struggling for existence *on their own*: it is an interpretive *problem* to relate this *Dasseinstreben* picture to the conception of a beneficent creative will.[15] In fact, the notion of incompossibility becomes crucial to maintaining a gap between the actual and the possible, just insofar as one *abstracts* from the divine power and beneficence.

Thus, on the one hand, I do not think that D'Agostino succeeds in showing that a logical conception of (in)compossibility is necessary for Leibniz's strategic purposes. But, on the other hand, I agree with his contention that frequently mentioned arguments against the opposite, analytic view are not compelling.

12. For present purposes I go along with what I take to be a problematic interpretation of Spinoza's necessitarianism.

13. See, for instance, Bertrand Russell, *A Critical Exposition of the Philosophy of Leibniz* (London: George Allen and Unwin, 1937 [2d ed.; 1st ed. 1900]), pp. 183–85.

14. I think that Brown's paper, while ostensibly focused on the explication of (in)compossibility, is really fundamentally concerned with providing a positive answer to the question whether, under the Principle of Perfection, God could rationally decide to create *less than* the maximum number of possibles.

15. See, for instance, David Blumenfeld, "Leibniz's Theory of the Striving Possibles," in Woolhouse, *Leibniz*, pp. 77–88 (this paper was originally published in 1973).

One such argument rests on the claim that logical incompatibility between any two possible entities is hard to conceive—or is even unintelligible—in Leibniz's system. For Leibniz himself rules out logical incompatibility among primitive concepts. The following early passage is often cited:

> It is yet unknown to me what is the reason of the incompossibility of things, or how it is that different essences can be opposed to each other, seeing that all purely positive terms seem to be compatible.[16]

As D'Agostino points out, this passage does seem to show that Leibniz was *thinking of* incompossibility in the logical way when he wrote it—a far from negligible point. But many critics have taken the view expressed in this passage to show that such a notion of incompossibility is, at best, deeply problematic for Leibniz.[17] (They differ on whether or not some form of "analytical" reading can be salvaged.)

To me it seems rather strange that the "positive primitive concept" issue has so readily been taken as weighty, either with respect to the interpretation of Leibniz's notion of incompossibility or with respect to its cogency. The early passage just does not take us that far with respect to understanding Leibniz's mature views about compossibility.[18] Further, the postulation of (logically) incompossible possibles—whatever its difficulties—seems easy and almost obvious in comparison with the doctrine that all concepts are analyzable into primitive positive properties (identical, as Leibniz also says, with the attributes of God).[19] Why should one suppose that the latter element in Leibniz's early thought came to repel the former? Or, if we have to abandon, on Leibniz's behalf, one doctrine or another, why not the primitive positive concepts one? D'Agostino gives fairly detailed reasons for discounting the positive primitive concepts "problem" for the analytic interpretation; I will not take time to retrace them here.

But even if one discounts the primitive positive concepts issue, it seems

16. G VII, 194.
17. See Louis Couturat, *La Logique de Leibniz* (Hildesheim: Georg Olms, 1961 [2d ed.; 1st ed. 1901]), p. 219; G.H.R. Parkinson, *Logic and Reality in Leibniz's Metaphysics* (Oxford: Clarendon Press, 1965), pp. 83–85; Hide Ishiguro, *Leibniz's Philosophy of Logic and Language* (Ithaca, N.Y.: Cornell University Press, 1972), p. 47; C. D. Broad, *Leibniz: An Introduction* (London: Cambridge University Press, 1975), pp. 161–62; Hacking, "A Leibnizian Theory of Truth," p. 192; Mates, *The Philosophy of Leibniz*, p. 76. See also Russell, *Critical Exposition*, pp. 19–21.
18. As I have already indicated, the same reservation holds with respect to the early passage on the compossibility of (immortal) minds with all other things, also stressed by Hacking.
19. See Brown, "Compossibility, Harmony, and Perfection," pp. 181–83, for references. (Brown mentions a passage as late as 1696 in which Leibniz identifies primitive ideas with the attributes of God.)

that there is another, connected reason for doubting that an analytic interpretation of incompossibility is available for Leibniz. For logical incompossibility would require irreducible relations, whereas Leibniz is widely thought to have denied such things (for reasons to some extent distinct from the primitive positive concept theory). Thus D'Agostino (among others) notes that irreducible relational predicates, together with negation, "seem to be necessary and sufficient conditions for solving the incompossibility problem" within a logical framework.[20] He illustrates how incompossibility can be achieved, assuming negation and irreducible relations, by the following example:

> If it is part of the complete individual concept of one substance A that it stands in a certain symmetric relation R to every other substance, *and* if it is part of the complete individual concept of another substance B that it does not stand in the relation R to any other substance, then A and B are clearly incompossible substances.[21]

One can more intuitively (and trivially) illustrate incompossibility, given relational predicates, by drawing on Leibniz's theory that there is for every possible substance a "complete concept" containing all the predicates of that substance, and that all the predicates are essential to the identity of the substance in question.[22] That is, part of the reason our world can have only one of the many "possible Adams" Leibniz discusses in the Arnauld correspondence—and not a whole slew of them—is that there cannot, logically, be two "first men." Because there cannot, logically, be more than one "fastest thrower on the Mets in the late 1980s," "our" Doc Gooden and George Plimpton's Sidd Finch cannot both be on the pitching staff at that time.

D'Agostino (following Rescher and Hintikka) backs up his example by arguing that Leibniz is not, after all, committed to the irreducibility of relational predicates. The latter issue remains, however, a focus of ongoing debate in the Leibniz literature: it is certainly a dauntingly complex as well as a controversial one. I want to avoid committing myself to any view on the subject, as much as possible.[23] For present purposes, I think it is sufficient to make three rather general points. First, the very difficulty in

20. D'Agostino, "Compossibility and Relational Predicates," p. 97. D'Agostino acknowledges that he is following Hintikka's reasoning in the article cited above. See also Rescher, *Leibniz's Metaphysics of Nature*.

21. D'Agostino, "Compossibility and Relational Predicates," pp. 96–97.

22. I assume for present purposes a "superessentialist" interpretation. (See, for instance, Mates, *The Philosophy of Leibniz*, pp. 75, 92.)

23. Note, though, that 'incompossible' is itself a relational term.

making out just what Leibniz's position on relations is (or positions are) indicates that it may be acceptable to interpret it (or them) in a way consistent with the logical understanding of (in)compossibility, if we have good reasons for wanting to do so. (Once again, there is more than *one* way to resolve any conflict that might arise.) Second, in any case, the synthetic approach to compossibility has to help itself to relational predicates, too: laws themselves, obviously, have to do with relations among entities.[24] Finally, as I shall explain later, even logical incompossibility may not strictly require irreducible relational predicates after all, given certain tenets of Leibniz's metaphysics.

II

Now I want to indicate briefly the simple reasons in *favor* of understanding incompossibility in terms of freedom from contradiction. The first has to do with the context in which the term 'incompossibility' typically occurs. When Leibniz tells us that not all possibles are compossible, we naturally assume that 'possible' means the same following 'com' as it does on its own, in the same sentence—and Leibniz (it seems) never explicitly says anything to forestall this assumption. But in all the contexts I have seen cited, 'possibility' is used in the logical or metaphysical sense.

The second consideration has to do with some (admittedly exiguous) textual evidence. As we saw above, Leibniz's very worry about the primitive positive concept theory in connection with incompossibility suggests that he was thinking of the latter notion analytically. Further, Leibniz at one point actually defines a *compossible* as "what, when taken with another does not imply a contradiction."[25]

Finally, constraints of lawfulness and order of *some* kind are needed to define the "pre-established harmony." Invoking them to account for compossibility as well risks collapsing what seem to be intended as distinct concepts into each other.

24. Brown, noting this, pauses in his exposition of a version of that reading to point out that there is a "growing consensus" that Leibniz did not regard relational predicates as necessarily reducible to nonrelational ones ("Compossibility, Harmony, and Perfection," p. 194).

25. Grua, vol. 1, 325; quoted by Brown, "Compossibility, Harmony, and Perfection," p. 178. Brown cites Grua's dating for this passage of 1683–94; R. C. Sleigh, Jr., however, indicates that more recent scholarship has tentatively resulted in a much earlier date range of 1679–85. See his *Leibniz and Arnauld: A Commentary on Their Correspondence* (New Haven, Conn.: Yale University Press, 1990), pp. 172–73.

III

This cannot be the end of the story, however. For there is, after all, good textual reason to suppose that Leibnizian incompossibility has *something* to do with laws. I am not really persuaded by Hacking's argument to this effect, but I do find Russell's impressive. I will first take a look at Hacking's—a major source in the literature for the "synthetic" interpretation—and then take up Russell's more compelling textual point.

Hacking mentions Leibniz's late discussion of the novel *Astrea*, where Leibniz links compossibility with "connections with the rest of the universe," as indicating that Leibniz understood incompossibility as depending on synthetic laws. In a letter to Louis Bourguet Leibniz remarks:

> I do not agree that "in order to know if the romance of 'Astrea' is possible, it is necessary to know its connections with the rest of the universe." It would indeed be necessary to know this if it is to be *compossible* with the universe, and as a consequence to know if this romance has taken place, is taking place, or will take place in some corner of the world, for surely there would be no place for it without such connections. And it is very true that what is not, never has been, and never will be is not possible, if we take the *possible* in the sense of the *compossible*, as I have just said.[26]

Hacking asks: "Now let us suppose that *Astrea* is pure fiction, and contains no identifying reference to anything historical. Then how could *Astrea* fail to be compossible with the existing universe?" He goes on to propose that *Astrea*'s incompossibility derives from its events not happening to relate in a lawlike way to any spatiotemporal arrangement of the actual world—rather than from any logical inconsistency between entities of the fable and actual beings.

It strikes me, however, that there is more than one way that a proponent of the analytic line of interpretation could reply to Hacking's rhetorical question. One might suggest, for instance, that it is a matter of logical or metaphysical necessity that a series taking place in the world must have a suitably specified spatial and temporal location within the world. Compossibility (with actual substances and events) can be achieved only by satisfying these logical conditions.[27] Or, one could draw on the complete concept

---

26. G III, 572 (L 661).

27. In *Leibniz's Metaphysics of Nature*, pp. 86–92, Nicholas Rescher maintains that differences in the "spaces" of different possible worlds *derive from* the analytic incompossibility of their respective substances: "Substances are located in different spaces *because* they contradict one

account of substance, and the accompanying theory of truth: if both are taken as logically necessary, then, one might argue, *Astrea* is logically incompossible with us substances in the actual world if *our* concepts contain no identifying connection with *it*. (A substance, I assume, is *not in a world*, unless there are "truths" relating it to other substances of that world.)[28] Leibniz's reference to the need for "connections" between a possible entity and actual ones can, in other words, be interpreted in logical terms as easily as in terms of lawfulness.

Russell, though, gives more compelling reason for thinking that Leibniz connected compossibility with (synthetic) lawfulness. He cites the following passage from the Arnauld correspondence:

> There were an infinity of possible ways of creating the world, according to the different designs which God might form, and each possible world depends upon certain principal designs or ends of God proper to itself, i.e. certain free primitive decrees (conceived *sub ratione possibilitatis*), or laws of the general order of this possible universe, to which they belong, and whose notion they determine, as well as the notions of all the individual substances which must belong to this same Universe.[29]

Fortunately, one can accommodate such passages as this, incorporating some of the benefits of the synthetic reading, without giving up the analytic or logical understanding of incompossibility. This is the approach I want to attribute to Russell himself. His resolution turns on, as he puts it, "the necessity for *some* sufficient reason of the whole series." He continues,

> Although this or that sufficient reason is contingent, there must be some sufficient reason, and the lack of one condemns many series of existents as *metaphysically impossible*. (emphasis added)[30]

another . . ." (p. 87). Rescher provides considerable support for his reading—though it does seem that in the *Astrea* passage Leibniz is representing compossibility as dependent on spatial connection (rather than the other way around).

28. ". . . it is in the nature of an individual substance to have such a complete concept, whence can be inferred everything that one can attribute to it, and even the whole universe because of the connexions between things" (Leibniz-Arnauld Correspondence, G II, 41; LA 44).

29. G II, 51; Russell, *Critical Exposition*, p. 67.

30. Russell, *Critical Exposition*, p. 67.

He then quotes the passage from the Arnauld correspondence I have given above, and concludes:

> This passage proves quite definitely that all possible worlds have general laws, which determine the connection of contingents just as, in the actual world, it is determined by the laws of motion and the law that free spirits pursue what seems best to them. . . .[31] Possibles cease to be compossible only when there is no general law whatever to which both conform. What is called the "reign of law" is, in Leibniz's philosophy, *metaphysically necessary*, although the actual laws are contingent. If this is not realized, compossibility must remain unintelligible. (emphasis added)

Russell's repeated stress on metaphysical necessity in this passage seems to have been overlooked. He is not saying *merely* that A's incompossibility with B is a matter of A's not being linked with B through suitable general laws (as Hacking suggests). He is saying further that the obtaining of such general laws, as a possible sufficient reason for the series' existence, is *metaphysically necessary*. Thus it is *metaphysically* impossible for both A and B to exist. And I take it this means—as it generally does in Leibniz—*absolutely* or *logically* impossible.[32] Russell's point is that the impossibility is not generated by considering A and B *alone*, in abstraction from the metaphysical necessity of a sufficient reason. His reading serves to accommodate the textual indications that "laws" figure in the partitioning of possible worlds, without (ultimately) giving up the "analytic" understanding of (in)compossibility.

There is, however, a problem for this reading that derives from a well-known passage from the *Discourse on Metaphysics* (vi), where Leibniz says that "one cannot even feign" something "absolutely irregular." No matter how apparently chaotic the data one starts with may be—say, a scattering of dots on a page—it will always be possible to subsume them under *some* law of interrelation. (That is, I take it, there will be a formula allowing us to predict the whole set, given one of its members.) He continues:

31. I have omitted a sentence that reads, "And without the need for *some* general laws, any two possibles would be compossible, since they cannot contradict one another." This sentence derives from Russell's acceptance of (a version of) the primitive concept worry, which I tend to reject. Note, though, that this sentence, too, indicates that Russell *understands* compossibility as a logical relation, just as Leibniz's expression of that worry indicates that *he* does.

32. On the previous page (66) Russell explains a "possible world" as a world "internally free from self-contradiction." I take it his subsequent appeal to Sufficient Reason is a way of maintaining a logical understanding of compossibility, while giving up the notion that it is entirely a question of "internal" factors.

> Thus one can say that in whatever way God had created the world, it would always have been regular and in a certain general order. But God has chosen the one which is the most perfect. . . .[33]

So, it seems, *any* putative group of possibilities must conform to some law or other; the Russellian formulation turns out to be *vacuous* on Leibnizian principles.[34]

This objection can be met, however, if we may suppose that not just any "law of the general order" qualifies as representing "a design which God might form," and hence as providing a possible sufficient reason for creating a given set of possible substances. I admit that this proposal requires a rather strained reading of the relevant section of the *Discourse*. But, on the other hand, it does seem consonant with certain passages of the Arnauld correspondence, including the one on which Russell particularly relies. When Leibniz says that "each possible world depends upon certain principal designs or ends of God proper to itself, i.e. certain free decrees . . . or laws of the general order," his language does not at all suggest the follow-the-dots model of *Discourse* vi. In similar vein he writes:

> . . . as there exists an infinite number of possible worlds, there exists also an infinite number of laws, some peculiar to one world, and some to another, and each possible individual of any one world contains in the concept of him the laws of his world.[35]

So,

> for instance, if this world were only possible, the individual concept of a body in this world, containing certain movements as possibilities, would also contain our laws of motion . . . but also as mere possibilities.[36]

33. G IV, 431; trans. P. G. Lucas and L. Grint (Manchester: Manchester University Press, 1953), p. 10.

34. Gregory Brown, "Compossibility, Harmony, and Perfection," emphasizes this difficulty for Russell's position.

A similar point is sometimes made with respect to Leibniz's concept of "expression." If 'expression' is understood in a broad way, so that *any* "constant and regular relation" is sufficient, any two possible substances will express each other, on Leibniz's principle. If it is understood more narrowly, as requiring *simple* relations, then it seems to collapse into harmony.

35. G II, 40; LA, 43.

36. Ibid.

I take it that Leibniz is here talking about something at least close to laws of nature in the standard sense. It may be, in other words, that the requirement that individuals, to be compossible, must conform to possible basic designs and primitive free decrees of God expresses a *metaphysical* condition that is not trivially satisfied by *just any* group of possible substances.[37] That is, he may be assuming that only possible substances linked by fairly simple lawful generalities present a world that God could, logically, have sufficient reason to create.[38]

But maybe the passage just quoted also shows us an *alternative* way of relating analytic compossibility and law—one that avoids the potential complexities inherent in Russell's appeal to sufficient reason. For, as I read the passage, it seems to indicate that each individual substance concept contains in itself a set of world laws in a quite determinate way. That is, if we think of laws as *facts* (of a certain kind), then individual substance concepts imply these possible facts. Then incompossibility can be (partly) explained as follows. Possible substances S and T will be (analytically) *incompossible* if the complete concept of S contains a fact, F, concerning the laws of nature of any world in which S might find itself, and the complete concept of T contains a fact that is (directly) logically inconsistent with F. For example, S's complete concept might contain the "fact" that $e = mc^2$, while T's complete concept includes the "fact" that $e = 2mc$. To suppose that S and T are both created is to suppose that, in actuality, $e = mc^2$ *and* $e = 2mc$—a *logically* self-contradictory assumption, we may suppose.[39] While lawlike relations of this sort may not be *all* that incompossibility consists in, we may still allow that the incompossibility of substance S and T has *partly* to do with the laws included in the concepts of the two substances respectively.

This way of construing the analytic conception of incompossibility involves an important departure from Russell, in that it requires us to hold that, after all, the incompossibility of two possible substances A and B *can* be established by considering A and B alone. But it does preserve the

37. Earlier I suggested (section II) that the analytic interpretation has the advantage of preserving a clear-cut distinction between compossibility and harmony. Insofar as one begins to build considerations of *simplicity of laws* into the interpretation, one does tend to lose this advantage.

38. Sleigh, *Leibniz and Arnauld*, pp. 52–53, argues for a sharp distinction between "laws of the general order" and "laws of nature" in Leibniz. I am not sure that the distinction is really as sharp in the texts as he suggests, but certainly his claim deserves fuller consideration than I have been able to give it here.

39. One might seek less anachronistic examples in Leibniz's conception of the laws of impact, and the conservation of "vis viva."

relevance of "laws of a world" to (in)compossibility judgments, while preserving the "analytic" intent of Russell's account (as I understand it).[40]

It also suggests the interesting point, in relation to the notion mentioned above, that incompossibility requires irreducible relational predicates. Once one allows substances to contain propositions, one can provide examples of incompossibility that do not rely on relational predicates—not even on "laws." For instance, if (substance) S is p; and T is q; and T "contains" the proposition 'If anything is p, nothing is q,' S and T are analytically incompossible.[41]

IV

In conclusion, I mention and concede that the views about compossibility I have proposed on Leibniz's behalf are tightly bound up with some pretty esoteric aspects of his metaphysics. For instance, the notion of possible *substances* containing *facts* (lawlike or otherwise) seems to get things more or less the wrong way round from the point of view of much traditional metaphysics. I admit it seems bizarre to me, even if it is (as I think) strongly suggested by certain Leibnizian texts. And ideas about incompossibility

40. I suppose it is debatable how far this reading can accommodate the spirit of the passage from the Arnauld correspondence on which Russell principally relies. It might help, though, to propose that while compossibility with respect to laws is analytic in the way just suggested, the issue of God's choice among worlds raises a separate question about the potential attractiveness to God of the various systems of laws reflected in the substances belonging to the worlds thus partitioned.

No doubt any description of incompossibility that relates the concept to *lawfulness* should take account of Leibniz's distinction between the primitive and the derivative predicates of a possible substance concept. It seems to be generally accepted that laws are what make possible the deduction of the latter from the former. So we must ask whether compossibility enters at the "primitive" level, or only after the laws are "added." Or does a combination of primitives—a collection of not-yet-complete substance concepts—automatically generate its own laws? (Russell does not deal with this issue, and to that extent his treatment of compossibility must be judged incomplete; Brown treats it in detail in "Compossibility, Harmony, and Perfection.") The only observations I want to make on the point here are that, first, I have not claimed that incompossibility has to do *exclusively* with laws; and, second, to the extent that it *does* have to do with laws, it will obviously come in at the level of primitive concepts, just in case they do *determine* laws (as opposed to the laws being "added on").

41. I owe this point (down to the exact phrasing, as far as I can recall) to Robert Sleigh, who raised it in discussion. If Sleigh's suggestion is, as I think, compelling, it perhaps deserves an essay in itself, given the prominence in the interpretive literature of the contrary assumption—that analytic compossibility requires irreducible relations. (For a similar example, see Nicholas Rescher, *A Theory of Possibility* [Oxford: Blackwell, 1975], pp. 78ff. Rescher, however, does not draw the same conclusion from the example as did Sleigh.)

based on Leibniz's (supposed) "superessentialism" seem contrary to main-stream conceptions of essence, both traditional and contemporary. Thus, as I pointed out earlier, one seems to get logical incompatibility between possible Adams, within Leibniz's system, by noting that there cannot, logically, be *two* first men. (While this notion may sound sophomoric, I do suspect it underlies what sense one may have of intuitive understanding of Leibniz's "possible Adams" talk.) But, of course, a more Kripkean notion of individual essences would allow us to say that "our" Adam could very well have existed without being "first." And Dwight Gooden just might have had the Mets' *second* fastest fastball in the late 1980s. If there is any "intuitive" explication of the notion of incompossible entities (and I am not sure there is), it may very well have much more to do with lawfulness than logic.[42]

42. Versions of this chapter were read at the New School for Social Research and at Rutgers University. I am grateful to all the participants in the discussions for their comments; I particularly thank Robert Sleigh, Dorothy Stark, Sarah Stroud, and Martha Bolton. The discussions made me all too aware of more problems and complexities in what I say here than I have been able to address in revision.

Donald P. Rutherford

Natures, Laws, and Miracles: The Roots of Leibniz's Critique of Occasionalism

Leibniz regarded his theory of preestablished harmony as offering the only plausible explanation of the remarkable agreement of the soul and the body: the agreement whereby physical stimuli give rise to appropriate sensory perceptions and volitions of the will terminate in appropriate bodily motions. According to his account, there is no real communication between the soul and the body, for neither is capable of exerting a real causal influence on the other. Instead, the soul and the body are to be conceived on the analogy of two perfectly synchronized clocks: each is responsible for the production of all its own states, yet the two nevertheless manage to agree or "harmonize" as a consequence of the consummate skill of the watchmaker who first set them in motion.

I thank Thomas M. Lennon and Steven Nadler for their helpful comments on an earlier draft of this chapter.

Since its conception, the theory of preestablished harmony has confronted the charge that it is at bottom indistinguishable from the doctrine of occasionalism.[1] Like preestablished harmony, occasionalism denies any causal influence of one created substance on another. By its account the only real causal agent is God, who causes thoughts to arise in the soul on the occasion of the appropriate motions in the body, and movements of the body on the occasion of the appropriate volitions of the will.[2] Now, fairly clearly, this is not a position to which Leibniz himself subscribes. Critics of preestablished harmony, however, are little moved by this fact. They allow that occasionalism may make a more direct appeal to divine action than does preestablished harmony; nevertheless, they contend that the two theories share the crucial feature that a prima facie natural phenomenon is ascribed to a supernatural cause: either God's immediate production of all the states of the soul and the body, or his creation of two substances that are programmed to instantiate just those states that will ensure their perfect agreement. From the critic's point of view, the similarities between occasionalism and preestablished harmony far outweigh their differences. Whether God actually deals the cards or merely stacks the deck, the result is the same.

In certain moods, Leibniz is happy to acknowledge the common ground the theory of preestablished harmony shares with occasionalism. Despite his concessions on this point, however, he remains adamant that there are important problems with the doctrine of occasionalism that his theory avoids.[3] Among the most prominent objections he raises to it are the following: (1) occasionalism is inconsistent with the supposition of finite substances; (2) occasionalism presupposes the occurrence of "perpetual miracles"; and (3) occasionalism requires that God "disturb" (déranger, troubler) the ordinary laws of nature. The first of these objections has received considerable attention in the literature. It has generally been acknowledged that Leibniz faults occasionalists for transferring all power to God on the grounds that such a move leads inevitably to the denial of finite

1. This criticism was first made by Arnauld; see his letter to Leibniz of 4 March 1687 (G II, 84/LA 105–6).

2. As Leibniz himself notes, the occasionalist theory is not limited to an account of soul-body relations, but extends also to causal interactions among bodies: "since the communication of motions also seemed inconceivable to them, they believed that God imparts motion to a body on the occasion of the motion of another body" (G IV, 483/AG 143). For recent reassertions of this point, see Thomas M. Lennon, "Philosophical Commentary," in LO, 810, and Steven Nadler, "Occasionalism and the Mind-Body Problem," Oxford Studies in the History of Philosophy 2 (forthcoming).

3. For examples of Leibniz both affirming and qualifying the relation of this theory to the doctrine of occasionalism, see his letters to L'Hospital (30 September 1695; GM II, 299) and Remond (26 August 1714; G III, 625).

created substances, that is, to Spinozism. At issue here is the proper understanding of divine omnipotence, and of the relationship between the power of God and that of created things. In this essay, I will not be directly concerned with this topic, although in the next section I will sketch the main lines of Leibniz's argument. My focus instead will be on objections (2) and (3). I will argue that both of these objections derive from a particular conception of the intelligibility of nature, a conception to which Leibniz is firmly committed and that occasionalists like Malebranche no less firmly reject. I will further suggest that this division is rooted in a deeper disagreement about the correct interpretation of divine wisdom as it figures in the respective theodicies of Leibniz and Malebranche.

I

Leibniz's theory of substance is constructed around two main claims: first, any substance is endowed with an intrinsic force or power sufficient to determine all its own states or modifications; second, the determinations of this active power are in agreement or harmony with those of the active powers of all other substances. It is the first of these claims that bears directly on his critique of occasionalism, for it is the occasionalist view that created beings lack all activity and that God alone has the power to bring about things in the world. Nevertheless, it is at least worth noting here the significance of the idea of universal harmony that animates Leibniz's thought from his earliest days.[4] It is a fundamental thesis of his philosophy that harmony, or the unity and agreement of a multiplicity of diverse beings, is a defining characteristic of metaphysical perfection. Consequently, insofar as it is accepted that God has been motivated to select this world for existence on account of its superior perfection, such a harmony must be a key component in our understanding of the world. The doctrine of the preestablished harmony of substances is but a refinement of this basic theme.[5]

4. Leibniz's attachment to this idea can be traced to his early (c. 1663–66) acquaintance with the writings of Johann Heinrich Bisterfeld (see A vi.I; 151–61).

5. It is important to distinguish Leibniz's arguments *against* occasionalism from his arguments *for* preestablished harmony. In this essay, I am concerned solely with the former, which do not directly involve the doctrine of harmony. Arguments against occasionalism form an essential component of one of Leibniz's main defenses of preestablished harmony. Briefly, he contends that there are only three ways of accounting for the agreement of the soul and the body: interactionism, occasionalism, and preestablished harmony. Neither interactionism nor occasionalism is tenable; preestablished harmony is possible; therefore, preestablished

That any substance is endowed with an intrinsic force or power appears in many places as a necessary truth for Leibniz. Commenting on Locke's debate with the Bishop of Worcester in the Preface to the *New Essays*, he says unequivocally that "activity is the essence of substance in general" (NE 65). Similarly, in a letter to De Volder, he writes that it is "metaphysically necessary" that any substance possess an intrinsic activity (G II, 169; cf. G VI, 598/AG 207). Again, he writes to Bayle in 1702 that "[w]ithout an internal force of action a thing could not be a substance, for the nature of substance consists in this regulated tendency, from which phenomena are born in order" (G III, 58). As I read these remarks, they involve more than a mere stipulation on Leibniz's part. Rather than simply fixing what is to be called "substance," he is working from a complex, historically rooted conception of what it is to *be* a substantial being, and is subsequently arguing that these conditions can only be satisfied if substance is conceived as being by nature a principle of activity. We may see him as claiming that substance could not fulfill its prescribed metaphysical roles—as an ultimate explanatory principle, as a being that is dependent for its existence on no other created being, as a being that persists through change, and as a true unity—unless it is also conceived as a principle of activity: a source productive of changes in its states or modifications, which nevertheless persists as itself through those changes.

Now, the occasionalist response to this line of reasoning will be to reassert the essential dependence in Christian metaphysics of all created being on God. As Malebranche interprets this dependence, created beings are conserved in existence only because God continues to will their existence. Thus, while from the side of creatures there appears to be a difference between creation and conservation, "in reality, creation does not pass away, since in God conservation and creation are one and the same volition, which consequently is necessarily followed by the same effects" (OC XII–XIII,

---

harmony must be accepted (cf. the "New System of the Nature and Communication of Substances" [G IV, 477–87/AG 138–45] and the Postscript to his 1696 letter to Basnage de Beauval [G IV, 498–500/AG 147–49]). In addition to this "argument from elimination," Leibniz also advances an *a priori* argument for preestablished harmony based on his concept of substance (cf. G IV, 494/P 126). Here the doctrine of harmony, or at least the weaker doctrine of universal expression, plays a central role in his reasoning. Starting from the premise that "God originally created the soul (or any other real unity) in such a way that everything must arise for it from its own depths, through a perfect *spontaneity* relative to itself, and yet with a perfect *conformity* relative to external things," he concludes in the "New System" that "[i]t is this mutual relation, regulated in advance in each substance of the universe, which produces what we call their *communication*, and which alone brings about *the union of soul and body*" (G IV, 484–85/AG 144). For a full discussion of both these arguments, see R. C. Sleigh, Jr., *Leibniz and Arnauld: A Commentary on Their Correspondence* (New Haven, Conn.: Yale University Press, 1990), pp. 161–80.

157/D 153). The dependence of creatures on God, moreover, extends not only to the conservation of their existence but to the conservation of their particular modalities.

> [God] cannot will what cannot be conceived. Hence, He cannot will that this chair exist without willing at the same time that it exist in some place or other and without his will putting it there, since you are unable to conceive that this chair exists and that it does not exist in some place, there or elsewhere. (OC XII–XIII, 156/D 153)

The upshot of the occasionalist position is that creatures essentially dependent on God are *completely* dependent on him for the production of all their states and effects. They possess no power to bring such things about themselves.[6] This is the conclusion that Leibniz rejects, emphasizing instead the connection between the claim of substance to an existence that, while dependent, is nonetheless distinct from that of God and its status as a persisting principle of activity.[7] In the absence of such a connection, he argues, the occasionalist position comes dangerously close to Spinozism. If created beings are denied a persistent force capable of producing (with the concurrence of God) their own modifications, and if instead those modifications are ascribed exclusively to the action of God, it ceases to make sense to talk about the modifications as being *theirs* rather than God's. Without a force of some duration, Leibniz writes in the 1698 essay *De ipsa natura*,

> no created substance, no soul would remain numerically the same, and thus, nothing would be conserved by God, and consequently all things would be only certain vanishing or unstable modifications or phantasms, so to speak, of the one permanent divine substance. Or, what comes to the same thing, God would be the very nature or substance of all things. (G IV, 508–9/AG 160)[8]

6. The above is not intended as a full account of Malebranche's arguments for this last claim. See Lennon, "Philosophical Commentary," in LO, pp. 809ff.; and Robert C. Sleigh, Jr., "Leibniz on Malebranche on Causality," in *Central Themes in Early Modern Philosophy*, ed. J. A. Cover and Mark Kulstad (Indianapolis, Ind.: Hackett, 1990), pp. 161–93.

7. The precise nature of the dependence of created substances on God in Leibniz's philosophy—the content of his doctrine of divine concurrence—is a vexed issue. See Sleigh, *Leibniz and Arnauld*, pp. 183–85, and "Leibniz on Malebranche on Causality."

8. See also his letter to Lelong of 5 February 1712:

> [F]orce is one of the principal perfections, which being removed there will remain nearly nothing of [substance], or soon nothing at all. And I dare to say that without force, there will be no substance; and one will fall, despite oneself, into the opinion of Spinoza, according to whom creatures are only passing modifications. It is necessary, therefore, to say that God gives the force, and that he does not replace it, in order to preserve the substances outside of him. (ML 421)

Compare G IV, 515/AG 165; G IV, 567–68/L 583.

Leibniz's first, and in many ways most compelling, response to occasional-ism, then, is to claim that to deny causal activity to substances is to deny that they satisfy the conditions of persistence and independence constitutive of substantial being. Thus, rather than solving the problem of how two distinct substances like mind and body appear to communicate with one another, occasionalists eliminate the problem by, in effect, denying that there are two such substances.

In the essay *De ipsa natura* Leibniz offers a further argument for the intrinsic activity of substance. He is principally occupied in this text with criticizing the occasionalist view, defended by Johann Christopher Sturm, that the motion of bodies occurs solely "by virtue of the eternal law God once set up." As it stands, Leibniz argues, this claim may be interpreted in one of two ways. On the one hand, it may imply that the motions of bodies come about as the result of a single original "volition or command" on the part of God, or "a divine law that . . . bestowed a mere *extrinsic denomination* . . . on things." On the other hand, this volition or command may be understood to have "conferred some kind of enduring impression" on things: namely, "an inherent law [*legem insitam*], . . . from which both actions and passions follow" (G IV, 506–7/AG 158). Leibniz strongly attacks the first of these alternatives, which he associates with occasionalists like Sturm, on the grounds that it destroys any intelligible connection between God's original volition and the present effects of things:

> For, since that past command does not now exist, it cannot now bring anything about unless it left behind some subsistent effect at the time, an effect which even now endures and is now at work. Whoever thinks otherwise, in my judgment, renounces all distinct explanation of things; anything could equally well be said to follow from anything else if something absent in place or time could be at work here and now, without an intermediary. And so, it is not sufficient to say that God, creating things in the beginning, willed that they follow a certain definite law in their change [*progressus*] if we imagine this will to have been so ineffective that things are not affected by it and no lasting effect was produced in them. (G, IV 507/AG 158)

The only coherent way to understand the connection between God's volition and the present effects of things, he argues, is to suppose that God's action has left some permanent impression on them: an "inherent law" that is sufficient to account for the pattern of their particular effects that itself involves an intrinsic force.

But if, indeed, the law God laid down left some trace of itself impressed on things, if by his command things were formed in such a way that they were rendered appropriate for fulfilling the will of the command, then already we must admit that a certain efficacy has been placed in things, a form or a force, something like what we usually call by the name 'nature,' something from which the series of phenomena follow in accordance with the prescript of the first command. (G IV, 507/AG 158–59).

This second argument provides a basis for rejecting at least one version of the occasionalist thesis and for recognizing in its stead the existence of beings endowed with an intrinsic force or activity. However, it is doubtful whether it proves telling against all versions of the doctrine. In criticizing Sturm, Leibniz begins from the assumption that God's will is exercised in the form of a single command prior to creation; from this he infers that such a command is either insufficient to account for the present effects of things, or that it issued in the creation of beings whose natures incorporate causal powers capable of producing the observed effects. An occasionalist might object, however, that Leibniz has omitted the possibility that God acts either by a continuous series of particular acts of will, intervening at each moment to secure a particular effect, or by an eternal or timeless will, which is sufficient to account for the effects of all things at all times, without the action of secondary causes. And, indeed, this latter view would seem to be the position of Malebranche, who writes in his *Dialogues on Metaphysics*: "From all eternity God has willed, and to all eternity He will continue to will—or, to speak more accurately, God wills unceasingly though without variation, without succession, without necessity—everything He will do in the course of time" (OC XII–XIII, 159/D 157).[9] Here, then, would seem to be a version of occasionalism that is at least prima facie resistant to Leibniz's charge that the doctrine assumes an unbridgeable gap between God's original volition and the present effects of things.

II

I turn now to Leibniz's second main criticism of occasionalism—his objection from the intelligibility of nature. The crux of his criticism here is that,

9. In "Occasionalism and General Will in Malebranche," *Journal of the History of Philosophy* (forthcoming), Steven Nadler argues that the former more accurately represents Malebranche's position: "that God always acts in accordance with the laws he has established in the realm of nature . . . does not rule out an infinite number of temporalized and individual acts of will on God's part" (pp. 20–21).

regardless of the mode of God's willing (whether it be singular or successive, in time or eternal), occasionalism is to be rejected on the grounds that
it assumes a natural order that is at odds with the *wisdom* God has exercised
in selecting this world for existence. Thus, in addition to the objection that
a world with no secondary causal powers would be a world in which there
would be no persistent substances, and hence no distinction between God
and creation, Leibniz claims that the occasionalist picture of God acting at
each instant to secure the continued progression of the world, or acting
timelessly to produce the totality of the world's effects, fails to support the
idea that God has chosen to create this world, as the best of all possible
worlds, because it best answers to the demands of his wisdom.

Essential to Leibniz's conception of this as the best of all possible worlds
is that it is a world in which the principle of sufficient reason is observed, a
world in which for anything that happens there is a reason that it happens
thus and not otherwise. A further dimension of this requirement, however,
which has not been widely recognized, is that within the "order of nature"
it is not enough simply that there be some reason for anything to happen
as it does; in addition, there must be what Leibniz calls a "natural reason":
a reason that displays the effect in question as following in an intelligible
manner from the nature or essence of some created being.[10] As Leibniz
writes in the Preface to the *New Essays*,

> within the order of nature (miracles apart) it is not at God's arbitrary
> discretion to attach this or that quality haphazardly to substances.
> He will never give them any that are not natural to them, that is,
> that cannot arise from their nature as explicable modifications. (NE
> 66)

In attempting to account for the phenomena of nature, Leibniz argues, we
may reject as insufficient any explanation that appeals either to supernatural
causes or to unintelligible "occult qualities": forms or faculties that are
postulated solely for the purpose of accounting for a particular phenomenon
(e.g., gravity, magnetism), without an attempt being made to explain how
such a quality follows from the nature of its subject. We must instead begin
from the assumption that the properties of things can in general be
conceived as modifications of attributes that partly define the natures of
their subjects.[11] I will return later to the deeper motivations, associated with

---

10. Compare G III, 519. I discuss this requirement in detail in my essay "Leibniz's Principle
of Intelligibility" (*History of Philosophy Quarterly*, forthcoming).

11. This is the objection that Leibniz raises against Locke's notion of "thinking matter":
   As for thought, it is certain, as our author more than once acknowledges, that it cannot

his understanding of divine wisdom, that attract Leibniz to this "principle of intelligibility." For the moment, I want to examine how it is applied in his critique of occasionalism.

We may begin with Leibniz's claim that occasionalism employs God as a deus ex machina, and that it consequently resorts to miracles in its attempt to account for the agreement of the body and the soul.[12] The first of these charges rests squarely on the principle just described. Espousing a conception of nature's order in which an explanation of the effects of any thing is always to be sought in that thing's intrinsic nature, Leibniz is hostile to all attempts to account for features of the natural world through appeal to divine action. A similar line of reasoning supports the claim that occasionalism transforms a natural circumstance like the agreement of the body and the soul into a "perpetual miracle." Pierre Bayle, who had commented on Leibniz's "New System" in his *Dictionnaire Critique et Historique* of 1697, argues that Leibniz had simply misunderstood the occasionalist position in bringing this objection against it.[13] According to Bayle, occasionalism does not require that the actions of God occur miraculously. For an occasionalist like Malebranche, God acts in the world, but he ordinarily acts only by "general volitions" or "according to general laws"; hence, the natural order of things does not amount to a continual miracle.[14]

In his 1698 reply to Bayle, Leibniz reiterates his charge against occasionalism, while taking care to distinguish his own understanding of the notion of a miracle from that assumed by Bayle:

> be an intelligible modification of matter and be comprehensible and explicable in terms of it. That is, a sentient or thinking being is not a mechanical thing like a watch or a mill: one cannot conceive of sizes and shapes and motions combining mechanically to produce something which thinks, and senses too, in a mass where [formerly] there was nothing of the kind—something which would likewise be extinguished by the machine's going out of order. So sense and thought are not something which is natural to matter, and there are only two ways in which they could occur in it: through God's combining it with a substance to which thought is natural, or through his putting thought into it by a miracle. (NE 66–67).

Compare his letter to Lady Masham of 30 June 1704 (G III, 355/AG 290).

12. Compare the "New System":

> It is quite true that, speaking with metaphysical rigor, there is no real influence of one created substance on another, and that all things, with all their reality, are continually produced by the power [*vertu*] of God. But in solving problems it is not sufficient to make use of the general cause and to invoke what is called a *Deus ex machina*. For when one does that without giving any other explanation derived from the order of secondary causes, it is, properly speaking, having recourse to miracle. (G IV, 483/AG 143).

13. See "Remark H" to the article "Rorarius" in Pierre Bayle, *Historical and Critical Dictionary: Selections*, trans. Richard H. Popkin (Indianapolis, Ind.: Hackett, 1991), p. 238.

14. Compare *Traité de la Nature et de la Grace* I, lix (OC V, 63); and *Dialogues on Metaphysics* VIII, iii (OC XII–XIII, 177–78/D 175).

[L]et us see whether the system of occasional causes does not in fact assume a perpetual miracle. Here it is said that it does not, because according to this system God would only act through general laws. I agree, but in my opinion this does not suffice to remove the miracles; even if God should do this continuously, they would not cease being miracles, taking this word, not in the popular sense of a rare and marvelous thing, but in the philosophical sense of what exceeds the powers of created things. It is not enough to say that God has made a general law; for besides this decree there must be a natural means of executing it; that is, it is necessary that what happens can be explained through the nature that God gives to things. (G IV, 520/L 494)[15]

In this passage, as in many others like it, Leibniz links his understanding of the miraculousness of events to his conception of the intelligibility of nature. What qualifies an effect as "extraordinary" or miraculous, he argues, is that it cannot be explained by the natures of created things. Occasionalism, in interpreting all change as the direct effect of God's action, denies that such explanations can be given for natural effects. Hence, it renders them miraculous. From Leibniz's perspective, it matters not whether occasionalists interpret God as intervening only in a regular manner or according to "general volitions." The point is that on their view God *does* intervene in the world, rather than granting created things natures sufficient to account for their effects.

In claiming that the system of occasional causes assumes a "perpetual miracle," then, Leibniz does not fault occasionalists for advancing a theory in which no provision is made for natural regularities. His objection is instead directed at how occasionalists account for such regularities. According to Malebranche, a law of nature exists just in case God wills that a certain sort of event should regularly follow another sort of event. On his account, God's nature places important constraints on the form that natural laws can take. Most significantly, such laws will always be simple and will guarantee the maximum uniformity of nature, since these qualities reflect the perfection of God's "ways."[16] Beyond this, Leibniz argues, occasional-

15. Similar statements appear in the *Theodicy*, §207 (G VI, 240–41/H 257) and § 355 (G VI, 326/H 338–39), in his comments on Lamy (G IV, 587–88, 594–95), and in his letters to Basnage de Beauval, c. 1696 (G III, 122), and Conti, 9 April 1716 (GB 277). Leibniz does not deny the possibility of God's extraordinary intervention in the world, but only claims that it is necessary to draw a clear distinction between the ordinary course of nature, which can be understood through the natures of created things, and genuine miracles. Thus, he writes to Lady Masham in 1704 that "the ways of God are of two sorts, the one natural, the other miraculous" (G III, 353).

16. See section III below.

ists regard natural laws as products of divine convention. All things being equal, there is no reason that bodies should tend to move along a tangential path, rather than a circular one, except that God has decreed it to be so. Likewise, there is no reason that minds and bodies should not interact (in the occasionalist's sense), so long as God chooses that such a regularity should be observed in nature. It is precisely this suggestion of the potential arbitrariness of God's choice concerning the laws of nature that Leibniz finds objectionable.[17] For properties or events to be characterized as natural, it is not enough that they conform to lawlike generalizations. In addition, it must be possible to understand how such properties or events follow from the nature of their subject. The debate between Leibniz and the occasionalists thus comes down to the question of what it is to be a genuine law of nature (and, conversely, what it is to be a miracle or an exception to such a law). According to occasionalists, a law of nature exists just in case God wills, in a manner consistent with his nature, that a certain regularity should occur. According to Leibniz, for a generalization to qualify as a law of nature it must, in addition, be possible to conceive of the effects it describes as "explicable modifications" of the nature of their subject. To put the point succinctly, for Leibniz, laws of nature are laws of *natures*: exceptionless sequences of events that are explainable by the intrinsic natures of *types* of being.[18]

17. Responding to François Lamy's critique of the doctrine of preestablished harmony in his *Connaissance de soi-même* (1699), Leibniz writes that according to occasionalists "a miracle is only an exception to general rules or laws that God has established arbitrarily. Thus once God has made it a general law or rule that the body should always agree with the soul, and vice versa, there would be no miracle about it; and in this sense, a miracle would only differ from another action of God by an external denomination, that is, by its rarity" (G IV, 594). There is no question that in Leibniz's mind occasionalists are committed to the arbitrariness of the laws of nature, insofar as they do not see God as constrained to will contingent events "in conformity with" the eternal natures of things (cf. G III, 529; G IV, 594–95). Malebranche would obviously contest this charge. Not only, he believes, is God "obliged to act always in a manner worthy of Him, by ways which are simple, general, constant and uniform" (OC V, 49), but all of his actions are subordinated to the highest aim of creation—the Incarnation of the Word in the person of Jesus Christ; cf. *Traité* I, i, and Additions (OC V, 12–13), and Lennon, "Philosophical Commentary," in LO, 824. For more on this issue, see section III.

18. Sleigh remarks that, for Leibniz, "Laws of nature are . . . characterized as generalizations that are true of created substances in virtue of their natures" (*Leibniz and Arnauld*, p. 162). I believe that this account needs to be emended slightly. As I read Leibniz, laws of nature are in the first place expressive not of the individual natures of substances, but of the natures of *types* or *species* of being (e.g., body or soul), only some of which are, strictly speaking, substances. What needs to be emphasized, I think, is the conceptual relation for Leibniz between the idea of a "law of nature" (including the laws that govern corporeal phenomena) and the notion of intelligibility (or explainability in terms of natures) described above. I take it to be consistent with my position that the causal powers of any given species of being (e.g., material being)

The establishment of this point helps us to understand Leibniz's further charge that on the system of occasional causes God would be guilty of "disturbing" the respective laws of the soul and the body:

> [R]ather than saying with [occasionalists] that God has made it a law always to produce in a substance changes conforming to those of another substance, which disturbs [*troublent*] at every moment their natural laws, I would say that God has given to each of them from the start a nature whose own laws bring about its changes, in such a way that in my view the actions of souls neither increase nor decrease the quantity of moving force which is in matter, nor even change its direction, as M. Descartes believed. (G III, 122)

The basis of Leibniz's criticism in this case is not that occasionalists like Malebranche commit themselves to mistaken views about the laws of nature (e.g., they ignore the principle of the conservation of force). Nor does he take issue with their failure to acknowledge the existence in nature of certain types of causal sequences.[19] He is instead concerned with the tendency of occasionalists to conceive of God as arbitrarily imposing natural laws on created things otherwise undetermined in their effects, rather than giving each thing "from the start a nature whose own laws bring about its changes." The objection that God "disturbs" or "interferes with" the natural laws of things is just that on the occasionalist account natural laws are not conceived as the lawful expression of the natures of created things.[20]

---

supervene on the causal powers of individual substances—the only true sources of activity for Leibniz.

19. This is how Sleigh understands the criticism. He sees Leibniz as objecting to "Malebranche's belief that some physical events have as their sole immediate quasi-cause a mental event" ("Leibniz on Malebranche on Causality," pp. 167–68; cf. *Leibniz and Arnauld*, pp. 164–68) on the grounds that it is inconsistent with his "great principle of physics"—that "a body never receives a change in motion except by another body in motion that pushes it" (G VI, 541/L 587). On Sleigh's account, Malebranche is guilty of no more than a mistaken belief about the sequences of events that in fact obtain in the world: namely, that there are some physical events for which there are no identifiable physical causes. And this is a belief that Malebranche could easily have given up while preserving his system of occasional causes. I see Leibniz's criticism as going beyond this.

20. I take this point to be implicit in the following version of Leibniz's "elimination argument" (see above, n. 5):

> [H]aving assumed that ordinary things must occur naturally and not by miracle, it seems that one can say that according to this my hypothesis is demonstrated. For the two other hypotheses necessarily make recourse to miracle. . . . And in all one can find no other hypothesis than these three. For either the laws of bodies and of souls are interfered with [*troublées*], or else they are conserved. If these laws are interfered with (what must come about from something outside), it is necessary either that one of these

Now, obviously, one of the principal points at issue here concerns the economy of power: whether God is to be accorded all power, or whether power is to be shared in some manner with finite created beings. On this question, there is a clear division between Leibniz and the occasionalists: he believes that there exist secondary causal powers, while occasionalists like Malebranche deny it.[21] The issue I want to emphasize, however, which in my view occupies at least as prominent a place in Leibniz's reasoning, concerns the provision made for the intrinsic intelligibility of the created world. On my reading, Leibniz faults Malebranche not simply for denying created things the power to produce their own effects but also for his failure to insist that created things be endowed with natures through which their properties and effects can be rendered intelligible. Extensionally, these objections might seem to amount to much the same thing, for it is plausible to think that the effects and properties of things will be explicable by their natures just in case their natures include powers sufficient to produce them. For two reasons, however, I want to resist the move to run these two lines of argument too closely together. First, they bear on what are manifestly different aspects of the created world: on the one hand, its intrinsic intelligibility; on the other, its degree of causal self-sufficiency.[22] Second, the intelligibility objection plays an important dialectical role in Leibniz's thought that is independent of the attribution of real causal powers. He deploys this objection in many contexts where it enjoys no obvious basis in a view about what sorts of created things are in fact endowed with force or activity. Instead, his point in these contexts is limited to the claim that, with regard to certain species or types of being, only certain effects can be conceived as following in an intelligible manner from their natures: namely, only those that can be conceived as "explicable modifications" of them.

This type of reasoning figures centrally in Leibniz's discussion of the soul-body relationship. He relies on it in attacking the Cartesian hypothesis of interaction on the grounds that it is impossible to conceive how a material thing could bring about changes in a mental thing, or vice versa.[23]

---

two things interferes with the other, which is the hypothesis of influence common in the Schools, or that it is a third thing which interferes with them, that is, God, in the hypothesis of occasional causes. But finally, if the laws of souls and of bodies are conserved without being interfered with, that is the hypothesis of preestablished harmony, which is consequently the only natural one. (letter to Lady Masham, 30 June 1704 [G III, 355])

21. Malebranche's fullest defense of this position is in *The Search after Truth*, Bk. 6, Pt. 2, Ch. 3, and in the "Fifteenth Elucidation."

22. Likewise, they raise the question of the proper understanding of two different divine attributes: God's power and God's wisdom.

23. He writes to Jaquelot: "I have said to you that it is as far from reasonable to attribute to the soul an immediate physical influence on the body as to attribute to matter the faculty of

As we have seen, he employs it in criticizing occasionalists: their account makes no attempt to explain divine action in a way that is consistent with the natures of created beings. Finally, he cites it as an advantage of his own theory of preestablished harmony that it ascribes to the body and the soul only those effects that can be understood as following from the nature of each being: material effects from material things, mental effects from mental things. In each of these cases, we find Leibniz arguing purely on the basis of considerations of intelligibility: within the "order of nature" it must be possible to conceive how any effect follows in an intelligible manner from the nature of its subject.

At another level, however, considerations of intelligibility do become closely linked in Leibniz's mind with the idea that any substance is by nature a principle of force or activity. Applying the principle of intelligibility to the *individual* nature of a substance, he infers that a substance must not only be *a* principle of activity, but a principle that is sufficient to account for the production of all its particular natural effects. Together, then, the claims of activity and intelligibility lead to the conclusion that it is of the very nature of the soul (and, in an extended sense, of the body)[24] to be causally responsible for the production of all its own states in the order in which they occur. Rather than one substance influencing the other, or God influencing both, each has been created from the start such that through the exercise of its own natural powers there follows the entire sequence of its effects.[25] We may conclude, then, that in his discussion of

---

thinking. My reason is that the one is as inexplicable as the other by the modifications of the thing to which it is attributed" (G VI, 569; cf. 570).

24. The case of bodies raises special problems. Although I cannot argue the point here, on Leibniz's understanding of the body-soul relation any fundamental commitment to the substantiality of bodies is given up; instead, every body is, in the final analysis, an "aggregate" of soul-like monads. (On this, see my essay "Leibniz's 'Analysis of Multitude and Phenomena into Unities and Reality,' " *Journal of the History of Philosophy* 28 [1990]: 525–52.) Thus, while in many of his published writings Leibniz represents the theory of preestablished harmony as a response to the views of Descartes and Malebranche on the issue of mind-body interaction, this posture is to a degree deceptive. At a deeper level, the preestablished harmony of body and soul is revealed to be a preestablished harmony among the perceptions of a universe of unextended, soul-like substances.

25. Roger Woolhouse has argued that Leibniz's objection that occasionalism introduces a perpetual miracle "turns on his view of substances as active and as containing in their own natures the principle of their changes" ("Leibniz and Occasionalism," in *Metaphysics and Philosophy of Science in the Seventeenth and Eighteenth Centuries*, ed. R. Woolhouse [Dordrecht: D. Reidel, 1988], pp. 166–67). I see his position as largely consistent with my own, although it collapses the distinction between what I regard as two separate argumentative strategies in Leibniz—the one bearing on the nature of substances as persisting principles of activity, the other on the intrinsic intelligibility of nature as a whole. Again, I would stress the point made with respect to Sleigh: Leibniz's arguments concerning miracles and intelligibility are in the

the problem of soul–body agreement Leibniz draws on the principle of intelligibility in two quite different ways: on the one hand, to insist that from any given being there follow just those effects proper to the type of being it is; on the other hand, to insist that the effects of any particular body or soul are determined by, and hence are explainable in terms of, its individual nature or causal power. Both of these considerations can be seen as contributing to the case he makes for the superiority of the theory of preestablished harmony over the Cartesian and the occasionalist positions:

> [S]ouls or vital principles, according to my system, change nothing in the ordinary course of bodies and do not even give God the occasion for doing so. Souls follow their laws, which consist in a definite development of perceptions according to goods and evils, and bodies follow theirs, which consist in the laws of motion; nevertheless, these two beings of entirely different kind meet together and correspond to each other like two clocks perfectly regulated to the same time. It is this that I call the theory of *pre-established harmony*, which excludes every concept of miracle from purely natural actions and makes things run their course regulated in an intelligible manner. Instead of this, the common system has recourse to absolutely unexplainable influences, while in the system of occasional causes God is compelled at every moment, by a kind of general law and as if by compact, to change the natural course of the thoughts of the soul in order to adapt them to the impressions of the body and to interfere with the natural course of bodily movements in accordance with the volitions of the soul. This can only be explained by a perpetual miracle, whereas I explain the whole intelligibility by the natures which God has established in things. (G VI, 540–41/L 587)

The interpretation of Leibniz's position I have so far developed leaves one point untouched. This is the question of what, if anything, the theory of preestablished harmony has to tell us about the apparent *communication* of the body and the soul. What we had expected to account for in the ordinary course of things, after all, was not simply the fact that material things give rise to material effects and mental things to mental effects; we were initially puzzled by the problem of how material things appeared to give rise to mental effects, and vice versa. What we seem to be missing to this point is any explanation of why the soul and the body appear to be joined in a

---

first place concerned with the sorts of effects that can be conceived as following from the natures of different *types* of being.

functional union whereby it is reasonable to think of the two as communicating with each other.

In Leibniz's view, this impression that the soul is in immediate communication with the body—that it is capable both of influencing and being
influenced by the body—is a phenomenon that can be explained in a way
that is consistent with the assumption of nature's intelligibility. As he sees
it, it is part of the soul's intrinsic nature to "represent" each and every state
of its associated organic body.[26] To say that a soul is naturally representative
of its body means, among other things, that it perceives itself as being
located within a body that it identifies as its own, and that it perceives itself
as interacting with other bodies via the instrumentality of this body.[27]
Again, Leibniz takes this to be an essential property of any soul-like
substance. To posit a soul acting without representing the state of its body,
he suggests, would be to contravene the "order of nature." It would be to
accept

> a metaphysical fiction, as when one assumes that God destroys a
> body in order to create a vacuum; the one is as contrary to the order
> of nature as the other. For since the nature of the soul has been made
> in such a way from the beginning as to represent successively the
> changes of matter, the situation which we assume could not arise in
> the natural order. (G IV, 519/L 493)

Presented with this position, a critic might well raise the objection that
Leibniz has advanced what is fairly described as an ad hoc solution to the
problem of the communication of the body and the soul. While rejecting as
unintelligible the hypothesis that the two causally interact, as well as all
appeals to a supernatural influence, he has failed to explain how it happens

26. In his first reply to Bayle, Leibniz claims that "it is the soul's own God-given nature to
represent everything that takes place in its organs by virtue of its own laws" (G IV, 519/L 493).
Compare *Theodicy*, §355: "The true means whereby God causes the soul to have sensations of
what happens in the body have their origin in the nature of the soul, which represents bodies,
and is so made beforehand that the representations which arise one from another within it, by
a natural sequence of thoughts, correspond to the changes of bodies" (G VI, 326).

27. In the "New System," Leibniz writes that the "internal perceptions in the soul itself
must arise because of its own original constitution, that is, they must arise through the
representative nature (capable of expressing external things as they relate to its organs) given
to the soul from its creation, which constitutes its individual character" (G IV, 484/AG 143).
He further remarks that the "organized mass" of the body contains the "point of view" of the
soul, and that "the soul has its seat in the body by an immediate presence" (G IV, 484–85/AG
144). For reasons of space, I omit here any discussion of the special sense Leibniz gives to the
terms 'expression' and 'representation'. Such a discussion would obviously be necessary for a
complete account of his position.

that two things as different as the body and the soul nevertheless appear to operate in complete agreement in the confines of a single human being. Leibniz's response seems to take us no further than: It happens because that's the sort of beings they are; God has created each from the start such that it appears to communicate with the other. Yet this seems uncomfortably like the notorious pseudoexplanation that opium sedates by virtue of its intrinsic dormitive power.

In answering the criticism that the system of preestablished harmony is in some way an ad hoc theory of the soul-body relation, what needs primarily to be stressed, I think, is the common methodology that informs the development of Leibniz's own system and his objections to occasionalism. In both cases, he is principally motivated by the requirement that it must always be possible to account for natural effects as intelligible consequences of the nature of some created being. As we have seen, in his discussion of the problem of soul-body agreement, he employs this principle in two quite different ways: sometimes critically, in order to undermine a given philosophical theory; at other times constructively, in formulating positive hypotheses about the natures of things. On the critical side, he draws on the idea of intelligibility in attacking a wide range of rival philosophical positions: the doctrines of interactionism and occasionalism, the supposition of atoms in a vacuum, the notion of a primitive force of attraction, and, in general, any hypothesis that invokes so-called occult qualities.[28] On the positive side, the assumption of intelligibility plays a complementary role in inspiring that part of Leibniz's philosophy that takes as its primary task the construction of a general theory of the natures or essences of created things. It is in this context, I think, that we can best understand the assertion that it is part of the nature of the soul both to be causally responsible for the production of its own internal states and to represent the states of its own body. We may see this claim as being in the first place a hypothesis about the intrinsic nature of any substantial being, which, consistent with the assumption of intelligibility, suffices to account for the apparent communication of the soul and the body.

Hypotheses about the natures of things are often defended by Leibniz on the grounds of their capacity to save the phenomena. Ultimately, however, such hypotheses end up being more than mere conjectures in his system, insofar as they are supported by the *a priori* consideration that the character of God's wisdom would in fact have inspired him to create a world that manifested just this sort of rational order. This brings us at last to the deepest level of Leibniz's disagreement with the occasionalist philosophy:

28. For more on this topic, see my essay "Leibniz's Principle of Intelligibility."

what he sees as occasionalism's negative consequences for the project of theodicy.

III

We have seen how Leibniz's charge that occasionalism implies a "perpetual miracle" draws on the assumption of nature's intelligibility. In rejecting the demand for intelligibility, he argues, occasionalism promotes the elimination of any coherent distinction between the natural and the miraculous, and with it any notion of what Stuart Brown has called the "autonomy of nature."[29] For Leibniz, this is a result with profound consequences for the project of theodicy. As he sees it, the principle that the ordinary effects of things must always be explicable by the natures of those things stands in a critical relationship to God's wisdom.[30] As he writes in his 1709 response to Lamy: "the wisdom of God appears more clearly in the system of harmony, in which all is connected through reasons drawn from the natures of things, than in that of the occasionalists, in which everything is compelled by an arbitrary power" (G IV, 594).[31]

We can conceive of the relationship between God's wisdom and the

29. "Leibniz's 'Crossing from Occasional Causes to the Preestablished Harmony,' " in *Leibniz: Tradition und Aktualität. Vorträge, V. Internationaler Leibniz-Kongress*, ed. I. Marchlewitz (Hannover: Schlütersche Verlagsanstalt, 1988), pp. 116–23.

30. A forceful statement of Leibniz's concern on this issue appears in the Preface to the *New Essays*:

> I acknowledge that we must not deny what we do not understand, but I add that we are entitled to deny (within the natural order at least) whatever is absolutely unintelligible and inexplicable. . . . The distinction between what is natural and explicable and what is miraculous and inexplicable removes all the difficulties. To reject it would be to uphold something worse than occult qualities, and thereby to renounce philosophy and reason, giving refuge to ignorance and laziness by means of an irrational system which maintains not only that there are qualities which we do not understand—of which there are only too many—but further that there are some which could not be comprehended by the greatest intellect if God gave it every possible opportunity, i.e. [qualities] which are either miraculous or without rhyme or reason. And indeed it would be without rhyme or reason for God to perform miracles in the ordinary course of events. So this idle hypothesis would destroy not only our philosophy which seeks reasons but also the divine wisdom which provides them. (NE 65–66)

31. Compare his letter to Lady Masham of 30 June 1704: "[T]he very reason and order of divine wisdom determines that one not have recourse to miracles unless necessary. . . . Thus it seems that my hypothesis is something more than a hypothesis, being not only entirely possible, but also the one which is most in conformity with the wisdom of God and the order of things" (G III, 353–54).

intelligibility of nature as being established in the following way. We know that within Leibniz's theodicy there is an important connection between the character of this world as the best of all possible worlds and God's wisdom as the attribute determining his selection of this world for existence. If we now assume that the idea of nature's intelligibility plays an essential role in Leibniz's attempt to conceptualize the rational order that marks this as the best of all possible worlds, we may infer that any hypothesis that challenges the assumption of intelligibility also contains a concealed attack on the notion of God's wisdom. Given the capacity of occasionalism to pose just such a challenge, we may conclude that Leibniz's opposition to this doctrine is again ultimately motivated by theological concerns. In addition to placing in jeopardy the vital distinction between God and his creation, Malebranche's theory denies the condition of intelligibility by which the natural world is rendered compatible with God's wisdom, and thus worthy of his choice for creation.

At first sight this conclusion might seem a surprising one, for we know that Malebranche and Leibniz agree on the basic point that God has chosen this world for existence because its production represents, overall, the creative act of greatest possible perfection. There remains, however, a significant disagreement between them on the issue of how God's perfection is communicated in creation. Malebranche repeatedly asserts that it is not enough simply to look at the end of creation, the intrinsic perfection of the created world, but that it is also necessary to consider the means of God's volition. Accordingly, on his view, a world of greater perfection might have been created, but this would have required that perfection be sacrificed in the mode of God's willing. For Malebranche, God acts in ways that are "the most simple, the most general, the most uniform" (OC V, 28); and the result is a world in which there are intrinsic imperfections and evils, but in which the elimination of any of these imperfections would have interfered with the "simplicity of God's ways," that is, the general laws by which he brings about all that happens in the world.[32]

32. Compare *Traité* I, xiv:
   God could undoubtedly make a world more perfect than the one we inhabit. He could, for example, make it in such a way that the rain, which serves to render the earth fertile, should fall more regularly on lands that are worked than in the ocean where it is not so necessary. But in order to make this world more perfect, it would have been necessary for him to have changed the simplicity of his ways, and to have multiplied the laws of the communication of motion by which our world subsists; and then there would no longer have been between the action of God and his work that proportion which is necessary in order to determine an infinitely wise being to act, or at least there would not have been the same proportion between the action of God and this world, however perfect, as there is between the laws of nature and the world we inhabit. For our world, as imperfect one may want to imagine it being, is founded on laws of

As Catherine Wilson has emphasized, Leibniz, particularly in his early writings, shows signs of being strongly influenced by Malebranche's approach to the theodicy problem.[33] Arguably, this is an influence that persists through the publication of the *Theodicy*, in the view that the metaphysical perfection of a world is to be regarded as a function of both the plenitude of its existence and the simplicity of its laws. Despite these points of contact between the views of the two philosophers, however, the fact remains that while Malebranche sees the perfection of God's creation as essentially dependent on the perfection of his "ways" or modes of willing (their simplicity, uniformity, etc.), Leibniz is concerned exclusively with the perfection that a world possesses by virtue of its own intrinsic nature. This is most immediately apparent in his image of God surveying the domain of all possible worlds, weighing their respective degrees of perfection, and only then choosing to create that world which is by its own nature the best of all possible worlds (cf. *Theodicy*, §225). Within this model there is no room for an independent weighing of the particular mode of God's willing. Instead, God brings into existence the possible world of greatest perfection by virtue of a "moral necessity, which constrains the wisest to do the best" (*Theodicy*, §367; G VI, 333/H 345).[34]

---

motion so simple and so natural that it is completely worthy of the infinite wisdom of its author." (OC V, 29)
See also *Dialogues* IX, x (OC XII, 213–14/D 213).

33. "Leibnizian Optimism," *Journal of Philosophy* 80 (1983): 765–83, and *Leibniz's Metaphysics: A Historical and Comparative Study* (Princeton, N.J.: Princeton University Press, 1989), pp. 281–88.

34. A somewhat subtle distinction is involved here. My claim is not that the mode of God's willing (God's "ways") is irrelevant for Leibniz in determining the perfection of a world, but only that it is not a factor that is set against the perfection of the "work," as in Malebranche. According to Leibniz, God's assessment of a world's degree of perfection requires that he foresee the results of certain free decrees of his will. (In the Arnauld correspondence, Leibniz says that God considers these decrees *sub ratione possibilitatis*; cf. G II, 51–52/LA 56–58.) These free decrees are responsible for the specific causal order of any world, and thus contribute to determining its intrinsic perfection. The difference between the positions of Leibniz and Malebranche is that for Leibniz the mode of God's willing is relevant to the assessment of the perfection of God's creative act only insofar as it contributes to the intrinsic perfection of the *product* of creation. For Malebranche, by contrast, the mode of God's willing becomes a factor that is in competition with the perfection of the work. The apparent similarity between their two positions allows Leibniz to claim (when it suits him) that he is really just saying the same thing as Malebranche. Reading carefully, however, the distance between the two becomes clear. In the *Theodicy* (§208), for example, Leibniz defends the Malebranchian view that the "ways of God are those most simple and most uniform"; but he immediately goes on to stress that these are also the means that are the "most productive" and that they lead "to a single advantage, which is to produce as much perfection as is possible" (G VI, 241/H 257; cf. ML 392). This is a point that is reiterated in a number of texts suggesting that God's decision in creation is to be seen not as a balancing of two competing sources of perfection—richness of

The conflict between the positions of Malebranche and Leibniz is not limited to this point alone. At bottom it extends to a set of basic disagreements concerning God's goal in creation and the character of the wisdom that he therein expresses. In Malebranche's view, God acts only for the sake of his own glory, and this he finds only if his work is sanctified by a divine person, Jesus Christ, the Incarnation of the Word.[35] "Separate Jesus Christ from the rest of creation," Malebranche writes in his *Traité*,

> and see if he who can only act for his glory, and whose wisdom has no limits, would not be able to carry out the plan of producing nothing externally. But if you join Jesus Christ to his Church, and the Church to the rest of the world, then you raise to the glory of God a temple so august and so holy that you will perhaps be surprised that its foundations have been set down so late. (OC V, 15)

We know, however, that for Malebranche the excellence of God's creation cannot be understood through its end alone; God must be honored both by his work and by his ways. It follows that while the Incarnation of the Word is the only end that justifies creation, insofar as it is the only end capable of ensuring God's glory, it is necessary that God also be glorified by the means he chooses to realize this end.[36] As Malebranche conceives them, the means God selects are chiefly distinguished by their being expressions of his unlimited wisdom.[37] To appreciate precisely how this wisdom is expressed in the created world, we must see Malebranche's theodicy from within the framework of his occasionalism. Within this framework, we have observed, there is no significant distinction between creation and conserva-

---

existence (perfection of the "work") versus simplicity of laws (perfection of the "ways")—but that a simplicity of laws is merely the means by which the greatest quantity of intrinsic perfection can be realized (cf. G I, 331/L 211; G VII, 303/L 487). Compare Martial Gueroult, *Malebranche*, 3 vols. (Paris: Aubier, 1959), vol. 2, pp. 194–207, and Geneviève Rodis-Lewis, *Nicolas Malebranche* (Paris: Presses Universitaires de France, 1963), pp. 310–12.

35. "[T]he Incarnation of the Word is the first and principal of the plans of God" (OC XII–XIII, 207/D 205). Compare *Traité* I, i–ii, and *Dialogues* IX, iii–vi. I am grateful to Thomas Lennon for making this point clearer to me; see his "Philosophical Commentary," in LO, p. 284; see also Gueroult, *Malebranche*, vol. 2, ch. 5.

36. "God wants His conduct, as well as His work, to bear the character of His attributes. Not satisfied that the Universe honor Him by its excellence and its beauty, He wants His ways to glorify Him by their simplicity, their fecundity, their universality, their uniformity, by all the characteristics expressing qualities which He glories in possessing" (OC XII–XIII, 214/D 213).

37. "God [is] obliged to act always in a manner worthy of him, by ways simple, general, constant and uniform, in a word, by ways conforming to the idea we have of a general cause whose wisdom has no limits" (OC V, 49).

tion: God's volition is a necessary condition for the existence of the world at each and every moment. God's wisdom is expressed through his willing the continued existence of the world according to those laws, or ways, that are "the most simple, the most general, the most uniform" (OC V, 28).

On the basis of this brief account, we may see Malebranche's theodicy as defined by two basic commitments. The first is his concern to uphold the tenets of orthodox Christianity—in particular the event of the Incarnation, which he deems necessary for the creation of a world worthy of God. The second is his determination to see God's wisdom and providence as actively expressed in the world through the simplicity of his ways.[38] With respect to both of these commitments, his position is at odds with the main tendencies of Leibniz's thought. According to Leibniz, God's sole aim in creation is the production of the maximum possible goodness; and this he conceives most basically as *metaphysical* goodness: that is, perfection or reality.[39] Working from a position that identifies goodness with being, Leibniz assumes that God is naturally disposed to create something rather than nothing, and that he is antecedently inclined to create any possible world in proportion to its degree of goodness.[40] Within his scheme, the issue of the worthiness of the created world vis-à-vis God receives a completely different treatment than in Malebranche. Quite simply, we can say that the only possible world worthy of God is that world which contains, in and of itself, the greatest perfection or reality.

The notion of divine wisdom plays no less central a role in the theodicy of Leibniz than it does in that of Malebranche; however, again, this wisdom is conceived very differently. Leibniz defines God's wisdom as his "knowledge of the good" (L 564), which is to say his knowledge of the perfection,

---

38. Compare *Traité*, "Premier Éclaircissement," III:
      On the basis of these definitions, one sees that far from denying providence I assume on the contrary that it is God who brings about everything in all things; that the nature of pagan philosophers is a chimera; and that properly speaking what is called *nature* is nothing other than the general laws that God has established in order to construct or conserve his work by means of very simple ways, by an action that is always uniform, constant, perfectly worthy of an infinite wisdom and universal cause. (OC V, 148)

39. On the first point, see *Causa Dei*, §§25–26: "The antecedent will of God tends toward actualizing all good and repelling all evil, as such, and in proportion to the degree of goodness and evil. . . . The consequent will arises from the concurrence of all antecedent acts of will. When the effects of all antecedent acts of will cannot be carried out together, the maximum effect which can be obtained by wisdom and power will be obtained" (G VI, 442–43/S 119). On the second point, see *Causa Dei*, §30: "*Metaphysical* good or evil, in general, consists in the perfection or imperfection of all creatures, even those not endowed with intelligence" (G VI, 443/S 120). In an appendix to the *Theodicy*, Leibniz defines a "perfection" as "any purely positive or absolute reality" (G VI, 383/H 384).

40. Leibniz maintains that God would only not create if it were impossible to fix on a single best possible world; see *Theodicy*, §8.

or positive reality, that is contained in the eternal natures or essences of things.[41] In the context of creation, God's wisdom is expressed in two principal ways. First, divine wisdom serves to determine God in his choice of which possible world to create. Motivated by the supreme goodness of his will to create the best world possible, God is informed by his wisdom, or knowledge of the good, as to which possible world contains the greatest perfection.[42] Second, in willing into existence a particular series of contingent events, God is constrained by his wisdom to act in accord with the principle of intelligibility, that is, to will only those events that can be explained by the natures of created things. The reason for this constraint, crucial to Leibniz's case against occasionalism, can be understood as follows. God's wisdom, according to Leibniz, is identical with his knowledge of what is positive or unlimited in the natures of things. Thus, God is guided by his wisdom insofar as he wills only those contingent events that can be explained through "limitations" of the perfections definitive of those natures. These, we may assume, will be just those events that can be conceived as "explicable modifications" of the attributes of created beings.[43]

Although our survey of the theodicies of Malebranche and Leibniz has not been exhaustive, we have established grounds for seeing the conflict between occasionalism and preestablished harmony as predicated on a much deeper disagreement concerning the wisdom that guides God's will in creation. When Leibniz criticizes Malebranche for advancing a theory that is at odds with the principle of intelligibility, he is in effect calling into question Malebranche's understanding of divine wisdom and its relation to the perfection of the created world. While Malebranche conceives of God as bestowing activity on a world of otherwise passive creatures, and thereby realizing perfection through the exercise of his wisdom or the simple and uniform mode of his willing, Leibniz conceives of perfection as resident in the essences or natures that are themselves constitutive of the world. God exercises his wisdom in Leibniz's view by acting in ways that conform to

41. Leibniz's standard examples of perfections are the attributes of power, knowledge, and will. The nature of any possible substance can be defined by limitations of these primary perfections. See "Monadology," §48, "Principles of Nature and of Grace," §9, Preface to the *Theodicy* (G VI, 27/H 51), and, especially, Grua, 126.

42. Compare *Theodicy* §225: "The wisdom of God, not content with embracing all the possibles, penetrates them, compares them, weighs them one against the other, to estimate their degrees of perfection or imperfection. . . . The result of all these comparisons and deliberations is the choice of the best from among all these possible systems, which wisdom makes in order to satisfy goodness completely; and such is precisely the plan of the universe as it is" (G VI, 252/H 267–68). See also "Observations on the Book Concerning 'The Origin of Evil,' Published Recently in London," §21 (G VI, 423/H 428).

43. I am here merely sketching a line of argument that needs to be filled out in greater detail.

his knowledge of the perfection of those natures. In addition to this specific point of disagreement, we have located a more general tension between the ways in which Malebranche and Leibniz each approach the problem of creation. Malebranche remains committed to constructing a metaphysics that is consistent with the fundamentals of Christian doctrine, one that acknowledges the central place of the Incarnation and the essential dependence of created beings on God. Leibniz, by contrast, develops his position largely under the influence of a conception of God as an infinitely skillful craftsman, one who is disposed to create that world which in and of itself contains the greatest possible perfection.

Given the theological distance that separates Leibniz from Malebranche, there is no easy way to judge the success of his critique of occasionalism. We can perhaps best see it as an attempt to push forward the program of rationalist metaphysics unencumbered by the demands of religious orthodoxy.[44] This is not to suggest that Leibniz rejects the significance of theological concerns—his philosophy is of course infused with them—but rather that his God is, to a more significant degree than Malebranche's, the God of a philosopher: the divine mathematician, the infinitely skillful artisan. Confronted with the occasionalist position, Leibniz will insist that in denying created things natures sufficient to account for their effects, Malebranche has effectively robbed God of the honor of having conceived and created that artifact which best displays his wisdom. Rather than being a worthy product of God's creative will, the world becomes no more than a continuous expression of God's personal power.[45]

---

44. Compare Wilson, *Leibniz's Metaphysics*, pp. 297–303. Wilson's book emphasizes another strand of Leibniz's thinking that is at odds with orthodox Christianity: his sympathy for a Neoplatonic account of creation as emanation (see pp. 275–81). Arguably, this is a point on which Malebranche's position is also at risk.

45. In a somewhat unlikely place, Hume's *Enquiry Concerning Human Understanding*, we find a compelling statement of this distinctively Leibnizian complaint. According to the occasionalists, Hume writes,

> every thing is full of God. Not content with the principle, that nothing exists but by his will, that nothing possesses any power but by his concession: They rob nature, and all created beings, of every power, in order to render their dependence on the Deity still more sensible and immediate. They consider not, that, by this theory, they diminish, instead of magnifying, the grandeur of those attributes, which they affect so much to celebrate. It argues surely more power in the Deity to delegate a certain degree of power to inferior creatures, than to produce every thing by his own immediate volition. It argues more wisdom to contrive at first the fabric of the world with such perfect foresight, that, of itself, and by its proper operation, it may well serve all the purposes of providence, than if the great Creator were obliged at every moment to adjust its parts, and animate by his breath all the wheels of that stupendous machine. (sec. vii)

Catherine Wilson

Constancy, Emergence, and Illusions: Obstacles to a Naturalistic Theory of Vision

The time is past when occasionalism and preestablished harmony were considered as nothing more than episodes of minor hilarity in the history of philosophy and as more or less interchangeable theories that differed only in a small detail: in the assertion of God's continuous activity by contrast with a unique nonrepeated command. To a certain extent, this more favorable and more differentiation-ready attitude toward both theories has been correlated with a decrease of attention to occasionalism, in particular, as a theory of mind-body interaction, and with increased attention to occasionalism as a theory about physical events and their relations. This shift has taught us a good deal about occasionalism's medieval roots, its theologically ambiguous status, and its relationship to the seventeenth-century attack on natures, forces, and powers.

Recent research has also shown how difficult it was, when it came down to specifying God's precise role in determining or expediting natural processes, to preserve his freedom and field of action while developing a scientific picture of the world as governed by fixed and immutable laws. If there is no difference between God's will and the regular, immutable course of nature, and if God never shows his power over nature by disrupting it, but only through nature by sustaining and maintaining it, theism collapses into Spinozism. One would expect, therefore, that sensitive and worried theists would turn their attention from the broader theater of nature where ostensibly miracles no longer occurred—and perhaps never had—to less familiar regions, little pockets, as it were, existing everywhere but revealed only to the eye of the most diligent researcher and not to the ignorant populace. Here God might act, if not against nature, at least in such a way as to avert catastrophes and make a genuine, nonredundant contribution to human life.

The thesis of this chapter is that Malebranche found such a region in the theory of perception. By rendering problematic the task of assigning a fixed, immutable relation between brain states and experiences, a task that the assertion of causal connections between brain and mind presupposes, he found a new realm for divine intervention. In doing so he called attention to a number of interesting and recherché psychological phenomena. Following the discussion of Malebranche's theory, I will say a little about Leibniz's somewhat strange adherence to both (a) a mechanical theory of mind, according to which experiences are generated by a machine, though not as direct products of the machine, and (b) a theory of preestablished harmony, according to which experiences are generated by the soul, bodily states by previous bodily states.

Occasionalism, on the view I am defending, presupposes that mind and body are separate substances, but it is above all a theory about their union. And it presupposes some kind of scientific reduction of the material world—though Malebranche has little vortices of fluid matter instead of corpuscles—but it is above all a theory about what physics cannot explain. Not only does Malebranche refer constantly to what he calls the "laws of the union of body and soul," his prose is full of terms like "bond," "society," and "relation": "What wisdom in the subordination of causes, in the linkage of effects, in the union of all the bodies of which the world is composed," says Ariste in the *Dialogues on Metaphysics*. "This earth which we inhabit is made only for the societies that are formed in it," Theodore confirms.[1] And Malebranche shows us over and over that between the Cartesian description of the world as matter in motion, with minds exercising here and there an influence over certain bodily machines, and the world of human society and everyday experience, there is a gulf that only God can

---

1. *Dialogues on Metaphysics*, XII, D 279 (OC XII, 278–79).

bridge. Occasionalism is, he thinks, the only possible solution to an antinomy noticed but not solved by Descartes. Descartes's semantic analysis of perception, which was meant to show how visual experience could occur naturally even in the absence of intelligible causal links, will not work. The facts of visual illusion and visual constancy that Malebranche studied intensively, along with the emergence of what we would call "physiognomic" qualities, seemed to him to exclude any naturalistic account of perception.

I. The Cartesian "Arbitrariness of the Sign"

It is well known that one of the prejudices that Descartes worked hard to eliminate in his readers was the doctrine of "little images" or visual species: something emitted from visible objects that got into the eye and made us see. As long as we have no way to see retinal images or brain traces that take the form of little pictures, images drop out as irrelevant to the explanation of vision.[2] It is true that he calls attention to the image projected through the lens onto the back of the eye, but this, he explains, is only to win the confidence of those attached to the older doctrine of transmissible visual species. "If in order to depart as little as possible from accepted views," he says, "we prefer to maintain that the objects which we perceive by our senses really send images of themselves to the inside of our brain," then we should at least recognize "that they do not exactly resemble in all respects the objects they represent."[3] The argument is extraordinarily clever. Descartes shows that little pictures are not the key to perception by pointing out that even real pictures are not simulacra but consist only of "a little ink placed here and there on a piece of paper," which can nevertheless succeed in producing an illusion of presence.[4] When I look at a picture, my eyes and brain are simply bombarded with certain pressures, and as a result I see an image of, I seem to see, a forest, a town, people, and even battles and storms. The picture, like any other object in the external world, has simply to be regarded as a way of stimulating the mind to conceive an object. This kind of stimulation happens all the time; the words that evoke in us ideas and images are also just stimuli: nobody thinks they are icons of meaning. Laughter and tears, Descartes points out, stimulate us to think of joy and sorrow, though the associated facial movements and ocular secre-

2. *Optics*, AT VI, 130 (CSM I, 167).
3. *Optics*, AT VI, 112–13 (CSM I, 165).
4. Ibid.

tions are something without any intrinsic connection with a state of inner emotion. Here he introduces his famous paradox—seeing objects is less like seeing pictures than it is like being blind and reaching, probing, and tapping with a stick.[5] Visual information is a code or a language that the mind succeeds in understanding in its own terms.[6]

It is perhaps the illusionism of the three-dimensional representation of space on a flat canvas—and the availability of tactual experiences of space— which suggested to Descartes that, since spatial depth and distance were artifacts, every visual quality dimension, including color, might be. If flat blotches of paint can be seen as a three-dimensional structure, some equally blotchlike sequence or pattern of impulses to the brain should generate a three-dimensional perception and some other pattern the perception of something green. In any case, he devotes considerable space to the problem of how the mind is brought to conceive position (orientation) and distance. The inversion of the retinal image does not provide reason for thinking that we ought to see the world upside down, for our knowledge of the orientation of the object "does not depend on any image, nor on any action coming from the object, but solely on the position of the tiny parts of the brain where the nerves originate," which gives us kinaesthetic information about the position of our limbs relative to the surface of the earth.[7] Nor does the flatness of the image create a problem about depth, for again "the seeing of distance depends no more than does the seeing of position upon any images emitted from objects."[8] It depends on a series of factors, including the effort needed to focus, calculations made involving the angle induced by binocular vision through our "natural geometry," the distinctness or indistinctness of the object seen, size, and occlusion.[9] Light itself, as might be expected, is only the force of movement, the different colors depending on the quantity of force with which each nerve fiber is moved.[10]

We need at this point to observe that Descartes, who is unsystematically interactionist in his theory of mind-body relations, finds nothing in the impossibility of a transmitted icon or the irrelevance of the retinal image to exclude a plain causal-semantic account. He speaks of bodies as "occasion-

5. There is still a good deal of nonarbitrariness, or analogical extrapolation, in Malebranche and Descartes: for example, from the softness of the fibers of the infant brain and the inflexibility of old people's brains to their supposed difficulties in accepting new ideas (*Search* II.1.vi: OC I, 230 [LO 110]).

6. *Optics*, AT VI, 84–86 (CSM I, 153–54).

7. Ibid., AT VI, 134–35 (CSM I, 169).

8. Ibid., AT VI, 137–38 (CSM I, 170).

9. Ibid., AT VI, 139–40 (CSM I, 172).

10. Ibid., AT VI, 132 (CSM I, 168).

ing" sensory perceptions, or as enabling the soul to have them[11] or as informing the soul,[12] but also as "causing them"[13] or as stimulating the mind to conceive them.[14] Interaction in a suitably loose sense occurs, just as it does when a person is reading a book, hearing a speech, poking around with a stick, or just looking at someone's facial expression. The antinomy of perception—how conscious experiences can be natural occurrences even if we cannot trace the causal chain that brings them about—is regarded as solved.[15] This happy indifference vanishes in Malebranche's reception of the optical theory that occupies the first chapters of his *Search after Truth*. Malebranche sees that the semantic model will not work; just as the icon theory required a homunculus who could see images, the semantic theory requires a code reader. It is not, however, that the brain code is per se indecipherable by the mind; it is that its details are too complicated for human beings.

II. The Discontinuity of Some Perceptual Processes: Malebranche

What persuades Malebranche that what Descartes took for a process needing no more specific divine assistance than a general maintaining of the laws of nature really demands something more? Is it really that there are no natural causal chains at all? If so, then the connection between physical states and experiences is no better than, but also no worse than, the connection between the motion of one billiard ball and the motion of another. Is it that the last step alone of the supposed causal chain running from object to retina to brain to soul is non-natural and so poses problems that billiard-ball interaction does not? Or does Malebranche have reason to think that some particular causal connections between body and mind make

11. Ibid., AT VI, 114 (CSM I, 166).
12. Ibid., AT VI, 135 (CSM I, 169).
13. Ibid., AT VI, 131 (CSM I, 167).
14. Ibid., AT VI, 112 (CSM I, 165).
15. The antinomy could be expressed as follows—*Thesis*: The relation between brain movements and experiences is natural, for particular movements are associated with particular experiences regularly, reliably, and immediately. *Antithesis*: The relation between brain movements and experiences is non-natural, for it is impossible that movements of matter should produce experiences. *Synthesis*: The relation between brain movements, or "traces," and experiences is semantic, and so entirely natural, even if we cannot see how the sign or stimulus gives rise to the mental content.

a particularly strong claim on God's attention and participation? "Motion in the brain," he says bluntly at one point, "cannot be changed into light or color,"[16] a remark that might lead us to think that it is simply the last step of the causal chain that creates the problem in Descartes's account. But this objection would not apply to the other possibilities in addition to a physical stimulus's being "changed into" an experience that Descartes entertains. Why should not brain movements enable the soul to form a representation, or stimulate it to do so, with the soul, as it were, fabricating its own representation on the basis of information supplied and thus being the causal agent? And this seems to be what Descartes really has in mind.

Some Cartesian critics objected to his semantic theory: If the chain of events terminating in the brain is to be only a code for, not an icon of, say, an object ten feet away, and if the code requires a calculation to unravel it, as Descartes's natural geometry requires, who or what does the calculating? The seeing homunculus has just been replaced by a calculating or decoding homunculus. The estimation of distance, Descartes says, "is done by a mental act which, though only a very simple act of the imagination, involves a kind of reasoning quite similar to that used by surveyors."[17] And it is often pointed out that Descartes's "natural geometry" presupposes either (a) unconscious mental calculation, which seems to be inconsistent with his claim that we are aware of all our genuinely mental processes, or (b) a nonmental, purely mechanical calculation of the brain, which he would not have allowed for, as he does not think that brains can reason and calculate. It seems to fall, in other words, between the stools of the deliberate and the automatic. However, this does not appear to be Malebranche's objection. He understands, first of all, that if Descartes is to be made consistent with himself, the soul cannot measure angles between observed external objects to determine their distance. For then the objects will already be a certain distance "out" before the soul has established their distance. Descartes's remark that our knowledge does not depend on any action coming from the object must be understood strictly. If something calculates in us or for us, it must take eye or brain traces as its raw material, not objects.

Here Malebranche finds reason to be specifically dissatisfied with the idea that the body-mind connection could be an invariable, hence natural one in some extended sense. The representation in our minds is based upon the internal state of the brain fibers, by contrast with the state of affairs existing in the external world. But there is no absolutely fixed correspondence between what we see and the exact state of our brains at any given moment.

16. *Dialogues on Metaphysics*, IV, D 87 (OC XII, 94).
17. *Optics*, AT VI, 138 (CSM I, 170).

"The same disturbances are followed by different perceptions and different disturbances are accompanied by the same perceptions."[18] Thus the laws that map brain states into experiences are not themselves physically instantiated. Only God knows what experience should be assigned to a particular brain state, and his derivation of the correct experience, though rule governed, is such a complex affair that it is beyond our capacities.[19] The information needed to derive a representation is "there" in the sense that it is given somehow by the total situation, but it is nowhere represented in a form available to the soul.

How this can be is explained in his treatment of the moon or sun illusion, presented in book 1, chapter 8, of the *Search*, and in expanded form in the *Dialogues on Metaphysics*. In the *Dialogues*, Malebranche repeats his gloss on Descartes's *Optics*: "God determines to act in our souls in a particular way only through changes which occur in our bodies. He acts on the soul as if He knew nothing of what is happening outside and only on the knowledge He has of what is taking place in our organs."[20] If depth perception raised doubts about whether either the mind or the brain was capable of making the necessary calculations, common visual illusions, according to Malebranche, settle the question in the negative. We see the sun's appearance as smaller at the zenith than at the horizon. This despite the fact that we not only have good reasons for believing that the size of the sun is constant, we can also keep the appearance constant by blocking out the context; for example, by looking at the sun in both locations through a piece of smoked glass. Both suns will then look the same size. And it can be inferred from the laws of optics that the "image" supposedly projected on the back of the eye by the lens will be the same in both cases. Why then does the sun on the horizon look larger? The answer given is that in order to rationalize an apparently farther away object's producing a "retinal image" of the same size as a nearer object, the object must be made, as it were, to grow. We are directly aware, then, not of the suns as they really are (in which case they would be equal) nor of the retinal images (which would also be equal). Yet there is a reason why we see the sun the size that we do. We have the sense impressions that "we would give ourselves if we had divine knowledge of Optics and if we knew exactly all the relations that hold among the shapes of bodies that are projected at the back of our eyes."[21] The size of the perceived sun really is entirely determined in the sense that there is one and only one correct apparent size for the sun to appear. Not only is there some

18. *Last Elucidation, Search*: OC III, 326 (LO 733).
19. For Malebranche's account of distance, see *Search* I.9.iii: OC I, 107ff. (LO 40–46).
20. *Dialogues*, XII, D 283 (OC XII, 284).
21. Ibid., XII, D 283 (OC XII, 282).

mapping that takes the state of our organs into that size of sun, but this mapping is privileged, because it preserves the rules of optics. Now, this does not show that our perception of the sun could not be a natural relation; why should not that mapping just occur in a direct causal manner? The implicit answer is that there are two possibilities: such a direct mapping could occur if the soul gave itself the sense impressions that would preserve those relations, or if the body supplied them directly to the soul.

For Malebranche, the knowledge required to generate the correct mapping is so comprehensive that the human mind cannot produce it itself. This seems indeed to be his main argument. "Besides the fact that matter is a purely passive substance, [and] cannot act on the mind," he tells us in the *Elucidations* (as though that consideration were a mere ornament!), "and that there is no necessary relation between certain disturbances of the brain's fibres produced by the light reflected off objects and the perceptions we have of them" (as though that argument, too, was just a sort of background consideration), what we see "is governed by inferences that depend on so great a knowledge of optics and everything happening in the body that there is no intelligence that can make them at the very instant that we open our eyes and look around."[22] Many simple experiments should convince the reader of the truth of this claim. For instance:

> [Y]ou bow your head, you turn your eyes, you look at a clock if you will from between your legs. You will not see it reversed from top to bottom. For although the image of the clock was reversed in your eyes or rather in your brain . . . your soul knows the disposition of your body by the change which this disposition makes in your brain and so it will judge the clock to be right side up.[23]

You will not just judge it to be right side up; you will see it as such and read the time with no trouble. This is not the case if you just hold a clock upside down in front of you. When you walk, Malebranche has just explained, the (projected) images of things change places on your retina, just as they would if they were moving past you. Yet you judge them to be stable.[24] This is because, he says, you have a *sentiment interieur* or kinaesthetic sensation of the movement of your body that renders a certain choice of hypothesis preferable. Optically the situation is the same, but your volitional apparatus will be engaged differently if you are a more or less stable object in a world of moving things, or a more or less moving object in a world of stable

22. *Last Elucidation, Search*: OC III, 327 (LO 733).
23. *Dialogues*, XII, D 285 (OC XII, 284).
24. Ibid.

things. Thus visual constancy, as much as visual illusion, implies a persistent sampling and assessment of a range of evidence. To see a white horse running at a gallop may, Malebranche points out, involve assumptions and deductions like the following: that it is about a hundred steps away; that it is a large horse (not just a closer horse); and that, because the space its image traverses on the retina is of a certain size per unit-time interval, the horse is running at full gallop.

> [I]f I incline my head or lie down on the grass while looking at the horse, its image will change place on my retina and no longer disturb precisely the same fibres in it; yet I shall always see it the same. Or assuming that it stops and I begin to run while steadily looking at it, its image will change place in the fundus of my eye, and yet I shall see it immobile.[25]

Curiously, Malebranche allows that whiteness is not an idea given by God, but one that the soul can make for itself: I know the horse is white because "I know what kind of disturbance the rays it reflects produce on my retina, and since I can act on myself, I give myself without ever erring, a given sensation when there is a given disturbance on my retina and through it, in my brain."[26] Yet even if I can both know what corresponds to color and produce myself the appropriate color, my mind is not capable of making all the judgments noted; of making them for all objects, constantly; of making them instantaneously and repeating them with the least movement of the eyes; and, finally, of duplicating them for both eyes. "Neither our soul nor any finite spirit can instantly make an infinity of inferences." "Therefore it is not we who make them but God alone who makes them for us, and if we call them natural or refer them to the soul, this is only to stress their regularity and reliability and to speak as others do."[27] So Malebranche appears to concede that the Cartesians would be right, that perception would be a purely natural process, if it required the soul to know only the figure-and-motion code of, for example, color. The soul could then produce by itself the appropriate experience. What renders Descartes's account impossible is the manifold complexity of perceptual experience. Needless to say, this is at variance with a common presentation of occasionalism—including Malebranche's own typical presentation—according to which the soul is helpless to produce the right experience without divine assistance.

25. *Last Elucidation, Search*: OC III, 345 (LO 745).
26. Ibid.
27. Ibid., OC III, 345 (LO 746).

Malebranche treads a fine line between a naturalistic and a supernatural-istic explanation of the psychology of perception. "I feel I must warn," he says, "that judgements about the distance, size, and so on, of objects are formed in the way I have just explained, not by the soul but by God according to the laws concerning the union of soul and body. I have therefore called these sorts of judgements *natural* in order to emphasize that they occur in us independently of us and even in spite of us."[28] Here "natural" seems to be a sort of synonym for "unconscious" or "automatic" by contrast with "conscious" or "deliberate." But there is no room in Malebranche's scheme, any more than in Descartes's, for unconscious automatic calculations and assessments. These unconscious, automatic events, then, are simply testimonies of a higher conscious intelligence at work.

Malebranche does not address the question of whether animals, which are unconscious according to the standard Cartesian doctrine (i.e., have no visual representations), might still experience illusions and constancy in a form that could be behaviorally manifested. If he had allowed for this, Malebranche would have had to suppose that the brain was able to summa-rize, weigh, and calculate, or that the range of possible sensory inputs for an animal was restricted enough so that behavioral outputs could be preestablished. In the former case, the brain itself would determine the uniquely correct visual representation to correspond to its own state, though this representation would not in fact occur. In the latter case, no processing would take place: the animal would respond in an entirely preprogrammed way. Now, as animals do seem to face new situations, their brains must, as Malebranche could have recognized, be able to perform some visual geometry in order to judge the distance to prey and predator. But how could constancy be wired beforehand? Malebranche understands that the visual system is functional, that it is organized in ways that make it useful to the animal possessing it. And he foreshadows the modern under-standing of illusions as by-products of constancy mechanisms. But the notion that the brain itself is capable of tremendous feats of synthesis is, for reasons that are understandable, beyond him.

III. The Emergence of Social Meanings

For Malebranche, there is something puzzling about the entire human world; it is not identical with the natural world of miniature whirling

---

28. *Search*, I.9.iii: OC I, 119 (LO 46).

vortices, nor is it a presentation to consciousness of just that world. How is it, he wonders, that wave disturbances of the air, a variegated black and white, certain combinations of facial features, can produce religious feeling, civil society, and friendship and loyalty? All sentiments experienced by individuals, the bond of fellow feeling that holds society together and that depends upon the proper reading and interpretation of writing, speech, gesture, and expression, are functions, he says, of the union of mind and body. So they depend on God. Human society could not have arisen or continued naturally, and God is its true foundation.

Again Malebranche's strategy is to show that what Descartes treats as natural and obvious is in fact a mystery and to show that, to the extent that these things seem natural and obvious, God's power and agency are at work. How am I able to perceive a face as friendly? "If I look a man in the face, I comprehend whether he is sad or joyful, whether he esteems me or despises me, whether he wishes me well or ill—all of this through certain movements of the eyes and lips which have no relation with what they signify."[29] When a dog shows me its teeth, I read its intentions as hostile; when a person shows me his teeth, however, I read his intentions as friendly.[30] Again Malebranche takes the lack of a correspondence between the external object per se (teeth, in this case) as an argument against any specific causal role for them. There is no doubt a brain state in which the teeth figure as part of a constellation of factors, but it is not we who are able to produce the appropriate mental reaction to this brain state. It cannot be inferred from, say, the teeth together with some other features of the external situation, for no conscious process of inference takes place; painters do not always know how to represent the various emotions by adjusting features and their relations. (So they learn from books and copy from each other.) "When a man is animated by some passion, everyone who looks at him notes it well, though they do not perhaps notice if his lips are raised or lowered, if his nose protrudes or recedes, if his eyes are open or closed."[31] And again we might wonder whether conscious inference on someone's part is really necessary: What about animals? Malebranche admits that a dog will respond to "certain motions in my body," which will produce in it a faithful attitude and a personal attachment. (He seems willing to allow in a non-Cartesian way that animals might experience emotions or have personality traits.) As a result, we might seem to be presented with something like Gassendi's fork; either admit that the readings of gestures and expressions can be accomplished naturally by the brain, or ascribe a

---

29. *Dialogues*, XII, D 287 (OC XII, 286).
30. Ibid., D 289 (OC XII, 286).
31. Ibid.

soul to animals as well as to men. Malebranche does neither; he simply explains that the bond between dog and master, like the bond between human and human, requires divine intervention to sustain it.

I do not think it is straining to see the problem of the meaningfulness of expressions and gestures as part of the problem posed by the Cartesian doctrine of the arbitrariness of the meaningful sign; Descartes clearly stated, as we saw, that as the word is to its meaning, and as laughter is to joy, so light considered as physical stimulus is to the light of experience. And as the relation in each case has something "arbitrary" to it, so, conversely, "meaningfulness" may be considered as a kind of physiognomic quality. The words belonging to a language I understand are like the face whose expression I am able to read; the difference between a meaningless ritual and one whose significance I understand may not involve the use of wholly unfamiliar objects or parts of the body, but only a combinatorial unfamiliarity. So, Malebranche would say, it cannot be the words or gestures or the patterns and sequence of the ritual themselves that give me an understanding of them. Something else must be operative at the same time. When children are educated, they are taught to perceive as meaningful or "shown the meaning of" certain constellations of events, times, places, and the like. They are taught to perceive as meaningful or "shown the meaning of" certain combinations of words that they would otherwise ignore. So, from what is an interesting and original point of view, Malebranche can claim that all human institutions—religion, education, or science—are "unnatural" in the same sense. Only God, by establishing the laws of union between soul and body that connect our responses in a regular, reliable way to inherently meaningless or ambiguous signs, events, and movements, can make our experience possible. Thus: "God himself is present in our midst, not as a simple spectator and observer of our good or bad actions, but as the principle of our society, the link of our friendship, the soul, so to speak of the relations and discussions we have together. . . ."[32]

The problem Malebranche is concerned with should thus be viewed as complementary to the problems of illusion and constancy described above. In both cases, unconscious principles of calculation and interpretation seem to be at work that issue in definite sensory or emotional impressions, or in the experience of meaningfulness, or in literal comprehension. We cannot trace these impressions back to their causes; we cannot derive them out of what we presume to be their causes (marks, stimuli, movements). It is of course impossible to speculate about what an occasionalism not developed in the context of propositions about the causal inefficacy of created things and the omnipresence and omnipotence of God would look like, and my

32. *Dialogues*, VII, D 167 (OC XII, 167).

suggestion is not that Malebranche was not motivated by general meta-physical considerations. It is rather that Malebranche's reflection on Des-cartes's semantic model for perception, combined with his own research and reflections on the problems of illusion, constancy, and emergence, led him to an antinomy he could not resolve without abandoning the Cartesian solution. Without God, words would have no meaning. The soul cannot understand the brain's interior language without God, any more than an exterior, social language is directly understandable by people. Language and the community that depends upon it are not the effects of particular powers of human beings. Whether Malebranche's claims here bear out or contradict the common perception of the rationalist philosophers as remote, abstracted, and hostile to values of community is another question en-tirely.[33] It is now useful to consider Leibniz's entry into the discussion.

IV. Leibniz's Mechanism and His Preestablished Harmony: Complementary or Contradictory?

When we turn to Leibniz, who is known to have read parts of the *Search*, we are led to wonder whether his views about perception show, as Male-branche's do, any coherent set of concerns, and any evidence of engagement with Descartes's antinomy and its proposed solution.

Here a large problem of interpretation faces us. Leibniz appears to have two theories, which have nothing to do with each other, about mind–body relations. The theory of preestablished harmony denies the existence of any reciprocal influence, including Malebranche's God-mediated influence. The second, more mysterious theory is that figures and motions can be "intel-ligible causes" of perceptions, even though we can never observe these causes actually producing their effects.

However we should explain Leibniz's adherence to it, the theory of preestablished harmony is not some trivial variant of occasionalism. For occasionalism is in spirit, if not in the letter, an interactionist theory; the occurrence of an experience follows, not from any previous experience, but from the underlying state of the brain. As Malebranche is a mechanist, presumably these brain states show a necessary order of progression; but

---

33. Thus Susan Bordo, in *The Flight to Objectivity: Essays on Cartesianism and Culture* (Albany: State University of New York Press, 1987), interprets occasionalism as a manifestation of separation anxiety and suggests that there is something "narcissistic" in this communicative insulation of the mind. But the main effect of Malebranche's discourse is to call attention to the ubiquity, strength, and so on of social and semantic relations.

there is no independent logic to the sequence of thoughts. The mind, as Malebranche always stresses, is continually adapting to the physical state. His scheme is, in the grammatical sense, a generative one: physical stimuli are transformed in accord with certain laws into brain states that are then mapped into experiences. Given a new physical configuration of objects, the brain and God together will invariably determine an experience for it. Every time I open my eyes there is something new for me to perceive, a new combination of objects, motions, problems, yet I succeed in seeing something, just as, although most of the sentences I hear are new, I manage to understand them. (Most of them.) An illusion is just a perception whose originating rules seem at first to conflict with other originating rules, only because we do not understand the complexity of the rules.

Now, this generativeness and interaction de facto if not de jure is just what is missing in preestablished harmony. We gain in compensation something else: the idea that the environment does not determine the content of our thoughts, our own natures do. The general aura of helpless waiting in Malebranche[34]—an aura that is not dispelled even by our knowledge that God always acts immediately—is replaced by the dynamic Leibnizian idea that the sequence of our perception is somehow ruled by our own appetitions, either through the tendency to move into a more desirable perceptual state or simply through a tendency to move into a state consonant with our own full identities.

But let us return to Leibniz's other theory. In an intriguing article of 1974, Margaret Wilson made the suggestion that Leibniz was at some points favorably disposed toward materialism.[35] She called attention to a passage in a late dialogue of his that concerns Malebranche's theories of perception and that ostensibly expresses Leibniz's view that sensory qualities "may at last be reducible to something measurable, material and mechanical."[36] The suggestion is that if you allow that qualities have some corpuscular basis, it should be possible for them to have a brain-movement basis. This suggestion unleashed something of a storm; many people thought that one could at best interpret Leibniz's naturalistic-sounding remarks about perception as a veiled threat: either accept monadology or you get materialism! But I think Wilson's insight was correct. The obstacles that Malebranche saw to a naturalistic theory of vision were not there for Leibniz. This was so for both positive and negative reasons; on the negative side, he was not

34. "Here you are in the world without any power, as incapable of motion as a rock, dumb as a log" (*Dialogues*, VII, D 161–63 [OC XII, 165]).

35. See M. Wilson, "Leibniz and Materialism," *Canadian Journal of Philosophy* 3 (1974): 495–513.

36. "Conversation of Philarete and Ariste," in L 623.

interested in illusions, constancy, and emergence and so failed to appreciate the difficulties. On the positive side, his philosophy was considerably more favorable to the idea that either the brain or the mind could, in the modern sense, process information, or, in seventeenth-century terms, use its knowledge of physical and optical laws and mathematics.

Leibniz's original understanding of the mind-body problem is firmly within the framework established by Descartes and Malebranche: he sees it, that is, as a problem about "arbitrariness," and he is fully aware of Descartes's semantic solution. In a set of Notes pertinent to the *Search* he puzzles over whether ideas (he mentions ideas of color, heat, sound, etc.) can be joined immediately to "traces" in the brain without thereby being joined naturally.[37] And he produces an interesting proposal. The difficulty the brain has in informing the mind or disposing it to form the correct idea is like the difficulty we have of making someone who does not speak our language understand us. Leibniz points out that if, for example, I want to give an American ("savage") the idea of "thinking" I will show him the posture of a thoughtful man, and he notes that a book has been published in Nuremberg, home of other curiosities, which provides little images for words, presumably a sort of all-purpose traveler's guide.[38] He seems to be interested in the idea that, even though the connection of word to referent is arbitrary, and so not naturally understandable to someone who does not speak the language, it is possible to communicate by simply doing the right things. The original, but very doubtful, suggestion is that the brain might teach the mind what it meant by certain traces, even if the mind does not immediately speak its language. It is difficult to see this line of thought as very promising, for the strategy presupposes that there is a common ground of understanding between brain and mind, as there is between his American savage and the European instructor. If Malebranche is right, all gestures are conventional anyway; the American and the European can use the gesture language only because God is helping them. But in this discussion we have at least some clue to Leibniz's views. He is always looking for ways to reduce arbitrariness, to replace it with intuitive continuity, and the mind-body problem is no exception. Even after he has had to concede a good deal to Locke about the arbitrariness of the linguistic sign, he is not prepared to accept Locke's teaching about the arbitrariness of the mind-body relation.

Sometimes, as a result, he seems to leave the preestablished harmony behind to develop a theory of perception that is simply naturalistic in the sense that Malebranche had rejected. Leibniz believed, at least in certain

37. *Zu Simon Fouchers Reponse*, A vi.III, 320.
38. Ibid., p. 321.

periods of his life, that it was possible that a machine could simulate all the activities of a live person, including thinking and communicating,[39] not surprising for the man who had designed a calculating machine and who believed that reasoning and speech were reducible to formal rules; he did not see Malebranche's semantic gulf. Nor could he have been troubled, as Malebranche was, by the worry that the soul lacked the resources to perform the calculations, assessments, and evaluations needed to make the visual scene appear. The mind contains at any moment an infinity of thoughts—the complexity of the task is not an obstacle—and it possesses a complete knowledge of the *a priori* sciences, so that the superficial mathematical-optical ignorance of the seeing peasant is not a problem either. Both the mind and the brain are suited to unconscious reckoning. All that seemed to be lacking, for Leibniz to be able to meet Malebranche's objections to a naturalistic theory, was an answer to the blunt Malebranchian claim that "[m]ovements cannot produce color."

Here, though, Leibniz thought he had at least a sketch of an explanation. The emergence of qualities can be natural rather than non-natural, despite the fact that the two termini cannot be simultaneously in awareness, as is normally the case with causal chains. In the case of emergent aesthetic or gestural qualities, the cause of the received impression is unidentifiable. In the case of sensory qualities generally, we may have hypotheses about the causes but be unable to watch them producing their effects. The example is the famous *transparence artificiel*. We identify the gaps of the teeth and the speed of the wheel as the cause of the phenomenon; we are in no doubt that they are productive of the phenomenon. Yet we cannot perceive cause and effect at the same time any more than we can appreciate the trompe l'oeil painting and be aware of the mechanism by which it is produced.

Applied to the case of sensation this means that the motions of the brain are really the cause of the impressions of pain, colors, heat, and so on. Why should not a motion produce a color in the same sense that a cog and a gap produce a transparency?[40] Leibniz shows himself remarkably unafraid of causal language: "if we had arrived at the inner constitution of certain bodies, these [sensible] qualities would be traced back to their intelligible causes and we should see under what circumstances they were bound to be present; even though it would never be in our power to recognize the causes acting sensorily, in our sensory ideas which are the confused effects of bodies on us."[41] We need to look at the famous, ambiguous mill passage

39. M. Schneider, "Leibniz ueber Geist und Machine" (manuscript).
40. NE 403.
41. Ibid.

from the *Monadology*[42] with these remarks in mind. When Leibniz says that perception is "inexplicable in mechanical terms" because, if we "pretended" that there was a machine as large as a mill that was able to think, feel, and perceive, we would not, by touring the inside of the mill, get to understand how it worked, is this meant as a *reductio* (because there can be no inexplicable mills)? Or is he just making the point that, though a machine might think, we could never explain how because we can never get both termini in view?

The thrust of the paragraph is admittedly toward the former, stronger interpretation. The concept of a machine seems to involve the notion of what might be called the "perspicuous production" of goods or effects. But although this shows that the brain could not be a machine *for* the production of thoughts, it perhaps does not exclude the possibility that the brain might be a machine that, while perspicuously producing or effecting something else—say, the survival of the organism—produced thoughts and experiences nonperspicuously. But what is particularly interesting about Leibniz's conception of mind–body relations is that he believes that the information the mind needs in order to know what visual experience to have is all there: it is fully determined by the physical situation, the very point that Malebranche denied. This is apparent, for example, in his treatment of the three-dimensional nature of perceived space, which he discusses in the context of the man born blind and made to see. Will such a man grasp that "the paintings of [objects] (as it were) that he forms at the back of his eyes, which could come from a flat painting on the table, represent bodies"?[43] Will he, in other words, be able to get a mapping—from in this case a retinal image—to a world beyond his eyes? He will not get to this immediately, Leibniz allows. But he can learn to in two ways: either through the use of his sense of touch or by working out the geometry and optics of the situation.

In either case, the man can, by his own unaided efforts, come to understand the difference between the cube and the sphere. He will figure out that the pattern of light rays means that something is blocking them. As soon as the cube and the sphere begin to roll, or when he or the light source begins to move, he will notice the different shadows and contours and conclude that they are objects. It is by so varying our position, Leibniz says, that we are able eventually to distinguish between the trompe l'oeil and the real object. There is no suggestion at all that the calculations needed are so difficult and complex that God must come to our aid; what the soul can accomplish consciously, she can also accomplish unconsciously.

42. *Monadology* 17 (L 644).
43. NE 138.

This leaves us with a critical question. Is the mill passage, which can be interpreted either as an illustration of the preestablished harmony or as an illustration of a causal-interactionist theory of mind based on the notion of "confusion," *deliberately* ambiguous? Are Leibniz's two theories just a system of mutual checks and balances? Is the preestablished harmony a check on the tendency of Leibniz's thought to advance to the conclusion that a machine could think, feel, and experience? Is the confusion theory a check on the tendency of preestablished harmony to tolerate a perfect "arbitrariness" in mind-body relations? Was preestablished harmony a way of attacking the Cartesians for their bad physics (*influxus physicus*) and their bad metaphysics (denial of forces), while the confusion theory attacked their advocation of "arbitrariness" and "voluntarism"? Or is there some unity of concern that relates them? My own view is somewhat pessimistic here. We do not merely need to reconcile the letter of preestablished harmony with the confusion theory and the notion of a calculating brain; we need to reconcile the spirit. With a free enough use of the notion of preestablished harmony it is easy enough to reconcile the letter: experiences are harmoniously related to brain states, previous experiences, other people's experiences, states of affairs external to the subject, and so on. But this is merely a superficial smoothing operation. Leibniz is clearly working from two opposing models. The first is a radically desemanticized Cartesian model, with the homunculus eliminated, according to which physical stimuli are naturally productive of experiences. The second is a different model, a nongenerative one in the grammatical sense suggested earlier, according to which the sequence of experiences is laid down in advance and physical events play no productive role.[44]

What has perhaps obscured recognition of these two different systems of explanation is the belief that Leibniz could not have assigned a productive role to physical stimuli in the first place. But this sidesteps the real issue. Both Leibniz and Malebranche believe that there are machines. Both reject causal influx. But Malebranche appears to deny, Leibniz to allow, that a machine can uniquely determine the experience it should have when set down in a particular environment.

V. Epilogue: The Ordinary and the Miraculous

"The air strikes our ears and you know what I am thinking"—this is the kind of thing that never fails to amaze Malebranche. Two opposed impulses

44. For Spinoza as a possible source of this model, see the chapter by Mark A. Kulstad in this book.

meet in him: the scientific, aiming at demystification, the laying bare of actual or probable causal chains; and the religious, which is at home amid disconnections and apparent impossibilities. In Malebranche's world, something wonderful and almost incredible is always happening: this is the countertheme to the theme of the fixity and invariability of the laws of nature

But Malebranche often worries about the stability of this form of theological-scientific discourse and about the possibility that his intentions will be reversed. His worry is that his audience will not see that God is always present and active even in the most ordinary events of life (such as looking around or walking or hearing speech or reading a book, thereby ennobling the mundane), that he will be read as trivializing the divine. He knows that he does not, cannot have complete control over this situation, and his dialogue partner keeps bringing the issue up. When Aristes in the *Dialogues* suggests that it is a mistake to talk so much about God, that we should not search for sublime truths, that there is a danger of dishonoring them by approaching too close to the divine perfections, he is serving as Malebranche's bad conscience. Similar self-warnings occur throughout Malebranche's physicotheology. His response is to undermine the objection by reminding Aristes of the conditions of their discussion. If God is the source of our human fellowship, and the true author of all human meaning, we cannot eliminate him from the conversation. "How will we inform one another in love if we banish from our discussions Him whom you have acknowledged as the soul of our association, as the bond of our small society?"[45]

Leibniz, as we know, was opposed to this, the saturation of the ordinary with the divine. His view of religion tended to the political and the practical; his view of institutions and practices was that they were historically explainable. Ordinary human dispositions created the social bond, political events shaped it, and though society might—if it were sufficiently improved—come to mirror the kingdom of ends, it was not suffused by it. His opposition to occasionalism was not based simply on his sense that it was unworthy of God to have to bestir himself in the creation, that he ought to do once and for all what he could. If he did read Malebranche with any attention, I suspect that he found highly unsympathetic the latter's view that our language, institutions, and customs, as well as our visual experience, have no intrinsic meaning.

45. *Dialogues*, D 169 (OC XII, 171).

Thomas M. Lennon

Mechanism as a Silly Mouse: Bayle's Defense of Occasionalism against the Preestablished Harmony

If Liebniz was the broadest and most consistent, indeed, most brilliant thinker of his time, Bayle was perhaps that period's deepest thinker. Alas, the attention Bayle nowadays draws is hardly commensurate with such alleged profundity. He is known, if at all, as a source exploited by later thinkers for some few arguments concerning the primary-secondary quality distinction and the infinite divisibility of space and time. Beyond that we have a vague notion of Bayle's use of skeptical arguments in an entertaining send-up of arid Scholasticism and as a basis for views on religious and political toleration that appealed to the Enlightenment. But none of this is sufficient for explaining the success of Bayle's *Dictionary* as the most popular book of the eighteenth century or his heroic status among the fashioners of the Enlightenment. Nor does it even begin to provide an interpretive key to the sprawling morass contained in the *Dictionary*'s four long volumes in-folio.[1]

Obviously, Bayle's neglect cannot be fully redressed here.[2] But the specific issue I shall discuss—Bayle's defense of occasionalism against Leibniz's preestablished harmony—does offer a broader perspective on Bayle's corpus.[3] For, given Bayle's skepticism, it is initially surprising to find him befriend so abstruse a metaphysical doctrine as occasionalism. Roughly put, my speculation is that the doctrine enables him to transcend the mechanism that he finds in Leibniz, the explanatory value of which for Bayle is at best severely limited. Occasionalism, by contrast, at least opens the way to a *narrative* account of human history, particularly when God is a part of it. Such an account is necessary, according to Bayle, because human history characteristically consists of unique events best instanced, in fact, by divine miracles. This primacy of place for narrative is the broader perspective that might be extended even to the whole of Bayle's corpus, although here I can develop that perspective only with respect to a single issue.

After a brief look at Bayle's Cartesianism and at his arguments for occasionalism, I turn to the exchange between Bayle and Leibniz between 1695 and 1702. There are seven stages in the exchange, but here I shall treat the material systematically rather than chronologically.[4] Each held the other

1. Because of its historical significance, quotations will be from the English translation of 1737 (London): *The Dictionary Historical and Critical of Mr Peter Bayle* (New York: Garland, 1984). The structure of the work allows easy collation with the French text.

2. There are exceptions to this general neglect: the work of E. Labrousse, noted below, H. M. Bracken, R. H. Popkin, P. Cummins, P. Dibon, R. Whelan, and some few others.

3. This issue in itself has not drawn much attention. The literature consists of a rich footnote in E. Labrousse's masterly *Pierre Bayle*, 2 vols. (The Hague: Martinus Nijhoff, 1964), vol. 2, pp. 208–10, and an article from A. Robinet, "La philosophie de P. Bayle devant les philosophies de Malebranche et de Leibniz," in *Pierre Bayle*, ed. P. Dibon (Amsterdam: Elsevier, 1959), pp. 49–65.

4. The seven stages are as follows. (1) Leibniz, "A new system of the nature and the communication of substances, and of the union of the soul and the body," *Journal des savants*, 27 June 1695; G IV, 477–87 (L 453–59; AG 138–45). Postscript of a letter to Basnage de Beauval, 3/13 January 1696; *Histoire des ouvrages des savants*, February 1696 (see also previous year), and *Journal des savants*, September 1696; G IV, 498–500; L 459–61; AG 147–49. (2) Bayle, *Dictionnaire historique et critique* (1st ed., Rotterdam, 1697), article "Rorarius," remark H. (3) Leibniz, "Clarification of the difficulties which Mr. Bayle has found in the new system of soul and body," *Histoire des ouvrages des savants*, July 1698; G IV, 517–24; L 492–97. (4) Bayle, *Dictionnaire* (2d ed., Rotterdam, 1702), article "Rorarius," remark L. (5) Leibniz, "Reply to the thoughts on the pre-established harmony contained in the second edition of Mr. Bayle's *Critical Dictionary*, article 'Rorarius' " (1702); G IV, 554–71; L 574–85. Also, to De Volder, 19 August 1702; G III, 63–64. De Volder conveyed to Bayle the ms of Leibniz's paper, which was first published in 1712 in S. Masson's *Histoire critique de la république des lettres*, vol. 2, p.78ff. Note that there is a discrepancy on this information among G, AG, L, and Labrousse. (6)

in high regard, and the exchange between them was as polite as it was philosophically rich.[5] The main part of this chapter is an extended discussion of my speculation about why Bayle should have been attracted by occasionalism. I then conclude with my argument, as part of this speculation, that he was attempting to resist physical and metaphysical mechanism.

I. Cartesianism

Labrousse has convincingly shown that Bayle saw Cartesian dualism, especially in the hands of Malebranche, as the great advance of modern over ancient metaphysics.[6] Its great advantage, according to Bayle, was to block the materialism that even among the Platonists led to an implicit denial of Providence and eventually to de facto atheism. For as the impeccable logic of the Epicureans showed, if matter is eternal and uncreated, it does not need even a demiurge to bring it to order. The upshot of the Cartesian radical distinction between organizing mind and lifeless matter is that only the omnipotent deity as creator and unique real cause can bridge the separation and account for the order we find in the world.

A concomitant advantage is to emphasize the transcendence of God by construing creation as inconceivable. In remark O of the *Dictionary*'s article "Spinoza," we read that

> a matter created out of nothing cannot be conceived, tho' we strive
> never so much to form an exact idea of an act of will, which changes

---

Bayle, to Leibniz, 3 October 1702; G III, 64–65. (7) Leibniz, to Bayle, 5 December 1702; G III, 65–69.

5. Said Leibniz in his first response: "Nothing is kinder than the consideration he shows for me, and I hold myself honored by the objections which he has put in his excellent *Dictionary*, in the article on 'Rorarius'. So great and profound a mind as his, moreover, cannot but instruct, and I shall strive to profit by the light which he has shed on these matters in this article and at many other points in his work" (L 492). This attitude prevailed until what must have been Leibniz's last statement on the matter (1716). It seems that Toland may have replied to Leibniz's "Reply to . . . the second edition . . ." (see note 4 above, stage 5, and AG 226, n. 273–74). Said Leibniz: "The author of these remarks appears to be a man of wit and learning, but he does not show here the exactitude and depth of thought that one recognizes in the writings of Bayle . . ." (AG 226). For his part, Bayle held Leibniz in the highest regard, saying at the end of remark L that "no body can travel more usefully and more safely than he in the intellectual world and that with his great genius he will smooth the rough parts of his system," and so on. Certainly these encomiums must to some extent be discounted by the formulaic politesse of the period, especially well observed by these protagonists; even so, one senses genuine respect between them.

6. Labrousse, *Pierre Bayle*, vol. 2, p. 187.

into a real substance what was nothing before. This principle of the Antients, *ex nihilo, nihil fit*, . . . offers itself continually to our imagination, and there appears with such evidence, that it stops us short, in case we have begun to frame any conception of creation.

If creation is inconceivable, yet actual, then we seem to have only the alternatives either of Spinoza, who, motivated also by the problem of evil, regarded matter as a necessary emanation from God, or of the occasionalists, who take God to be absolutely omnipotent and transcendent, even if inscrutable, and his creation a brute fact. An advantage of the latter from Bayle's perspective is that it leaves God free to govern the world according to his own Providence, which includes responsiveness to our prayers.[7]

These alternatives of either Spinoza or the occasionalists adumbrate Bayle's criticism of the preestablished harmony. For they point to the question Leibniz raised in, for example, his *Principles of Nature and Grace, Based on Reason*, namely, Why is there something rather than nothing?[8] to which he answered with his principle of sufficient reason, and to which Bayle rejects any rational answer, at least for finite existence.[9] Briefly, on Leibniz's system, the whole of creation is not only conceivable but follows—indeed, does so with at least moral necessity—from God's goodness. For the occasionalists, creation is inconceivable, yet actual, and thus is a brute fact that requires understanding in a way other than sufficient reason.[10]

II. Occasionalism

Bayle appears to give a number of arguments for the view that only God can be a real cause. (Whether this amounts to occasionalism for Bayle is, as we shall see, a separate question.)

(i) It is agreed on all hands, he thinks, that man does not have the power of creation, that is, of drawing substance out of nothing. But neither can he cause modifications—for either they are distinct from substance, as the Aristotelians think, in which case they are beings requiring creation, or they are not distinct from substance and thus require the same power

---

7. See Labrousse, *Pierre Bayle*, vol. 2, p. 194, n. 31.

8. L 639.

9. And perhaps for all of existence. See Labrousse on the ontological argument, in *Pierre Bayle*, vol. 2, p. 165.

10. This is so even if for Malebranche the connection between God's will and its effect is the only conceivable necessary connection. That God actually wills is a matter of sheer indifference to Him.

necessary to create substance.[11] The important point to note here is that all real causation for Bayle is creation ex nihilo.

(ii) *A fortiori* there can be no real physical causes, for a real cause must also be conscious. In various texts Bayle argues as follows. God is the cause of motion in the world because things cannot put themselves in motion and, lacking knowledge, cannot have a tendency toward it; lacking knowledge, bodies cannot determine what quantity of motion should be communicated;[12] and the specific motion a thing has cannot be determined by some general motor faculty it is alleged to have and thus can depend only on the free choice (*bon plaisir*) of God.[13] Bodies are indifferent to motion and rest, and, lacking knowledge, they cannot determine themselves to one or the other as more appropriate.[14]

We may note in passing that Bayle applies this sort of argument against the preestablished harmony as an account of the mind-body connection.[15] He asks us to imagine an animal created by God to sing constantly. If it is to change its tune, or even its tone, it must have a tabulature with all the appropriate notes before its eyes. Similarly, unless a man have the series of thoughts before his mind, he will be unable to produce them individually as necessary. Malebranche, of course, had used the same premise in his argument against the magazine theory of innate ideas.[16] But in neither case does the theory under attack require *conscious selection* of thoughts, only that the mind be programmed in a certain way. Thus, Leibniz's appeal to his theory of *petites perceptions* in this context rather misses the point, which is not that we should somehow be conscious of our thoughts, as both Bayle and Malebranche assume, but simply that the soul should have them.[17] There is a more interesting version of this issue to which we shall return in due course.

(iii) It may be that Bayle thinks that occasionalism follows from the Cartesian version of the theory of divine *concursus*.[18] Certainly it is hard to

11. *Dictionary*, article "Paulicians," remark F.

12. *Theses Philosophiae* X. *Oeuvres diverses de Mr. Pierre Bayle* (The Hague, 1727–31), hereafter OD; thus: OD IV, 138–40. He also argues the same case on the basis of projectile motion. It is a law that things in motion should continue in motion, but that law is the will of God, or depends on it for its efficacy (*Systeme Abregé*, OD IV, 323).

13. *Réponse aux questions d'un provincial*, IV, xxii. OD III, 1065. Compare Labrousse, *Pierre Bayle*, vol. 2, pp. 206–7.

14. *Theses* ix. OD IV, 138–39.

15. *Dictionary*, article "Rorarius," remark L (pp. 915–16).

16. *The Search after Truth*, LO 227.

17. "Clarification," L 495.

18. For a relevant discussion of this traditional concept vis-à-vis occasionalism, see Malebranche, *Elucidations of "The Search After Truth,"* XV, LO 676ff.

extract much more than this premise from the following argument in remark D of the article "Rodon":

> We must reject the clearest notions, or acknowledge that a Being made out of nothing by the infinite power of the Creator, cannot have any cause of its existence in itself; and therefore it cannot continue to exist but by the same power that produced it at first: it is therefore created in each moment of its duration, that is, it exists in each moment, only because God continues to have the same will that he had, when that Being began to exist. This act of the divine will cannot cease to create whilst it subsists, since it did create in the first moment that creatures began to exist.[19]

It is clear in any case that Bayle does not base his argument, as did Descartes, on the nature of time. According to Bayle, "the nature of time is a secret it has pleased God to keep hidden from us."[20] Indeed, "everything that has been said about time is so obscure and incomprehensible that it is perhaps better not to say anything about it."[21] Nor, as far as I can tell, does Bayle give Malebranche's definition of a real cause as that between which and its effect we perceive a necessary connection. In fact, in remark L of the article "Rorarius" he goes off in a non-Cartesian direction, claiming "not to know whether the Cartesians would presume to say, that God cannot communicate to our souls a power of acting." For Malebranche, at least, such a communication of power would be inconceivable. Bayle says, however, that he will not pursue this issue because it leads to opposition between freedom and moral responsibility on the one hand and occasionalism on the other. "If they say [that God could not do so], how can they own that Adam sinned? And if they dare not say so, they weaken the arguments, whereby they endeavour to prove, that matter is not capable of any sort of activity." But to abandon the issue is legitimate, in Bayle's view, because all philosophical systems lead to the same dilemma. It is in this article that Bayle turns to the preestablished harmony, to which we also may now turn.

III. The Preestablished Harmony

Bayle's tendency is to treat both occasionalism and the preestablished harmony as theories directed primarily to the mind-body problem. It is in

---

19. See also *Abregé*, OD IV, 478.
20. *Theses*, v–vi; OD IV, 136–38.
21. *Abregé*, OD IV, 328.

these terms that he characterizes the difference between them in remark H of the article "Rorarius."

> Those two systems agree in this point, that there are some laws, according to which the soul of man is [as Leibniz put it in his "*Clarification*"] to represent what is done in the body of man, as we experience it. But they disagree as to the manner of executing those laws: the Cartesians say, that God executes them: Mr. Leibniz will have it, that the soul itself does it.[22]

In arguing against it, Bayle concentrates only on "what is peculiar to the system of the pre-established harmony." Thus, he does not press the problem of human freedom in the face of a perceived fatalistic mechanism, which is a difficulty he sees for all philosophers, including, as just noted, the Cartesians. By the same means he outrageously sets aside Leibniz's main objection against occasionalism, namely, that it requires a continuous miracle in, for example, maintaining the mind-body connection. Bayle had replied to this objection that "it cannot be said that the system of occasional causes brings in God acting by a miracle, *Deum ex machina*, in the mutual dependency of body and soul: for since God does only intervene according to general laws, he cannot be said to act in an extraordinary manner."[23] He does not insist on this point about general laws, however, because he concedes that the preestablished harmony, by making individual substances active, also avoids universally miraculous divine action. That is, he does not respond to the objection to occasionalism because it is not also an objection to the preestablished harmony. The objection is not so easily ignored, of course, and will return to us later.

What, then, are Bayle's objections to the preestablished harmony? Sometimes, in what he obviously takes to be a reductio ad absurdum, Bayle draws out consequences of the preestablished harmony that Leibniz himself in fact happily accepts. For example, in a marginal note to remark L of "Rorarius" he points to the multiplicity of substances composing the body, each with its own principle of spontaneous activity. "Now this must needs

---

22. Bayle remarks elsewhere:
This system [of occasional causes] contains two suppositions; one that there is reciprocally a constant connection between modifications of the body and of the soul of man; the other, that the body physically produces nothing in souls, nor souls in bodies, and that God alone is the efficient cause of sensations, etc. and of the motions that follow the dispositions of our soul. The second of these two suppositions is the character that distinguishes the system of occasional causes from every other; the first is a sure fact known through experience. (*Réponse aux questions d'un provincial*, OD III, 1064)
23. *Dictionary*, article "Rorarius," remark H.

vary their effects. . . . For the impression of the neighbouring bodies must needs put some constraint upon the natural spontaneity of every one of them." For his part, however, Leibniz elsewhere regards the *conspiration universelle* as an attraction of his system, and certainly not as a reductio of it.

In another marginal note he argues that if, as Leibniz contends, there is a particular law for each mind—what we might call an individual concept— then no two people ever have the same thoughts even for two minutes, much less for a month.[24] He continues, more accurately perhaps, that as on the Thomist view on angelic natures, there will be as many species as there are individuals. Once again, however, we know that Leibniz holds up the identity of indiscernibles as an advantage of his system deriving from his principle of sufficient reason.

More relevantly, perhaps, Bayle gives what may be called the *a priori* implausibility argument. It is *a priori* implausible that the body of Caesar should spontaneously enter the Senate and produce the noises we associate with his ambitious plans, just as it is *a priori* implausible that a ship should by itself sail into a harbor and come to rest at a wharf. (Remember that Bayle is writing in Rotterdam.) We can understand how the ship is buffeted by winds on the high seas, but not how it might spontaneously enter the harbor. Such behavior would raise "the power and wisdom of the Divine art above whatever can be conceived," as Bayle puts it in theological terms; or, as he puts it nontheologically: "the actions of creatures must be necessarily proportioned to their essential state, and performed according to the character that belongs to each machine."[25] Leibniz would agree, of course, but there remains a difference between them. It would seem that for Bayle not everything has a reason, but all reasons are intelligible; whereas for Leibniz, everything has a reason, even if not all reasons are intelligible to us.

In remark H, Bayle had found himself unable to understand how, according to Leibniz, the perceptions in the soul of a dog (its hunger, for example) should arise from its own internal constitution in such a way that it would have just them even if it were alone in the universe with God, but that it nonetheless has them, like synchronized pendula, in conformity with things around it, for example, the states of its body. Bayle raises a number of difficulties. In particular, he cannot understand "the connection of internal and spontaneous actions, which would have this effect, that the soul of a dog would feel pain immediately after it felt joy, tho it were alone in the universe." He understands how if a dog happily satisfying its hunger is

24. P 916.
25. *Dictionary*, article "Rorarius," remark L.

suddenly struck with a stick, it feels pain; but that it should feel pain regardless of the stick, he cannot understand. The simplicity and indivisibility of the soul pose a further problem for the synchronized-pendula model of conformity with respect to *change* of states.

> It may clearly be conceived that a simple being will always act in an uniform manner, if no external cause hinders it. If it was composed of several pieces as a machine, it would act in different ways, because the peculiar activity of each piece might change every moment the progress of others: but how will you find in a simple substance the cause of a change of operation?[26]

Like Russell two centuries later, Bayle failed to discern Leibniz's version of the principle of sufficient reason that lay at the foundation of the preestablished harmony. In his reply, Leibniz at least implicitly appealed to this principle when he proposed that

> it is in [the] nature of created substance to change continually following a certain order which leads it spontaneously . . . through all the states which it encounters, in such a way that he who sees all things sees all its past and future states in its present. And this law of order, which constitutes the individuality of each particular substance, is in exact agreement with what occurs to every other substance and throughout the whole universe.[27]

Thus Leibniz naturally enough questions whether Bayle really does understand how the dog suddenly feels pain upon being struck with a stick, pointing out to him the lengths to which the defenders of occasional causes must go to explain such correspondences.

In response to the specific difficulty of a simple substance's change of operation, which he characterizes as "an objection worthy of Mr. Bayle," Leibniz drew the following distinction.

> If to act uniformly is to follow perpetually the same law of order or of succession, as in a certain scale or series of numbers, I agree that in this sense every simple being and even every composite being acts uniformly. But if uniformly means similarly, I do not agree. To explain the difference this meaning makes by an example, a movement in a parabolic path is uniform in the former sense, but not in

26. P 911.
27. L 493.

the latter, for the parts of the parabolic curve are not similar to each other as are the parts of a straight line.[28]

We may put the same point differently by saying that, for Leibniz, every change, either in simple or complex beings, is a function of some concept or law. Once we accept Leibniz's concept of a possible world, then everything by its very nature is—to use Bayle's term—*connected* with everything else.[29]

It was precisely on the issue of connectedness that Bayle was unconvinced by Leibniz's distinction. Construing Leibnizean substances as metaphysical atoms, he supposed that, like Epicurean atoms that uniformly change place, all their changes would have to be uniform, which is contrary to experience. He can understand continuity of the same thought in the soul of Caesar, or change of thought that "implies some reason of affinity"; "but one cannot apprehend the possibility of the odd changes of thoughts, that have no affinity with, and are even contrary to, one another, and which are so common in mens souls. One cannot apprehend how God could place in the soul of Julius Caesar the principle of what I am going to say."[30] For Bayle, in short, there are truly independent orders of causation and thus accidental events at least in the sense that independent orders of causation sometimes intersect.

The work of André Robinet has a contribution to make at this point. If I read him correctly, Robinet takes Bayle to argue ultimately against *both* occasionalism and the preestablished harmony on the basis of their failure to explain this intersection. In the *Pensées diverses* (1673) and, two decades later, in the *Entretiens de Maxime et Thémiste* (1707), Bayle argues that while physical law is uniform (i.e., universal), instances of causes and effect can be isolated (i.e., have no effect on each other). This means that miracles, or suspensions of physical law, can take place without a general upheaval. Thus, even if *required* by the moral order, miracles can occur as a result of God's *particular* volitions and not, as Malebranche and Leibniz both thought,

28. L 495.
29. The key premise here is that of a possible world as a maximal set of mutually compossible substances. The upshot is that no possible substance belongs to more than one possible world, which can be read off from the concept of each substance comprising it. See Benson Mates, "Leibniz on Possible Worlds," in *Leibniz*, ed. H. Frankfurt (Garden City, N.Y.: Doubleday, 1972), p. 354. Nothing like this key premise is cited here by Leibniz; nor is there even a mention of the concept of a possible world. Thus, as was suggested to me by Margaret Wilson, what might be another part of Bayle's concern, namely, the analysis of counterfactuals, is left unaddressed here by Leibniz.
30. *Dictionary*, article "Rorarius," remark L.

God's *general* (if unknowable) will.[31] In particular, the causal intersections on which Bayle insisted against Leibniz can come about as a result of God's particular will, the effect of which is indifferently described as accidental or miraculous. To show the importance of this point, I turn now to my speculation about the significance of occasionalism to Bayle and perhaps to others in the period.[32]

IV. Speculation

There is a wonderful line from the *Ars Poetica* that goes as follows: *parturient montes, nascetur ridiculus mus*—The mountains will labor; born, a silly mouse![33] Horace's point in context is that poets should not promise more than they can deliver. Nonetheless, he provides a nice image for what troubles Bayle about Leibniz's views, and more generally, I think, about mechanism by itself. And that is, that we are still left unable to understand the production even of a silly mouse, much less of anything grander.

31. Robinet, "La philosophie de P. Bayle," pp. 55–56. Thus, Bayle for the most part accepts Arnauld's insistence, against Malebranche, on the role of God's particular volitions. *Nouvelles de la republique des lettres*, August 1685, art. 3. OD I, 346–49. See also note 45 below.

32. The Christian view of miracles is that they indicate the special presence of God. Strictly speaking, only God can perform miracles. In the ecclesiastical context, they thus evidence the authenticity of Christianity. The Catholic position is that the age of miracles has not in principle ceased (even if belief in no miracle not contained in Scripture is required); the same attributes of the early church characterize the latter. Bayle is of course a Protestant, and the Protestant view is that the age of miracles has passed. Once the authenticity of Christianity was established, miracles were no longer needed and in fact ceased. An interesting text in this regard is *A Free Inquiry into the Miraculous Powers . . . .* , by Conyers Middleton, in his *Miscellaneous Works* (London, 1752). Middleton allows that until the time of the Reformation, the continuation of the age of miracles was universally accepted throughout Christianity. But then "the light of the Reformation dispelled the charm: and what *Cicero* says of *Pythian Oracle*, may be as truly said of the Popish miracles; *when men began to be less credulous, their power vanished*" (xxxii). Middleton cites a whole catalog of Protestant authors who pushed back the terminal date to the fourth or the fifth century, when the civil authorities began to support Christianity. But by then, according to Middleton, the whole array of Catholic superstitions had been established—monkery, images, relics, holy oils, and the like—and thus he endorses belief only in miracles attested to by Scripture, namely, those "wrought by Christ and his Apostles" (lxiii–lxiv). I am grateful to W. Abbott for drawing this text and others to my attention and for very helpful discussion. I have not yet determined where exactly Bayle stands in this debate; but it must be somewhere between the Leibnizian position, which seems to eliminate miracles, and the Catholic position, which for him would allow too many. My bet is that he would accept Middleton's position.

33. C. B. Brown has pointed out to me that the line is of interest for several reasons. See C. C. Brink, *Horace on Poetry*, vol. 2 (London: Cambridge University Press, 1971), pp. 214–16.

Occasionalism is the double thesis (a) that because there is a necessary connection only between God's will and his creation, only he can be a real cause, and (b) that because there is no necessary connection between finite events or things, they can serve as but occasions for the operation of the sole real cause. Modern investigations of occasionalism tend to focus on the second feature for the obvious reason that they are inevitably informed by what Hume took from occasionalism. Hume himself documents his debt to Malebranche,[34] and in this case he took over not only the view that there are no necessary connections between finite events or things, but even Malebranche's specific arguments against such connections between our volitions and what we will. But Hume of course took a further step by denying the intelligibility of necessary causal connections altogether and replacing them with constant conjunctions. The occasionalists' rebuttal of Hume's reliance on constant conjunction, which effectively construes occasions as real causes, would be that it fails to explain. We want to know why a pot of water we are heating boils, and we are told that when water is heated it boils. This is not very interesting, and it is not very interesting precisely because it ignores the first aspect of the occasionalist thesis. The sui generis relation between God and the world provides the vertical dimension of causation that, according to a long tradition of thinkers on the question, even an infinite series of horizontal causes (whether mechanical or not) can never provide. For, according to that tradition, we need to know that the mouse is *created* by God. Beyond this vertical dimension, occasionalism provides a conception of an immanent God, in whom we live and move and have our being, everywhere present and active. What is more, it is a God who acts, not mechanically, but as a character does in a story. What the appeal to God provides, according to occasionalism, is not the logical necessity that Hume failed to find between finite events (or anywhere else) but what might be called *narrative necessity*. "God said, let there be light: and there was light."[35] Had there not been light, God would have been acting out of character, not violating the law of noncontradiction. Had the darkness prevailed, the puzzle would have been, not logical, but narratological.

If this line of interpretation is at all correct, then according to Bayle, even if everything had its mechanical explanation, such explanation would be insufficient. Narratives are *not* designed merely to supply either our ignorance of a mechanical explanation or the lack, in principle, of such an

---

34. See R. H. Popkin, "So, Hume Did Read Berkeley," *Journal of Philosophy* 61 (1954): 773–78.

35. Genesis 1:3.

explanation. As it happens, however, not everything does have a mechanical explanation, in either of the two senses specified at the end of this chapter.[36]

So what is so special about narratives to somebody like Bayle? The answer, I think, is that they enable us to understand divine interventions in human history, which are unique events not open to generalization. Bayle's celebrated work *Pensées diverses sur la comète* is, after all, less about the mechanical explanation of comets than about the superstition they previously occasioned. It was important to circumscribe the false miracles he thought were being allowed to proliferate by Rome. Bayle's interest was not in exploring the mechanical explanations offered by physical astronomy, but in safeguarding the explanations offered by the Bible—the greatest story ever told, as United Artists called it. It is a story that perforce involves unique events like the incarnation of the only begotten Word of God. This specific instance of the Incarnation and Redemption, in fact, is why the plurality of worlds was such a big issue as to surface even in Descartes's *Principles*.[37] His claim there about the uniformity of matter follows from his doctrine on extension, but he uses it to enunciate the formula that denies any possible need for a Redemption in some other world, which are the terms in which the plurality issue was debated.[38] It was a plurality of worlds in this sense that made Cyrano de Bergerac's *Voyage dans la lune* (1657), for example, such a subversive work.[39]

36. I am grateful to Keith Yandell for pressing me to clarify the epistemic status of narratives vis-à-vis mechanical explanations.

37. II. 22. "Thus the matter of the heavens and of the earth is one and the same, and there cannot be a plurality of worlds" (CSM I, 232).

38. In a letter of 6 June 1647, Descartes discusses the place of man in the cosmological scheme of things. He concedes the point made by "preachers" that Christ in dying for all men did so for each as if each were alone;

> but, as that does not prevent Christ from having redeemed by this same blood a great number of other men, so I do not see that the mystery of the Incarnation, and all the other benefits that God has provided for man, prevent Him from providing an infinity of other great benefits to an infinity of other creatures. And although I do not infer from this that there are intelligent creatures among the stars or elsewhere, nor do I see that there is any argument to prove that there are not. (AT V, 54–55)

39. Later on, Fontenelle, in the preface of his [*Conversations on*] *The Plurality of Worlds* (1686; trans. J. Glanvill, London, 1688; reprinted in L. M. Marsak, *The Achievement of Bernard le Bouvier de Fontenelle* [New York: Johnson Reprint, 1970]) still worries about "those scrupulous Persons, who imagine, that the placing inhabitants any where, but upon the Earth, will prove dangerous to Religion" (Preface, unpaginated). His claim that the moon is inhabited may lead some "Church Men" to think him an atheist for thus supposing that since the moon was never colonized from earth, the men there would not be descended from Adam. It is not irrelevant that Leibniz subscribed, as one would expect, to the hypothesis of a plurality of inhabited worlds. Labrousse draws attention to a letter of his to Pierre Coste of 19 December 1707: "perhaps also there are spheres in which genii [*les Génies*] have greater leave than they have here below to interfere with the actions of rational animals" (G III, 403; AG, 198; Labrousse,

Occasionalism, then, is the view that best shows God to act meaningfully in the divine drama that is human history. If the necessity with which he acts is what I have called narrative necessity, then the interesting influence of Malebranche is not on Hume but (directly and perhaps indirectly through Bayle) on Berkeley. This general influence has been known about and investigated since Luce's pioneering work.[40] Here I shall only recall that when in the second of his *Dialogues Between Hylas and Philonous* Berkeley systematically sets out his differences from Malebranche, he not so much as mentions occasionalism. For that we must turn to his commonplace book: "We move our legs ourselves. 'Tis we that will their movement. Herein I differ from Malebranch [*sic*]."[41] This difference from Malebranche enables us creatures to speak, and not just hear, the language of the divine author of nature and thus to participate in the drama begun by Adam's fall.[42] That is, we are not merely passive recipients of messages from God; rather, we have an ongoing dynamic process of negotiation with him—in short, a conversation.

Incidentally, it seems to me no accident that the philosophical dialogue, largely in desuetude since Plato, is used with increasing effectiveness and centrality by Descartes, Malebranche, Bayle, and Berkeley, until with Hume, as with Plato, it is again unclear at points "who speaks for the author." The point of dialogical argument is to transcend the mere objective exposition of competing views, one of which the author happens to agree with—the *sic et non* binary opposition that one finds, for example, in Leibniz's "dialogues." (Nor is it surprising, on the other hand, that the incipient deist Locke, who in effect eliminates Revelation, also eschews the

---

Pierre Bayle, vol. 2, p. 249). (These *génies* will make a surprising reappearance below.) The contrast with the Cartesian position here is important. Roger Ariew points to "one of Leibniz's divergence[s] with Descartes. For Leibniz, the original creation produces all substances. There is no need for a special creation of man. These resulting Leibnizean substances (of the 1680's and 90's) do resemble Descartes's man, or informed matter, but they are everywhere in nature" ("Leibniz's Protogaea," in *Leibniz: Tradition und Aktualität*, V Internationaler Leibniz-Kongress [Hannover, 14–19 November 1988], p. 15).

40. A. A. Luce, *Berkeley and Malebranche: A Study in the Origins of Berkeley's Thought* (Oxford: Clarendon Press, 1934).

41. *Berkeley's Commonplace Book*, ed. G. H. Johnston (London: Faber & Faber, 1930), no. 553, p. 65.

42. One might have expected Berkeley to have been read this way by C. M. Turbayne, who more than anyone else has emphasized the significance of Berkeley's use of a linguistic model. But one looks in vain to *The Myth of Metaphor* (New Haven, Conn.: Yale University Press, 1962), at least, for even a mention of narrative; there, the conception of language is informed as much by 1950s ordinary-language philosophy as by anything in Berkeley. Language consists primarily of signs, things signified, and rules of grammar (pp. 69–70) put to the purposes primarily of signifying absent things and action about them (p. 93). Malebranche is mentioned only incidentally, Bayle not at all, and there is no mention even of biblical narrative.

dialogue altogether.) Bayle, in addition to using the dialogue, cannot resist a story of any sort, from his homely illustrations of dogs and singing birds, or even Caesar in the Forum, to such exotic sagas as that of the Mammilli-arians, for instance, which without the narratological background have been taken to be inexplicable aberrations.

V. Conclusion

But unless this narratological excursion itself be taken for a silly mouse, not to say an aberration, it must terminate at Bayle's critique of Leibniz. Recall, then, two threads left hanging from discussion earlier. One was the red-herring issue of conscious selection of thoughts as a condition for the mind-body connection; the other was the apparent requirement by occasionalism of a constant miracle in order to maintain the mind–body connection. At stake in both, of course, is Leibniz's principle of sufficient reason, which Bayle fails to engage—partly for the historical reason that Leibniz himself failed to make it explicit for him, but also because the principle would have violated the first condition for narrative, namely, time in which novel events take place. With Leibniz time is a matter of logical relations, which can be taken together to give us what Lovejoy called a *totum simul*—everything at once.[43] His principle of sufficient reason yields what we might call meta-physical mechanism—everything true of a thing, supernaturally no less than naturally, can be cranked out *a priori* from its individual concept, at least by God. For Bayle, by contrast, even if the outcome of history is assured by Providence, the path to that outcome is not laid out in advance, but is determined in time because of the intersection of independent orders of causation—interventions, the paradigm case of which is divine miracles.[44] The same point can be made at the epistemic level. By contrast with Leibnizian universalizable, *a priori* explanations that consist in the specifica-tion of a concept from which the explicandum logically follows, Bayle's explanations are (1) universalizable only in the way that parables, for

43. A. O. Lovejoy, *The Great Chain of Being: A Study in the History of an Idea* (New York: Harper & Row, 1960), ch. V, esp. pp. 154–55.

44. Labrousse puts it in even stronger fideist terms: "In a sense, God is not [merely] He who *performs* miracles, He *is* the miracle *par excellence*, the being who overwhelms and transcends all immanent lawfulness in the world, and who, having spoken to man, has opened to him a supernatural destiny—salvation or damnation" (*Pierre Bayle*, vol. 2, p. 298).

example, are relevant to more than one case, and (2) *a posteriori* in the sense that what comes *later* explains the significance of a previous event.[45]

With Leibnizian time, however, there is at least unidirectional ordering of events. Not so with physical mechanical processes, which of course are reversible. It matters not to Locke's famous clock at Strasbourg, or to the planetary system it models, whether it be run so that Tuesday follows Wednesday or conversely. But, so to speak, it sure as hell matters to human history as understood by Bayle whether Adam preceded Christ or conversely. Now, Bayle is generally quite sympathetic with mechanism—all change is change of motion, and motion changes only upon collision.[46] But the laws of the communication of motion are insufficient to explain all change. The growth, not just of animals, but of all living things is too complex to be explained by such laws. Yet an immediate appeal to God by itself would be no explanation. Instead,[47] an intelligent cause is required on the occasion of which God acts.

These intelligences cannot be human, and thus the hero of the Enlightenment and archopponent of desiccated Scholastic rationalism finds himself peddling angelology. Indeed, angels may even be appealed to as occasional causes in astronomical explanation. Given the criticisms of Newton and others, the laws of motion can no longer be held sufficient for the vortex hypothesis, so that "sooner or later" the followers of Copernicus will adopt the hypothesis of motor intelligences for their planets.[48] If Newton himself invokes the supernatural for the odd readjustment, Bayle does so for the

45. In his review of Arnauld's *Reflections philosophiques*, Arnauld's initial attack on Malebranche's *Treatise of Nature and Grace*, Bayle agrees with Arnauld's view that action through particular volitions is not incompatible with the idea of a perfect being. Among other considerations, he raises the case of those who attribute the irregularities in the world to the impossibility of correcting them except through particular decrees that would upset the simplicity of God's ways. In their ignorance of Providence, he says, they are like a man who leaves a play after the first scene and then gives a criticism of it (*Nouvelles de la republique des lettres*, August 1685. OD I, 346–47). I am grateful to Lois Frankel for urging me to sharpen the contrast between Bayle's position and metaphysical mechanism.

46. *System*, OD IV, 322.

47. *Dictionary*, article "Sennertus," remark C.

48. "Sir Issac Newton, and others, have so strongly assaulted the hypothesis of the Vortices, that the general laws of motion are not sufficient to account for the phaenomena. A particular direction of an intelligent Being would come in very seasonably" (*Dictionary*, article "Ricius," remark C). The French text makes clearer that Bayle is talking here of angels, not God: "La direction particulière d'une Intelligence viendroit ici fort à propos." R. A. Watson suggested to me that Bayle may here be speaking ironically. If so, my whole approach to Bayle is very much threatened. Labrousse, however, takes the passage at face value and points to correspondence and other articles of the *Dictionary* where Bayle argues the insufficiency of mechanism and proposes the hypothesis of angels as account of a variety of phenomena, including the astrophysical (*Pierre Bayle*, vol. 2, pp. 252–54).

continuous and regular operation of the universe. Occasionalist arguments thus represent for Bayle, not a philosophical *analysis* of mechanical causation, as they do perhaps for Malebranche and certainly for Hume, but a way of *transcending* mechanical causation in an effort to find the real significance of human history.

Lois Frankel

The Value of Harmony

The concept of *harmony* appears frequently in the history of philosophy. It is typically associated with notions of balance, proper proportion, justice, interconnection, sympathy, reconciliation of opposites, and goodwill. It is also used as a metaphor for an ideal society or ideal human disposition. Historically, harmony is closely associated with the Pythagoreans, Plato, alchemy,[1] and Renaissance Neoplatonism.[2] In the seventeenth century, two of harmony's strongest proponents were Gottfried Leibniz and Anne Con-

1. For alchemists, who believed that all things were related by a mutual affinity or sympathy, gold could be produced by a perfect natural harmony (John Roche, "The Transition from the Ancient World Picture," in *The Physical Sciences since Antiquity,* ed. Rom Harré [New York: St. Martin's Press, 1986], p. 35).

2. For additional discussion of harmony, especially in the context of medieval and Renaissance worldviews, see Carolyn Merchant, *The Death of Nature* (San Francisco: Harper & Row, 1980), esp. chs. 3–4.

way (author of *Principles of the Most Ancient and Modern Philosophy*, a work that had a significant influence on Leibniz's metaphysics).[3] Each sought to unify diverse methodologies, worldviews, models, and entities, and used the ideal of harmony both to advance their ethical views and to improve the intelligibility of their philosophical systems. In particular, both Conway's and Leibniz's versions of harmony provided ways to render causation— once taken for granted, now called into question as a consequence of a confusing assortment of competing models—more intelligible. Following a brief look at some applications of harmony to moral philosophy, particularly as manifested in Leibniz's and Conway's works, I will show how these authors apply their different but related concepts of harmony to the problem of the intelligibility of causation. Faced with the apparent inadequacy of any one model to cover all forms of causal interaction, Conway and Leibniz employ their versions of harmony to integrate some of the competing models into a more coherent account.

I. Harmony and Moral Philosophy

Harmony, as employed by Conway and Leibniz, is intended to unify elements that otherwise would appear to be diverse or even opposed, whether those elements be explanatory models, methodologies, individuals, societies, or pieces of the universe's furniture. Both authors are particularly eager to reconcile mechanism with earlier concepts of similarity, the latter sometimes expressed in terms of sympathy or kinship. Conway explicitly links similarity, sympathy, and kinship with respect and love. Sympathy and kinship, she believes, enable all creatures to love and respect one another, and to achieve a sense of unity:

> . . . as God made all Nations out of one Blood, to the end they might love each other, and stand in a mutual Sympathy, and help each other; so hath he implanted a certain Universal Sympathy and mutual Love in Creatures, as being all Members of one Body, and (as I may so say) Brethren, having one common Father, to wit, God in Christ, or the Word made Flesh; and so also one Mother, *viz.* that

3. For example, Conway used the term '*monad*' to refer to a living principle associated with a body. Leibniz began to use the term during the same period in which Van Helmont introduced him to Conway's work (Carolyn Merchant, "The Vitalism of Anne Conway: Its Impact on Leibniz's Concept of the Monad," *Journal of the History of Philosophy* 17 (1979): 255f.). See also *Principles of the Most Ancient and Modern Philosophy*, ed. P. Lopston (The Hague: Martinus Nijhoff, 1982) III.9, p. 163, and VII, p. 191.

Substance or Essence alone, out of which they proceeded, and whereof they are real Parts and Members; and albeit Sin hath in a wonderful Manner impaired this Love and Sympathy, yet it hath not destroyed it.[4]

Note the very literal use of kinship language in the above passage: all people, all nations, all creatures are portrayed as having common parentage so that they may have mutual sympathy and coexist harmoniously. That kinship, in turn, is based on similarity and common origin:

But now the Foundation of all Love or Desire, whereby one Thing is carried into another, stands in this, That either they are of the same Nature and substance with them, or like unto them, or both; or that one hath its Being from the other, whereof we have an Example in all living Creatures which bring forth their young; and in like manner also in men, how they love that which is born of them. . . . But besides this particular Love, there remains yet something of Universal Love in all Creatures, one towards another, . . . which certainly must proceed from the same Foundation, *viz.* in regard of their First Substance and Essence, they were all one and the same Thing, and as it were Parts and Members of one Body. Moreover, in every *Species* of Animals, we see how the Male and Female Love one another, and in all their Propagations (which are not Monstrous, and contrary to Nature) they respect each other; and that proceeds not only from the unity of Nature, but also by reason of a certain eminent similitude or likeness between them.[5]

For Conway, emanation is the most immediate form of causation and is a type of kinship relation. Thus she prefers to describe Christ's origin as a result of emanation or begetting, rather than of creation.[6] Leibniz also speaks of emanative causation, but more in the general context of the finite imitating the infinite than in Conway's specific context of God begetting Christ.

Unity, important both to premechanistic worldviews and to the ideal of harmony, can also have ethical connotations: Conway comments approvingly on the admiration that "good spirits" feel for the ideals of "Unity, Concord, and Friendship" among themselves.[7] She is also committed to

4. *Principles* VI.4, pp. 178–79.
5. *Principles* VII.3, pp. 198–99.
6. *Principles* V.4, p. 170. Conway considers this point important because a thing that is emanated or begotten has more in common with its cause than a thing that is created.
7. *Principles* VII.3, pp. 214–15.

reconciling opposing philosophical and religious views: the emanationistic and vitalistic tenets of the ancients (primarily the Greeks, the kabbalists, and Philo of Alexandria)[8] with the mechanistic philosophy of the moderns and with Jewish and Christian theology. This conciliatory motive is apparent when, in the first chapter of the *Principles*, she cites several "hypotheses of the Hebrews" as source material for her own views[9] and rejects the notion that God is three persons on the grounds that it is offensive to non-Christians.[10]

Leibniz also allows a more abstract form of 'sympathy' connecting all things,[11] manifested either in mutual correlation (monadic expression or mirroring) or in causal interaction (on the phenomenal level). For example, in the *Discourse* he writes that "all bodies of the universe are in sympathy with each other."[12] Writing to Arnauld, he associates sympathy with expression:

> Now this expression takes place everywhere, because every substance sympathizes with all the others and receives a proportional change corresponding to the slightest change which occurs in the whole world, although this change will be more or less noticeable as other bodies or their actions have more or less relationship with ours.[13]

Although Leibniz's notion of sympathy is primarily metaphysical, he considers metaphysics the foundation for moral philosophy, relating to it "as theory to practice."[14] This connection suggests the possibility of some corresponding moral principle. Leibniz connects the concepts of agreement, harmony, beauty, and love:

> Now unity in plurality is nothing but harmony [*Ubereinstimmung*], and since any particular being agrees with one rather than another being, there flows from this harmony the order from which beauty arises, and beauty awakens love.
>
> Thus we see that happiness, pleasure, love, perfection, being, power, freedom, harmony, order, and beauty are all tied to each other, a truth which is rightly perceived by few.[15]

8. *Principles* V.1, p. 167.
9. *Principles* I.Annotations, pp. 150–51.
10. *Principles* I.7, p. 150.
11. To De Volder, April 1702: G II, 240 (L 527).
12. *Discourse* 33: G IV, 459 (L 325).
13. To Arnauld, 9 October 1687: G II, 112 (L 339).
14. *New Essays* IV.viii.9: NE 432.
15. *On Wisdom:* G VII, 87 (L 426).

Leibniz associates virtue with "serenity of spirit" and "internal harmony."[16] He also assigns harmony considerable aesthetic value[17] and associates it with justice,[18] themes that can be found in the works of other seventeenth- and eighteenth-century authors. Spinoza, for example, claims that "things which bring it about that men live harmoniously, at the same time bring it about that they live according to the guidance of reason (by P35). And so (by P26 and P27) they are good."[19] He adds that harmony is a consequence of justice.[20] Although harmony is a common theme in moral philosophy, both Conway and Leibniz give it a central role in their metaphysics as well, where it allows them to give a more intelligible account of causation.

II. The Intelligibility of Causation

Prior to the seventeenth century, Western philosophy for the most part considered causation unproblematic—a suitable subject for description and classification, but one whose basic intelligibility was not at issue. However, during the seventeenth century, philosophers became more interested in questioning the intelligibility of specific types of causal interaction and of causation itself.[21] The occasionalists tried to circumvent direct interaction, because it was unintelligible under their model. Locke, on the other hand, accepted causal interaction, but decided to leave many details of how bodies cause sensations in us (or, for that matter, changes in other bodies) to the "good pleasure of our Maker," because so far as he could determine "there is no discoverable connexion between any *secondary Quality, and those primary Qualities* which it depends on."[22] An important, perhaps essential source of

16. Leibniz, *Reflections on the Common Concept of Justice:* L 569–70.

17. Leibniz to Wolff, 18 May 1715: C. I. Gerhardt, *Briefwechsel zwischen Leibniz und Christian Wolf* (Halle, 1860), pp. 170f. (AG 233).

18. *On the Ultimate Origin of Things* (1697): G VII, 307 (AG 154).

19. *Ethics* IV, P40: Edwin Curley, *The Collected Works of Spinoza* (Princeton, N.J.: Princeton University Press, 1985), vol. 1, p. 570 (C. Gebhardt, *Spinoza Opera*, 4 vols. [Heidelberg: Carl Winter, 1925], II, p. 241).

20. *Ethics* IV, Appendix XV: Curley, p. 590 (Gebhardt II, p. 270).

21. Louis Loeb recognizes this trend when he argues that Descartes, Spinoza, Malebranche, Berkeley, and Leibniz should be classified as "Continental Metaphysicians" because they are all willing to deny some form or other of causal interaction (*From Descartes to Hume* [Ithaca, N.Y.: Cornell University Press, 1981], pp. 17, 320–63).

22. *Essay* IV.iii.12 (John Locke, *An Essay Concerning Human Understanding,* ed. Peter H. Nidditch [Oxford, 1975], p. 545). See Lois Frankel, "How's and Why's: Causation Un-Locked," *History of Philosophy Quarterly* 7 (1990): 409–29, for further discussion of Locke's struggles with the intelligibility of causation.

these "discoverable necessary connections" was perceptible causal similarity. When one could observe similarity between phenomena, the mind could move easily between cause and effect and feel confident of their necessary connection. Descartes affirmed the importance of causal similarity in his Second *Replies*:

> The fact that 'there is nothing in the effect which was not previously present in the cause, either in a similar or in a higher form' is a primary notion which is as clear as any that we have; it is just the same as the common notion 'Nothing comes from nothing.' For if we admit that there is something in the effect that was not previously present in the cause, we shall also have to admit that this something was produced by nothing. And the reason why nothing cannot be the cause of a thing is simply that such a cause would not contain the same features as are found in the effect.[23]

Leibniz also endorses the concept of causal similarity, but explicitly treats it as more an analogous than a direct relationship:

> It must not be thought that ideas such as those of colour and pain are arbitrary and that between them and their causes there is no relation of natural connection: it is not God's way to act in such an unruly and unreasoned fashion. I would say, rather, that there is a resemblance of a kind—not a perfect one which holds all the way through, but a resemblance in which one thing expresses another through some orderly relationship between them. Thus an ellipse, and even a parabola or hyperbola, has some resemblance to the circle of which it is a projection on a plane, since there is a certain precise and natural relationship between what is projected and the projection which is made from it.[24]

Note that Leibniz interprets causal similarity as a kind of analogical correspondence or mapping relation. The relationship need not, so far as he is concerned, be obvious nor readily perceptible. This looser requirement is important because it fits well with Leibniz's hierarchical classification of reality, some of whose levels are perceptible while others (the most real levels) are not. Thus items may 'really' resemble one another in an appropriate way, even though such resemblance is not readily apparent.

23. *Second Replies*: CSM II, 97 (AT VII, 135); see also *Geometrical Exposition*: CSM II, 114 (AT VII, 162f.).
24. *New Essays* II.viii.13: NE 131.

Under premechanistic worldviews, causal similarity, whether direct or analogous, provided grounds for *deducing* cause from effect or effect from cause. Unfortunately, during the seventeenth century that relationship was becoming more difficult to observe. One factor that undermined confidence in causal similarity and hence in causation's intelligibility was the increasing popularity of mechanism as an explanatory and causal model. According to mechanism, causation is primarily a relation between bodies that occurs by means of motion or impact. This model can be useful for physical objects, all of which are capable of motion and are susceptible to impact, but it cannot account for any causal relation where these characteristics are absent—where cause or effect is nonphysical. Because of those and other limitations,[25] the mechanical model failed to render many cases of causation intelligible. It simply could not deliver everything desired of it: it could not account for many cases of causation, nor could it support causal similarity or perceptible necessary connections, both of which were still important components of the notion of causation.

A related factor was the "mind-body problem." If one accepted Descartes's argument for a real distinction between mind and body, it became difficult to comprehend, as Princess Elizabeth put it, "how the human soul can determine the movement of the animal spirits in the body so as to perform voluntary acts—being as it is merely a conscious substance." She wondered how, if contact were required in order to cause movement, and contact required extension, the unextended soul could be a cause of bodily motion.[26] More intelligible, in her view, was an account (rejected by Descartes) that allowed the soul to be extended and material.[27] Such an account would allow soul and body to be sufficiently similar to allow them to interact. He attempted to answer her question by appealing to one's everyday experience that the soul and body are united and *just do* interact (or, as Daniel Garber more charitably describes Descartes's response, mind-

25. For representative discussions of the limits of mechanism, see Margaret D. Wilson, "Superadded Properties: The Limits of Mechanism in Locke," *American Philosophical Quarterly* 16 (1979): 143–50; M. R. Ayers, "The Ideas of Power and Substance in Locke's Philosophy," in *Locke on Human Understanding*, ed. I. C. Tipton (Oxford: Oxford University Press, 1977); M. R. Ayers, "Mechanism, Superaddition, and the Proof of God's Existence in Locke's Essay" *Philosophical Review* 90 (1981): 210–51; and Alan Gabbey, "The Mechanical Philosophy and Its Problems: Mechanical Explanations, Impenetrability, and Perpetual Motion," in *Change and Progress in Modern Science*, ed. J. C. Pitt (Dordrecht: D. Reidel, 1985), pp. 9–84.

26. Elizabeth to Descartes, 6–16 May 1643, in *Descartes: Philosophical Writings*, trans. Elizabeth Ancombe and Peter Thomas Geach (New York: Bobbs-Merrill, 1954), pp. 274–75 (AT III, 661).

27. Elizabeth to Descartes, 10–20 June 1643, in Anscombe and Geach, *Descartes*, p. 276 (AT III, 663).

body unity and interaction are primitive notions, intelligible on their own terms).[28]

Among Elizabeth's concerns were the lack of similarity between mind and body (according to Descartes, mind does not share body's essential attribute of extension, and body does not share mind's essential attribute of thought) and the problem of applying the mechanical model to an immaterial substance.[29] In the Conversation with Burman, Descartes obliquely attempted to deal with the first difficulty: while agreeing that effects must resemble their causes in some way (a principle that was, after all, central to his Third Meditation argument for the existence of God), he stated that God's status as "being and substance" made it sufficiently similar to creatures for its causal role to be intelligible.[30] That is, Descartes's concept of similarity was quite broad: *all* substances counted as sufficiently similar to one another to allow causal interaction. Unfortunately, most readers considered Descartes's explanations unsatisfactory, and the mind–body problem persisted.

The mind–body problem in particular and the loss of confidence in causal intelligibility in general were symptomatic of the problem of finding an acceptable causal model. Each of the currently available models, not just the mechanical one, had difficulties and limitations. Other commonly used models included transfer, emanation, deduction, and volition. Of these, the transfer and emanation models were losing popularity to the logical, mechanical, and volitional models. According to the *transfer* model, the cause, in providing something to its effect (e.g., heat, motion, etc.), parts with that which it gives. According to the *emanation* model the cause possesses (in a higher form) whatever it gives to its effect (thus emanative causation is also eminent), and "radiates" what it imparts without diminishing itself in the process. Such causation is often described by metaphors of flowing fountains, reflection, and imitation of the higher by the lower. A variant of the emanation model might be called *contagion*, wherein the cause possesses what it shares with its effect in the same (rather than a higher) form.

Note that the emanation, contagion, and transfer models relied heavily on some kind of similarity, analogy, or something "in common" between cause and effect: the cause must either bestow something on the effect

---

28. Daniel Garber, "Understanding Interaction: What Descartes Should Have Told Elisabeth," *Spindel Conference 1983: The Rationalist Conception of Consciousness, Southern Journal of Philosophy* 24 (Supplement): 15–32; see 17ff.

29. Garber ("Understanding Interaction," p. 16) notes the prominence of impact as a mode of explanation but does not explicitly mention the issue of causal similarity.

30. *Descartes' Conversation with Burman*, trans. John Cottingham (Oxford: Clarendon Press, 1976), p. 17 (AT V, 156).

outright (as in the transfer model) or multiply something to share with its effect. Although these models made it easy to find many cause–effect relations intelligible (because many putative causes *are* observably similar to their effects), they encountered several difficulties. First, it was readily apparent that many putative causes appeared to be *dis*similar to their effects. Boyle and Locke, for example, each invoked the case of a sharp object piercing one's skin and causing pain, but without the object bearing any similarity to the pain.[31] Second, the almost physical imagery of transference and, to a lesser extent, emanation were troubling to some philosophers. Leibniz, for example, objected to the idea of accidents being "detached" from substances or "going about" on their own.[32] Finally, some of the putative causal relations sanctioned by these models were associated with concepts of sympathetic magic and occult qualities, both of which were losing favor to the more "modern" models: mechanical (discussed earlier), deductive, and volitional.

According to the *deductive* model, an effect follows or flows inevitably from its cause—logically, mathematically, or metaphysically. This model emphasizes the necessity of causal connections. It became attractive in connection with the increasing interest in logic and mathematics, but ran into difficulty, as Locke noted, when one attempted to make sense of the supposed necessary connections between individual causes and effects. If one could not perceive similarity between cause and effect, it was difficult to be confident of their necessary connection. The *volitional* model describes causation as the operation of an intelligent will, either finite or divine. This model suffers from a difficulty complementary to the one afflicting the mechanical model, namely, accounting for causes or effects that cannot readily be viewed as subjects or objects of volitions.[33]

Unlike the emanation and transfer models, the deductive, volitional, and mechanical models do not necessarily involve causal similarity. That indifference undermined confidence in causal intelligibility, for which most philosophers still expected some sort of similarity between cause and effect.[34] Consequently, the issue is not simply the adequacy of the mechan-

31. Boyle, *Origin of Forms and Qualities*, sec. V, in *Selected Philosophical Papers of Robert Boyle*, ed. M. A. Stewart (New York: Manchester University Press/Barnes & Noble, 1979), p. 31; Locke, *Essay* II.vii.13. Boyle was untroubled by this lack of perceived similarity, while Locke, as I argue in "How's and Why's," found it more disturbing.

32. Leibniz, *Monadology* 7: G V, 607–8 (AG 213).

33. Berkeley, who held to a volitional model of causation, was able to do so consistently only because he classified all entities as minds or ideas.

34. In addition to the passages quoted earlier from Descartes and Leibniz, see for example Spinoza, *Ethics* I, P3, Berkeley, *Principles of Human Knowledge* I.25. Locke's discomfort with the lack of observable resemblance he finds between causes and effects indicates that he, too,

ical model to explain mind-body interaction or causation in general. Rather, the problem involves the proliferation and confusion of, and ambivalence toward, available models.

In the next two sections I will show how the notion of harmony, including Leibniz's preestablished harmony and Conway's earlier, less abstract variety of harmony, may be used to provide a better foundation for causal intelligibility. Rather than forcing a single causal model to cover all cases, Leibniz and Conway develop inclusive models intended to handle all cases by employing analogies to incorporate other models. Each author uses the themes of unity, interconnection, and analogy to harmonize the sometimes-conflicting claims of the mechanical model and its predecessors.

III. Leibniz's Preestablished Harmony

Necessary connections are important to the notion of causal relations. One way to achieve causal intelligibility in that context is to invoke the necessity of a divine agent as ultimate cause. Leibniz claims that his system of preestablished harmony is the only way to render the universe intelligible. He argues that only the preestablished harmony, with its associated mathematical laws, including the law of continuity, can go beyond mere descriptions to genuine explanations of the universe, by "leading us to the reasons and intentions of the Author of things."[35] Leibniz's God serves as the ultimate source of causal laws and of harmonious 'expression', and is the model that other causes imitate. But God cannot simply provide necessary causal connections without also providing a sufficient reason for them. That reason must lie in the things themselves. Thus an important function of the preestablished harmony is to provide for causal similarity in the form of the mirroring relationship among monads.

Leibniz's interest in harmony and unity is fundamental. The following passage is one of his many strong endorsements of harmony in general, and of his system of preestablished harmony in particular, as means to unify a variety of philosophical systems:

> When we penetrate to the foundations of things, we observe more
> reason than most of the philosophical sects believed in. The lack of

---

has some unmet expectations of causal similarity and that he retains an assumption that causal intelligibility is associated with similarity.

35. *Reply to the Thoughts on the System of Preestablished Harmony Contained in the Second Edition of Mr. Bayle's Critical Dictionary, Article Rorarius*: G IV, 569 (L 583).

substantial reality in the sensible things of the skeptics; the reduction
of everything to harmonies or numbers, ideas, and perceptions by
the Pythagoreans and Platonists; the one and the whole of Parmeni-
des and Plotinus, yet without any Spinozism; the Stoic connectedness, which is yet compatible with the spontaneity held to by others;
the vitalism of the Cabalists and hermetic philosophers who put a
kind of feeling into everything; the forms and entelechies of Aristotle
and the Scholastics; and even the mechanical explanation of all the
particular phenomena by Democritus and the moderns; etc.—all of
these are found united as if in a single perspective center from which
the object, which is obscured when considered from any other
approach, reveals its regularity and the correspondence of its parts.
Our greatest failure has been the sectarian spirit which imposes
limits upon itself by spurning others.[36]

For Leibniz, ontological unity is achieved by setting up a system of
analogical hierarchies whereby all complex finite entities, including physical
objects, are reduced ultimately to nonphysical monads. As noted earlier,
similarity plays an essential role in causal intelligibility. For Leibniz, that
similarity is generally more analogical than direct. Analogy allows appar-

---

36. *Clarifications of the Difficulties Which Mr. Bayle has Found in the New System of the Union of
Soul and Body*: G IV, 523–24 (L 496); see also to Thomasius, 20/30 April 1669: L 98f.; to
Arnauld, 9 October 1687: G II, 115 (L 341); *Metaphysical Consequences of the Principle of Reason*:
P 174. Of special note is a passage from the *New Essays* that also refers explicitly to Conway:
> This system appears to unite Plato with Democritus, Aristotle with Descartes, the
> Scholastics with the moderns, theology and morality with reason. Apparently it takes
> the best from all systems and then advances further than anyone has yet done. I find in
> it something I had hitherto despaired of—an intelligible explanation of the union of
> body and soul. I find the true principles of things in the substantial unities which this
> system introduces, and in their harmony which was pre-established by the primary
> substance. I find in it an astounding simplicity and uniformity, such that everything
> can be said to be the same at all times and places except in degrees of perfection. I now
> see what Plato had in mind when he took matter to be an imperfect and transitory
> being; what Aristotle meant by his 'entelechy'; in what sense even Democritus could
> promise another life, as Pliny says he did; how far the sceptics were right in decrying
> the senses; why Descartes thinks that animals are automata, and why they nevertheless
> have souls and sense, just as mankind thinks they do. How to make sense of those who
> put life and perception into everything—e.g. of Cardano, Campanella, and (better than
> them) of the late Platonist Countess of Conway, and our friend the late M. Franciscus
> Mercurius van Helmont (though otherwise full of meaningless paradoxes) together
> with his friend the late Mr Henry More. How the laws of nature—many of which were
> not known until this system was developed—derive from principles higher than matter,
> although in the material realm everything does happen mechanically. (*New Essays* I.i:
> NE 71f.)

ently diverse elements to be integrated.[37] This analogical similarity functions among levels (God, finite substances, phenomena), among monads (the mirroring relationship), and among phenomena. The importance of monads in Leibniz's system and his commitment to analogy are exemplified by this passage from the *New Essays*, where he uses monads as the model for explaining all other things:

> I strongly favour inquiry into analogies . . . my views about monads will be found manifested everywhere—views about their endless duration, about the preservation of the animal along with the soul, about the occurrence of indistinct perceptions in a certain state such as that of death in simple animals, about the bodies which can reasonably be attributed to Spirits, and about the harmony between souls and bodies, such that each perfectly follows its own laws without being disturbed by the other and with no need for a distinction between voluntary and involuntary. It will be found, I claim, that all these views are in complete conformity with the analogies amongst things which come to our notice; that I am merely going on beyond our observations, not restricting them to certain portions of matter or to certain kinds of action; and that the only difference is that between large and small, between sensible and insensible.[38]

In Leibniz's preestablished harmony, the problem of the apparent interaction between mind and body, despite his arguments that they cannot interact, is solved by distinguishing between phenomenal and real levels of existence. At the phenomenal level, where bodies reside, interaction occurs; at the real level, consisting of unextended windowless monads, it does not. Monads are self-contained, and each is the source of all its own states: its appetitions or volitions express its complete concept. On each level the causation involved is reasonably intelligible: volitional activity for mental entities, mechanical causation for physical phenomena. But in order for these schemes to be *jointly* intelligible, some unifying theory is needed. The

37. See *New Essays* II.viii.13: NE 131, quoted earlier. See also *On The Elements of Natural Science* (c. 1682–84): L 287–88, where Leibniz rejects claims of explanatory value for the Scholastic concept of sympathy. For a more detailed discussion of how Leibniz's analogical hierarchies illuminate his views on causation, see Lois Frankel, "Causation, Harmony, and Analogy," in *Leibnizian Inquiries,* ed. Nicholas Rescher (Washington, D.C.: University Press of America, 1989).

38. *New Essays* IV.xvi.12: NE 473f.

preestablished harmony provides that unity by allowing the physical appearance to supervene on the monadic reality.[39]

Monads are simple substances, "true unities." Complex entities, such as bodies, are not true substances. This is not to say, however, that Leibniz ignores physical objects. Even though he considers them mere (albeit well-founded) phenomena, he devotes considerable attention to the mechanical details of their operation. Leibniz clearly wants to give bodies and mechanism "their due," using harmony to incorporate them into the larger framework of his system.

The preestablished harmony provides two sorts of unity. First, it gives a single ultimate cause for all entities and events (God), which also pulls together all types of causal relations among finite beings.

> [J]ust as in animated bodies what is organic corresponds to what is vital, motions to appetites, so also in the whole of nature efficient causes correspond to final causes, because everything proceeds from a cause which is not only powerful, but also wise; and with the rule of power through efficient causes, there is involved the rule of wisdom through final causes. This harmony of corporeal and spiritual is one of the finest and most evident arguments for a Divinity; for, since the influx of one kind on another it inexplicable, a harmony of things which are entirely different can arise only from the one common cause, that is, God.[40]

Second, Leibniz's metaphysical hierarchy, starting with God, proceeding through monads, and ending with phenomena, portrays each element as analogically similar to the others, and the lower elements as ultimately imitative of God. Monads' universal mirroring is analogous to the mutual relations among phenomena. Leibnizian bodies follow laws of motion, which in turn are based on metaphysical laws. Further, motion is the material analogue of monadic appetition, which is itself a finite analogue of the divine will, emanated from God, who, as common cause, unifies the diverse elements of reality. Just as Leibniz's primary finite substance is the monad, his primary mode of causation for finite substances is volition (appetition, a closely related concept, being the primary activity of mo-

---

39. Notice how this passage describes a harmonizing parallelism between monad and world, and between representation and reality: "The representation of the present state of the universe in the soul . . . will produce in it the representation of the following state of the same universe, just as the objects in the preceding state actually produce the following state of the world. In the soul, the representations of these causes are the causes of the representations of these effects" (G IV, 532–33).

40. *Metaphysical Consequences*: P 174 (C 13).

nads). All physical motions are reduced ultimately to appetitions, monadic volitions, or "active force," all of which imitate the divine will.

> [S]ome connection, either immediate or mediated by something, is necessary between cause and effect. . . . If . . . the law set up by God does in fact leave some vestige of him expressed in things, if things have been so formed by the command that they are made capable of fulfilling the will of him who commanded them, then it must be granted that there is a certain efficacy residing in things, a form or force such as we usually designate by the name of nature, from which the series of phenomena follows according to the prescription of the first command.[41]

To sum up, Leibniz's system is one in which, at the most real (monadic) level, each substance is a unity with its own distinct essence, from which all its qualities flow deductively, but which nonetheless abstractedly reflects ('expresses') every other substance by virtue of the preestablished harmony. On the monadic level, each substance is the sole cause of its states, while on the phenomenal level (including bodies) causal interaction proceeds along mechanical lines. The volitional and deductive models of causation compatible with monads are harmonized with the mechanical model compatible with bodies, thus alleviating any difficulties associated with trying to use a model on incompatible objects. Leibniz preserves causal necessity by referring everything ultimately to the divine nature as ultimate cause and model, or to divine laws as ultimate causal laws. He also preserves a form of causal similarity both by insisting on monadic expression (so that there is something in each monad that corresponds to and is loosely similar to every other monad) and by permitting a looser, analogical understanding of similarity. Thus Leibniz's preestablished harmony enhances the intelligibility of causation in his system: it provides a consistent method of describing causation depending on the kind of entity under discussion, while using analogies to link the diverse methods of description into a larger hierarchical

---

41. *On Nature Itself* 6: G VI, 507 (L 501). Leibniz mentions the imitative and emanative aspects of his hierarchical structure more explicitly when, in the *Discourse on Metaphysics*, he writes of the "imitation or image of the divine essence, thought and will" being in finite things (*Discourse on Metaphysics* 28: G IV, 453 [L 321]). Another allusion to emanation may be found in his mention of "continuous creation" in a letter to De Volder (24 March/3 April 1699: G II, 168 [L 515] and 21 January 1704: G II, 264 [L 535]). For a more detailed discussion of this issue, see Frankel, "Causation, Harmony, and Analogy." In the *Principles of Nature and Grace* Leibniz invokes the concept of eminent causation, writing that "this simple primary substance must include eminently all the perfections which are contained in the derivative substances which are its effects" (G VI, 602 [P 200]).

pattern. Further, the system allows for necessary connections, mechanistic behavior for bodies, and volitional behavior for souls, and preserves the intuition that causes have something in common with their effects.

IV. Conway's Universal Interconnections

Many of the features of Leibniz's system that enhance the intelligibility of causation are previewed in Anne Conway's *Principles of the Most Ancient and Modern Philosophy*. Of special note for our current purposes is her strong interest in unity and harmony. Other themes in Conway's work suggest Leibniz's "no windows" principle, which denies causal interaction on the monadic level, replacing it with the more abstract notion of expression: according to Conway, the 'atoms' that constitute a creature neither have internal motion nor receive motion or perceptions from outside themselves.[42] However, both Conway and Leibniz permit interaction among composite (for Leibniz, phenomenal) entities. Conway describes that interaction as a "Society of Fellowship among Creatures in giving and receiving, whereby they mutually subsist one by another,"[43] while Leibniz describes it in more mechanical terms.

Like Leibniz, Conway is strongly interested in harmony as a means of reconciling apparent opposites. Conway is well aware of the "new science" and the resultant popularity of mechanistic explanation—the explanation of all events through motion and impact. Her desire to reconcile mechanism with earlier approaches results in a system in which every created being is alive, shares its essence with every other created being, and is capable of motion, and in which motion and similarity are both central explanatory devices. Thus, she intends her system to provide equal room for mind and body, life and motion, causal similarity, and mechanism. Each element is to have its due. While Leibniz treats unity in a relatively abstract way, through hierarchical analogies anchored by God, Conway's concept of unity is very direct and literal: she states that "the whole creation is still but one substance or entity, neither is there a vacuum in it,"[44] meaning that all

42. *Principles* VII.4, pp. 208–9.
43. *Principles* VII.4, pp. 209–10. For further discussion of Conway's influence on Leibniz, see Merchant, *The Death of Nature*, ch. 11; Jane Duran, "Anne Viscountess Conway: A Seventeenth Century Rationalist," *Hypatia* 4 (1989): 64–79; and Lois Frankel, "Anne Finch, Viscountess Conway," in *A History of Women Philosophers*, ed. Mary Ellen Waithe (Dordrecht: Kluwer, 1991), vol. 3, pp. 41–58.
44. *Principles* VII.4, pp. 206–7.

creatures share a single essence, even though each creature is itself a multiplicity of bodies and spirits.[45]

Conway prefers to avoid what she considers excessive distinctions among substances, acknowledging only three distinct types of substance: God, Christ, and Creatures. Christ serves as an intermediary between the other two, having qualities in common with each of them.[46] By providing such an intermediary, Conway avoids Elizabeth's objection to Descartes concerning causal interactions among distinct substances. Because each essence, on Conway's view, includes several qualities, it is easy for substances with different essences to have something in common. All creatures share a single essence. Consequently, mind (or spirit) and body are not really distinct, but rather extremes on a continuum, and can be converted from one to another.

> Creature is but one Essence or Substance, as to Nature or Essence, as is above demonstrated, so that it only differs *secundum modos existendi;* or, *according to the manners of existence;* among which one is a Corporeity; whereof also there are many degrees; so that a Thing may more or less approach to, or recede from the State and Condition of a body or a Spirit; but because a Spirit (between these two) is more excellent in the Natural Order of Things, and by how much the more a Creature is a Spirit . . . so much the nearer it approaches to God, who is the chiefest Spirit.[47]

Spirit and body are so essentially similar that the only way to distinguish them is by means of their varying degrees of subtlety or grossness:

> [E]very Man, yea, every Creature, consists of many Spirits and Bodies . . . and indeed every Body is a Spirit, and nothing else, neither differs any thing from a Spirit, but in that it is more dark; therefore by how much the thicker and grosser it is become, so much the more remote it is from the degree of a Spirit, so that this distinction is only modal and gradual, not essential or substantial.[48]

45. *Principles* VI.11, p. 190; VII.4, pp. 209–10.
46. She remarks that

> [Christ] is a natural *Medium* between [God and creatures] by which the Extreams are united, and this *Medium* partakes of both Extreams, and therefore is the most convenient and proper *Medium;* for it partakes of the one Extream, *viz.* Mutability, to wit, from Good to a greater degree or measure of Goodness, and of the other Extream, *viz.* that it is altogether unchangeable from Good into Evil; and such a *Medium* was necessarily required in the very Nature of Things; for otherwise there would remain a Chasm or Gap. (*Principles* V.3, p. 169)

47. *Principles* VII.1, p. 192.
48. *Principles* VI.11, p. 190.

Conway holds that every body is connected to some spirit, and vice versa[49] (similar to Leibniz's claim that each monad is associated with a body),[50] and that just as every body is composed of numerous bodies, so is every spirit composed of "innumerable" spirits.[51] Thus in addition to claiming that spirit and body are "interconvertible," Conway maintains an isomorphism between them. The interaction of body with body, and of body with soul (or "Spiritual Body") occurs by means of the "links and chains" formed by several bodies/spirits of varying degrees of "subtlety."[52]

To complete the idea that the functions of spirit and body are unified, Conway argues that life (a mode of spirit) and figure (a mode of body) are "distinct, but not contrary Attributes of one and the same substance"[53] and cooperate in the activity of life. For Conway, motion imitates divine and finite volitions in being always *active* and alive; not, as in the pure mechanistic model, passive in material objects. She writes that "Sense and Knowledge" are the "Motion or Action of Life" and use the local or mechanical motion of bodies as their instrument.[54] But all motion is ultimately spiritual,[55] in analogous imitation of God.

Like Leibniz, Conway sees analogy as a means of harmonizing the older and newer models, similarity and mechanism. She views motion, volition, and emanation as analogous concepts:

> . . . that in [God] which hath an Analogy or Agreement with the Motions or Operations of Creatures, is the Government of his Will, which (to speak properly) is not Motion, because every Motion is successive, and cannot have place in God, as is above demonstrated.[56]

49. Ibid.

50. *Principles of Nature and Grace* 3: G VI, 599 (AG 207).

51. *Principles* VII.4, pp. 207–8.

52. *Principles* VII.3, pp. 214–15. Note that although the model of grossness and subtlety is physical, thus suggesting some epistemological preference for the physical side of things, Conway considers spirit to be more metaphysically "excellent" because it is closer to God, also considered a spirit.

53. *Principles* IX.8, p. 226.

54. *Principles* IX.9, pp. 227–28.

55. ". . . every motion and action, considered in the abstract, hath a wonderful subtilty or spirituality in it, beyond all created substances whatsoever, so that neither time nor place can limit the same; and yet they are nothing else but modes or manners of created substances, viz. their strength, power, and virtue, whereby they are extendible into great substances, beyond what the substance itself can make" (*Principles* IX.9, p. 229).

56. *Principles* III.8, p. 161. Consider also this passage: "But every motion, proceeding from the proper life and will of the creature, is vital; and this I call a motion of life, which is not plainly local and mechanical as the other, but hath in it a life and vital virtue" (*Principles* IX.9, pp. 229–30). In addition, Conway describes sin, or an evil will, as *"ataxia, or an inordinate*

Conway offers a fairly direct account of the intelligibility of causation, based on the concepts of similarity and mediation. When, as in the case of body-body causation, there is a "true agreement that one hath with another in its own Nature," the causation is directly intelligible, "because Things of one, or alike Nature, can easily affect each other." But because a soul is a "Spiritual Body," it may still interact with physical bodies by making use of intermediaries, "middle Spirits," or "certain Bodies, partaking of subtilty and grossness, according to diverse degrees, consisting between two Extreams," which form the "Links and Chains" between the most gross (matter) and the most subtle (spirit).[57] The notion of intermediaries facilitating the interaction of distantly related entities first appears in Conway's portrayal of Christ (who is not created, but "begotten," "generated," or "emanated") as the intermediary between God and creatures.

Conway is committed to the view that all elements of the universe are strongly interconnected, "inseparably united" by means of the intermediary function of "Subtiler Parts," which are the "Emanation of one Creature into another." These mediated connections facilitate action at a distance, and form "the Foundation of all Sympathy and Antipathy which happens in Creatures." Conway hopes that this view of things as unified by intermediaries will render intelligible "the most secret and hidden Causes of Things, which ignorant Men call occult Qualities."[58] Universal interconnection implies that there is no great mystery behind causal interactions, nor do such interactions require elaborate explanations, because they are the natural condition. That implication contrasts markedly with the mechanistic model's demand for detailed explanations employing matter and motion, rather than interaction, as primitives.

Conway hopes to bolster the intelligibility of causal connections further by showing that they involve both motion and "sympathy" (or similarity)—both the newer model and the older one. She affirms the importance of similarity for causation when she denies the existence of dead matter, because it could in no way resemble its divine cause. Thus, because the ultimate cause is alive, and because effects resemble the most important features of their causes, everything must be alive.[59] She also endorses a transfer model of causal connection, and ties it to the principle that cause

---

determination of motion, or the power of moving from its due place, state, or condition into some other" (*Principles* VIII.2, p. 214). See also *Principles* VII.4, IV.1–2, V.2, V.4, V.5.

57. *Principles* VII.3, pp. 214–15.

58. *Principles* III.10, p. 164.

59. "Now what attributes or perfections can be attributed to dead matter . . . we shall find none at all; for all [God's] attributes are living; yea, life itself . . . I demand, in what dead matter is like unto God? If they say again in naked entity, I answer, there is none such in God or his creatures: And so it is a mere *non ens*, or nothing" (*Principles* VII.2, p. 197).

and effect must be similar—must have something in common, and can exchange parts. To exchange parts, she argues, all creatures must be "manifold" rather than singular. Conway describes causal exchanges in terms of nourishment, interdependence, and friendship.[60] By contrast, Leibniz, who rejects any transfer or "influx" between substances, holds that substances are unities, rather than Conway's "multiplicities." His system replaces the direct-transfer model and the universal-causal interconnection with his more indirect preestablished harmony, universal mutual expression, and unfolding of individual complete concepts.

Relation and/or interconnection are important elements in Leibniz's and Conway's thought, but in quite different ways. For Conway, harmonious interconnection is basic to the nature of reality; for Leibniz, interaction (or its appearance) is a well-founded phenomenon made possible by the preestablished harmony, which maintains logical and metaphysical connections in the absence of causal ones.[61] Although 'real' finite substances (monads) do not interact, mere phenomena—specifically, bodies—can and do just that.[62]

Conway and Leibniz each employ models incorporating similarity, motion, and volition. Both authors use analogies: Conway's system is centered more in the physical sphere, includes physical causal links and "influxes," and accords full reality to physical objects; Leibniz's is centered in the mental sphere, denies full reality to physical objects, and prefers logical/metaphysical links. Both Leibniz and Conway employ hierarchies headed

60. She observes that
    a Creature, because it needs the assistance of its Fellow-Creatures, ought to be manifold, that it may receive this assistance: for that which receives something is nourished by the same, and so becomes a part of it, and therefore it is no more one but many, and so many indeed as there are Things received, and yet of a greater multiplicity; therefore there is a certain Society of Fellowship among Creatures in giving and receiving, whereby they mutually subsist one by another . . . by consequence every Creature which hath Life, Sense, or Motion, ought to be a number, or a Multiplicity. (*Principles* VII.4, pp. 209–10)
61. The following is a classic statement of his position:
    It is impossible for the soul, or any other true substance, to receive any influence from without, except by the divine omnipotence . . . [but] God has originally created the soul, and any other real unity, in such a way that everything in it must arise from its own nature through a perfect *spontaneity* with regard to itself; yet by a perfect *conformity* to things without. . . . So there will be a perfect accord between all these substances which produces the same effect that would be noticed if they all communicated with each other by a transmission of species or of qualities, as the common run of philosophers imagine. (*New System of Nature* I.14: G IV, 484 [L. 447–48])
62. "[T]he very smallest body receives some impression from the slightest change in all the others, however distant and small they may be, and must thus be an exact mirror of the universe" (*Reply to the Thoughts:* G IV, 557 [L 576]).

by God. For Leibniz, God's role is even more central. His preestablished harmony, though specifying that things *act* from their own natures, depends on God—an external agent—to prearrange it all, and denies any interaction on the real level. Conway's brand of harmony involves God and Christ (as the intermediary), but allows real things to *interact* by their own nature. Conway emphasizes the essential similarities and interdependence of all finite substances. Leibniz emphasizes their essential differences and isolation, despite the mirroring and expression relationship, plus their self-sufficiency and independence.

In either case, harmony—whether Conway's general and direct harmony of interconnection or Leibniz's preestablished harmony—succeeds in promoting causal intelligibility because it uses the strengths of each of the competing models of mechanism, kinship (similarity, emanation), and volition, relating them through analogies so that the explanations, like that which they hope to explain, can coexist harmoniously.

Index